Networks for Social Impact

Networks for Social Impact

Michelle Shumate and Katherine R. Cooper

OXFORD
UNIVERSITY PRESS

OXFORD
UNIVERSITY PRESS

Oxford University Press is a department of the University of Oxford. It furthers
the University's objective of excellence in research, scholarship, and education
by publishing worldwide. Oxford is a registered trade mark of Oxford University
Press in the UK and certain other countries.

Published in the United States of America by Oxford University Press
198 Madison Avenue, New York, NY 10016, United States of America.

CIP data is on file at the Library of Congress
Names: Shumate, Michelle, author. | Cooper, Katherine R., author.
Title: Networks for social impact / Michelle Shumate, Katherine R. Cooper.
Description: New York : Oxford University Press, 2022. |
Includes bibliographical references and index.
Identifiers: LCCN 2021015835 (print) | LCCN 2021015836 (ebook) |
ISBN 9780190092009 (paperback) | ISBN 9780190091996 (hardback) |
ISBN 9780190092023 (epub)
Subjects: LCSH: Business networks—Management. | Organizational behavior. |
Social networks. | Social change.
Classification: LCC HD69.S8 S548 2021 (print) | LCC HD69.S8 (ebook) |
DDC 658.4/08—dc23
LC record available at https://lccn.loc.gov/2021015835
LC ebook record available at https://lccn.loc.gov/2021015836

DOI: 10.1093/oso/9780190091996.001.0001

1 3 5 7 9 8 6 4 2

Paperback printed by LSC Communications, United States of America
Hardback printed by Bridgeport National Bindery, Inc., United States of America

MS: For my parents, who showed me that a life of service is the highest calling

KRC: For Belle and Charlotte, the next generation of impact-makers

Contents

Figures

Tables

Foreword

Michelle Shumate and Kate Cooper have written a book the network field badly needs. Networks are often portrayed as solutions to problems of collaboration as if the absence of collaboration is the problem, and not the social problem that compels collaboration in the first place. Shumate and Cooper call our attention to the social impact of the collaborative activity. Their view is that networks of various forms and types allow us to both solve collective action problems and allow us to have a social impact on wicked problems like homelessness, mental health, and natural disasters. That is the theme of this book. Shumate and Cooper use their own research, case studies, and an exhaustive review of the research on networks to answer that question. The answer does not lie in choosing a template or a set of "best practices" that apply to any network or any problem; rather they define the kind of networks that can achieve social impact and several pathways these networks use to produce a social impact based on the nature of the social problem or issue, the goals of the network, and the network's environment.

The goals of this book are to bring together "siloed" scholarship on networks from both social science and management, breaking it into configurational and process approaches. More importantly, the book engages students and network leaders in an accessible manner that retains fidelity to the research. To my mind, this is what the field of collaborative networks needs badly. There are plenty of self-proclaimed network gurus or consulting firms selling commercial products that claim to have the solution to the collaborative dilemma based on their experience or one or two examples. There is work that seriously reviews the research literature and distills the practice implications from it.[1] What we have not had until now is work that seriously reviews the research literature, classifies it, separates out what is germane for social impact, and gives readers the tools to build networks and evaluate them, both in the service of social impact in our communities. Shumate and Cooper present the reader with five axioms of networks for social impact.

1. Outcomes are interdependent.
2. Networks for social impact are sensitive to their environment.

---

[1] J. K. Popp et al., "Interorganizational Networks," Collaboration across Boundaries Series (Washington, DC: IBM Center for the Business of Government, 2014).

3. Networks' dilemmas are never solved, just managed within constraints.
4. Not all networks organized for social impact actually achieve that impact.
5. There is more than one path to social impact.

These axioms serve as the organizing framework for the book as the authors explore the subtle ways these axioms play out in specific examples. "Not all networks organized for social impact actually achieve that impact" (axiom 4) calls our attention to failure as well as success. We can learn a great deal from networks that fail to achieve their goals so we can avoid these problems in the future. Networks that aren't successful may fail in multiple ways that are very helpful to network architects. Several years ago, I evaluated two Collective Impact networks that were viewed as successes. United Way had originally funded four and I asked what happened to the other two. "They failed." "How did they fail?" I asked. "It doesn't matter," was the reply. It matters greatly, because how can we avoid pitfalls and problems if we only have a theory of success?

Network architects need failures and successes to construct networks that are recursive and path-dependent. These qualities present themselves to network leaders as managerial dilemmas. Dilemmas that represent opposing values can never be solved, only balanced better or worse. The trade-off that the network leader makes at one time may cause a problem with the other value somewhere down the road. Too much integration of the network at one point may create tensions that lead to calls for differentiation at another point, thus a temporary equilibrium is the most a network leader can hope for.

It is obvious that I like this book a lot. It is smart, nuanced, well-written and faithful to the research. All that is true, but what I like most about it is that it treats the reader as a partner in the enterprise of building networks for social impact. Shumate and Cooper say, "Here are your tools, let's get going, this is going to be fun."

H. Brinton Milward
Melody S. Robidoux Foundation Fund Chair in
Collaborative Governance, University of Arizona

Preface

In 2012, when Kate began to write her dissertation on Community Reach, we started a journey together to understand the collective impact movement. Michelle had been researching networks of nonprofits for about a decade. Still, there was something new and exciting about the idea of organizations working together across sectors to impact their communities. Since then, we have been privileged to work with and study many networks for social impact. Some of these networks got their start as part of the collective impact movement; others had been around for decades. Many networks do not adhere to the collective impact model or consider themselves part of it at all.

Eric Nee, the editor-in-chief of *Stanford Social Innovation Review*, when describing our research developing the Community Systems Solution Framework, wrote that we need a repertoire of approaches that "can be adopted when appropriate."[2] In many ways, his call sums up the reason why we wrote this book. Collective impact, or any of the models in the Community Systems Solutions Framework, for that matter, is not a one-size-fits-all solution. Instead, as we argue in this volume, there are many pathways to social impact. The critical factors that determine whether networks will make a social impact are making the right choices for the context and managing network dilemmas that never go away.

We wrote this volume to lay a foundation for study and practice; we identify the dead ends, network dilemmas, and pathways on the road to social impact. We combine the best academic research and case studies of successful networks to identify the appropriate decisions networks make and manage. Networks are not the solution to every social problem, and there are many cases where they are inappropriate. But we believe that networks, appropriately designed and managed, have the potential to move the needle on previously intractable social issues.

We had two audiences in mind as we wrote this volume. We hope that academic researchers and students will learn from how scholars across disciplines have studied social impact networks. In each chapter, we include a case study where students of social impact can apply the ideas presented. We

---

[2] Eric Nee, "A Flexible Framework for Going Beyond Collective Impact," *Stanford Social Innovation Review*, n.d., https://ssir.org/articles/entry/a_flexible_framework_for_going_beyond_collective_impact.

also hope that this book is a reference guide for network leaders who want to make the right choices for their context. In each chapter, we include Tools for Network Instigators. We designed the tools sections to help leaders implement the lessons from the text.

Our relationship as co-authors of this book is indicative of our long-term work together. Our partnership began in 2008 when Kate joined the master's and later PhD program at the University of Illinois Urbana-Champaign, where Michelle was a faculty member. Kate started graduate school after working with an international nonprofit; she hoped that the program would help her address some of the recurring problems she saw in her professional work. Over the years, many joint projects, including establishing the Network for Nonprofit at Social Impact at Northwestern University, blossomed. We discussed and debated what different networks for social impact ought to do over lunches and conference tables. We decided to capitalize on those years of conversations and joint research projects to produce this book.

We have many people to thank for their support, collaboration, and mentorship along the way. Among them are Janet Fulk, Michelle's doctoral advisor at the University of Southern California, who encouraged her transition from corporate knowledge management to nonprofit network scholar; and Em Griffin of Wheaton College. He encouraged Kate to pursue a career in research. We are also grateful to Marshall Scott Poole at the University of Illinois for his mentoring during our early careers; we are both better scholars because of him.

We are indebted to the funders that supported much of this work, including the National Science Foundation, Bill and Melinda Gates Foundation, and the Army Research Office. Without their support, we would not have conducted the foundational studies on networks and nonprofit capacity, implementing evidence-based practice across organizations, and comparative network effectiveness described in this book. We are also thankful to Northwestern University for their support of the Network for Nonprofit and Social Impact and funding a research leave for Michelle that made writing this book possible. We are also thankful to the Delaney Family for their generous gift supports Michelle's University Research Professorship.

We are also indebted to the many collaborators on these projects. They include Yannick Atouba, Andrew Pilny, Macarena Peña-y-Lillo, Ari Sahagun, Rong Wang, Zachary Gibson, Anne-Marie Boyer, Jiawei (Sophia) Fu, Joshua Paul Miles, Jennifer Ihm, Reyhaneh Maktoufi, Kaitlyn Childs, John Harris, Shaun Doughtery, Julia Carboni, Catherine Annis, Karen Smilowitz, Noshir Contractor, Leslie DeChurch, Paul Leonardi, Laurence Prusak, Miranda Richardson, Hannah Kistler, and Brint Milward. We are also grateful to the many undergraduate research assistants who aided us with data collection, including Fallon Parfaite, Ali Wilt, Alexander Furuya, Jessica Suratkal, Lindsey Pape, Emily Comstock, Michelle Lee, Hansuh Rhee, Avery Keesee, Tiara Swartz, Soteria Reid, Danielle Reiser, Jiyoon Song, Andrew Wayne, Alexa Bagamian, Will Deschler, Yunling Ding, Victoria Ham, Yerim Kim, Ren MacLean, Gloria Mao, Esther Park, Anna Petraskova, Kevin Qiu, Cara Savin, Sumin Woo, Nicole Tong, Hui-Ling Chen, Jailene Ochoa, Harriet Zhao, Camille Garcia-Mendoza, Lauren Thomas, and Jacob Jones.

Many scholars and thought leaders offered insights, wisdom, and critiques that were important to this volume. We are grateful to the scholars and thought leaders who attended the Collective Impact Summit we hosted in 2016; we developed many of the critical insights we had about the collective impact movement there. They included Brian Christens, Jeff Cohen, Marya Doerfel, Kirsten Foot, Vincent Francisco, Beth Gazley, Eric Glaser, Matthew Koschmann, Kathy Merchant, Monique Miles, Brint Milward, Chrystal Morris Murphy, Larry Pasti, Elizabeth Farley Ripple, Mary Kingston Roche, Tim Sass, John Selsky, Valerie Shapiro, and Danielle Varda. We are also indebted to Patrick Kenis and Joerg Raab for their help in developing the axioms of this book; they were both gracious hosts to Michelle as a visiting faculty member at Tilburg University in fall 2018. We have appreciated the feedback that scholars and practitioners at the Conference on Cross-Sector Social Interaction (CSSI) have provided. We tested many of the ideas from this book in early conference papers presented there.

We are indebted to the many network leaders who spent time telling us about their networks, among them: Heather Rowles, Rolf Wegenke, Anna Henderson, Quisquella Addison, Mark O'Brien, Gail Francis, Illene Rinn, Alexis Mancuso, Mary Anne Foley, Dana Gold, Genna Wirth, Jana Jones Halls, Delia Farquharson, Jackie Campbell, Stephanie Townsend, Florence Young, Jennifer Burns, Bela Mote, Partheev Shah, Matt Snyder, Derran Wimer, Traci Stanley, Lori Bass, Karen Vogel, Robert Kret, Janet Meeks, David Obedzinski, Kim Russo, Nicholas Armstrong, Sarah King, Hadass Sheffer, Traci Wirtanen, Annette Bakker, Simon Vukelj, Karen Peluso, and Shelley Richards, as well as those individuals and communities that appear under a pseudonym.

We are also indebted to our families for the support, love, and needed laughter they provided while writing this book. Lynn Cooper and Elissa Cooper provided ongoing encouragement and invaluable childcare support to Kate's family, as did Jackie and Fran Mongeon. We are thankful for our spouses, Michael Vila and Matt Mongeon, who embodied patience and support while they shouldered the extra parenting duties of young children when "mommy was writing." Thank you for believing in us, and we hope this book makes you proud. We are grateful for our children, Oliver and Alexander, and Belle and Charlotte, who *sometimes* played quietly, *occasionally* took longer naps than expected, and *always* made us laugh. We hope that this book helps make the world you will inherit better.

We are grateful to the editorial staff at Oxford University Press, especially our editor David Pervin, who believed in our project at the beginning. We are incredibly thankful to Brint Milward, a dear friend and colleague, for writing the foreword to this volume.

We hope that this volume inspires scholars and network leaders to work together to move the needle on social issues. To realize all the potential of networks for social impact, we will need bridge builders to close the academic-practice divide.

Michelle Shumate and Katherine R. Cooper

Acronyms

AIDS	Acquired Immunodeficiency Syndrome
AJLI	Association of Junior Leagues International
ASPIRE	Advisory System for Processing, Innovation and Resource Exchange
CSIRO	Commonwealth Scientific and Industrial Research Organisation
EPIC	Every Person Influences Children
GONGO	Government-Oriented Nongovernmental Organization
HIPAA	Health Insurance Portability and Accountability Act
HIV	Human Immunodeficiency Virus
INGO	International Nongovernmental Organization
MAAC	Multi-Agency Alliance for Children
NF	Neurofibromatosis
NGO	Nongovernmental Organization
NORC	Nationally Occurring Retirement Communities
R&D	Research and Development
SWOT	Strengths, Weaknesses, Opportunities, Threats
USAID	United States Agency for International Development
WAICU	Wisconsin Association of Independent Colleges and Universities Collaboration Project
WIN	Westside Infant-Family Network in Los Angeles

1

What Are Networks for Social Impact?

In Chattanooga, Tennessee, the Tennessee Aquarium, the Creative Discovery Museum, and the Hunter Museum of American Art formed the Chattanooga Museums Collaborative to save expenses by combining back-office functions and administrative responsibilities. Having achieved some organizational savings by sharing a wireless network and pooling insurance plans, the museum leaders considered whether they could leverage their partnership to support the community. With some collaborative success to build on and community champions' support, the museums joined the city in a public-private partnership for a joint capital campaign to revitalize the Chattanooga community and raised $120 million.

A group of six nonprofit organizations came together in Chicago to form the Chicago Benchmarking Collaborative. The purpose was to share data related to their work on youth and education. The organizations collectively agreed on ways to measure success, implemented a joint evaluation program, shared a database, and used their pooled data to make decisions about their plans. Partners acknowledged that the clients and neighborhoods' differences made it challenging to scale their efforts across the city. However, they all benefited from comparing their program outcomes to others.

In Melbourne, Australia's National Science Agency, CSIRO, strove to help its community fulfill the U.N. Sustainable Development Goals. They created a new online marketplace, known as ASPIRE, that served as a "matchmaker" between companies to divert commercial and industrial waste from landfills. Paired companies created new arrangements where one company's industrial waste served as the input for another company's production. ASPIRE was recognized as a model for system change, even though most organizations that log into the system never seek out new ways to dispose of their industrial waste.

In Pittsburgh, Pennsylvania, three agencies serving senior citizens were brought together by the Jewish Community Foundation to form AgeWell Pittsburgh. After a few iterations, they embraced a model that involved coordinating their services, removing duplication, and shared staff training. Through

Networks for Social Impact. Michelle Shumate and Katherine R. Cooper, Oxford University Press. © Oxford University Press 2022.
DOI: 10.1093/oso/9780190091996.003.0001

their efforts, seniors served by their agencies have significantly better outcomes than the national average.

This book is about how nonprofits/nongovernmental organizations (NGOs),[1] corporations, and government agencies come together to achieve social impact. We consider when sectors work together in cross-sector partnerships and when they work alone, as in NGO networks and government alliances. As illustrated in the earlier vignettes, there are many ways that network leaders make that impact. Some, like AgeWell Pittsburgh, are integrated partnerships—where agencies partner to coordinate services, share fundraising activities, or operate joint programs. Like in the Chicago Benchmarking Collaborative, others may operate under a different model in which organizations maintain distinct services and goals but come together to learn from one another. Sometimes these partnerships are long-lasting, but a network's success and survival depend on the environment in which it operates. Many times, collaborative ventures dissolve, or participants are not sure that their efforts made any difference at all.

Networks rarely achieve the promise of social impact, despite the encouragement of funders and social impact leaders' valiant efforts. This book describes the conditions, processes, and resources that networks need to achieve social impact. It is not a one-size-fits-all formula. Instead, we define several paths that networks use to produce social impact depending on the nature of the social issue, their aims, and the environment in which they operate.

We draw from research across disciplines—each of which has taken up the topic in their way. Also, we situate our research over the past 15 years within this body of work. This book is neither a Pollyannaish, pro-collaboration account of the benefits of cross-sector or interorganizational collaboration nor a critical view of these efforts. Instead, we walk the middle ground, highlighting networks' opportunities and challenges, and noting when networks are not worth the cost. We introduce a model that explains how networks make a social impact, and when they are unlikely to do so.

We have two goals in writing this book. First, this book brings together the previously siloed scholarship. We review research from business, communication, community psychology, public administration, network science, organization studies, social work, and social policy. And although this book brings

---

[1] In this text we generally refer to NGOs when describing nonprofit-nongovernmental organizations outside of the United States and nonprofit when we describe their activities in the United States. We consider the terms interchangeable.

together each of these perspectives, we draw most heavily from research on network governance,[2] orchestration,[3] processes,[4] and coalition management.[5] This interdisciplinary body of research provides a foundation for the systems perspective on social impact networks that this book introduces. In short, we contend that networks, if resourced, configured, and managed well, can transform inputs into social impact.

Second, but no less important, this book offers an accessible guide to students and network leaders who want to understand how organizations work together to achieve social gains. We chart several pathways that networks take to social impact and identify dead ends where networks fall short of their aspirations. Throughout this book, we rely upon interviews and case studies to bring to life some of the most challenging concepts from network and public policy research. These cases offer a realistic look at what it takes to make a social impact.

Social impact

Ultimately, this book is about social impact. Social impact reflects how communities benefit from the collaborative work of organizations, which we describe as networks. We use the term "social" to differentiate this impact from analyses of networks that form for commercial purposes (e.g.,

[2] Daniela Cristofoli, Josip Markovic, and Marco Meneguzzo, "Governance, Management and Performance in Public Networks: How to Be Successful in Shared-Governance Networks," *Journal of Management & Governance* 18, no. 1 (February 1, 2014): 77–93, https://doi.org/10.1007/s10997-012-9237-2; Keith G. Provan and Patrick Kenis, "Modes of Network Governance: Structure, Management, and Effectiveness," *Journal of Public Administration Research and Theory* 18, no. 2 (June 29, 2007): 229–52, https://doi.org/10.1093/jopart/mum015; K. G. Provan and H. B. Milward, "A Preliminary Theory of Interorganizational Network Effectiveness: A Comparative Study of Four Community Mental Health Systems," *Administrative Science Quarterly* 40, no. 1 (1995): 161–190; Jörg Raab, Remco S. Mannak, and Bart Cambré, "Combining Structure, Governance, and Context: A Configurational Approach to Network Effectiveness," *Journal of Public Administration Research and Theory* 25, no. 2 (April 1, 2015): 479–511, https://doi.org/10.1093/jopart/mut039.

[3] Raymond L. Paquin and Jennifer Howard-Grenville, "Blind Dates and Arranged Marriages: Longitudinal Processes of Network Orchestration," *Organization Studies* 34, no. 11 (November 1, 2013): 1623–53, https://doi.org/10.1177/0170840612470230.

[4] Barbara Gray and Jill Purdy, *Collaborating for Our Future: Multistakeholder Partnerships for Solving Complex Problems* (Oxford: Oxford University Press, 2018); Brian D. Christens, *Community Power and Empowerment* (Oxford: Oxford University Press, 2019).

[5] Valerie B. Shapiro, Sabrina Oesterle, and J. David Hawkins, "Relating Coalition Capacity to the Adoption of Science-Based Prevention in Communities: Evidence from a Randomized Trial of Communities That Care," *American Journal of Community Psychology* 55, no. 1 (March 1, 2015): 1–12, https://doi.org/10.1007/s10464-014-9684-9; Valerie B. Shapiro, J. David Hawkins, and Sabrina Oesterle, "Building Local Infrastructure for Community Adoption of Science-Based Prevention: The Role of Coalition Functioning," *Prevention Science* 16, no. 8 (November 1, 2015): 1136–46, https://doi.org/10.1007/s11121-015-0562-y.

biotech research and development networks, licensing networks). Networks for social impact attempt to address some of the world's most pressing social problems. In the following chapters, we illustrate many of the points through cases in which networks focus on a wide range of social issues, including educational outcomes for opportunity youth, elder care, veterans' benefits, improving early childhood outcomes, and improving outcomes for survivors of gender-based violence. Although each of these initiatives requires resources, including economic resources, their focus is on addressing social problems.

We also distinguish social impact from other beneficial network outcomes. First, *individuals* may benefit from their participation in networks. They might gain new knowledge, more significant professional opportunities, or a sense of satisfaction from their efforts. However, these individual outcomes are distinct from social impact. Second, we describe the ways that networks may benefit the *organizations* involved. These benefits can include greater legitimacy, better services for their clients, organizational learning, and better relationships with other organizations. Under the right conditions, these organizational benefits can translate into social benefits for communities and the environment. However, organizational gains are not social impact. Third, we examine the ways that *networks* can benefit from these efforts. Network benefits include reduced costs through efficiencies and cost sharing, attracting shared funding and recognition, and better referral systems or coordination among organizations that are part of the network. But network outcomes are not social impact.

Instead, social impact refers to how the network's work impacts people or environments most affected by the problem. In our research, such outcomes include improved kindergarten readiness in a community, lower rates of emergency room visits for seniors, and improvement in post-secondary educational attainment. A policy change that positively impacts those most affected is also a social impact. We provide some examples of how groups of organizations have collectively raised their voices to affect policy. We'll talk more about the types of social impact that networks make in Chapter 2.

Networks

One of the challenges of academic research on networks for social impact is the variety of names scholars have used to describe these partnerships.

They include but are not limited to, cross-sector social partnerships,[6] multi-organizational cross-sector social partnerships,[7] multistakeholder partnerships,[8] collaboration,[9] public-private partnerships,[10] collective impact,[11] coalitions,[12] and networks.[13] Although each has distinct definitions, for this book, we will regard each of these terms as a form of collaboration that we will describe as a network.[14]

Collaboration itself is a highly contested term.[15] Both in academic research and our experience conducting interviews with hundreds of social leaders, collaboration is in the eye of the beholder. Scholars have tried to address the various dimensions of partnerships by proposing collaboration continuums.[16] Although the typologies vary, each one tries to distinguish the interdependence level meant by "collaboration" between organizations. At the lowest level, each of the continuums takes up a simple exchange of resources or information. However, some scholars argue that financial exchange, such as contracting[17] or philanthropic donations,[18] should not be considered true collaboration. Scholars place highly integrated partnerships

[6] John W. Selsky and Barbara Parker, "Platforms for Cross-Sector Social Partnerships: Prospective Sensemaking Devices for Social Benefit," *Journal of Business Ethics* 94, no. 1 (July 1, 2010): 21–37, https://doi.org/10.1007/s10551-011-0776-2.

[7] Amelia Clarke and Mark Fuller, "Collaborative Strategic Management: Strategy Formulation and Implementation by Multi-Organizational Cross-Sector Social Partnerships," *Journal of Business Ethics* 94, no. 1 (July 1, 2010): 85–101, https://doi.org/10.1007/s10551-011-0781-5.

[8] Barbara Gray and Jill Purdy, *Collaborating for Our Future: Multistakeholder Partnerships for Solving Complex Problems* (Oxford: Oxford University Press, 2018).

[9] James E. Austin, "Strategic Collaboration Between Nonprofits and Businesses," *Nonprofit and Voluntary Sector Quarterly* 29, no. 1_suppl (March 1, 2000): 69–97, https://doi.org/10.1177/0899764000291S004; Chao Guo and Muhittin Acar, "Understanding Collaboration among Nonprofit Organizations: Combining Resource Dependency, Institutional, and Network Perspectives," *Nonprofit and Voluntary Sector Quarterly* 34, no. 3 (2005): 340–61; Sharon Lynn Kagan, *United We Stand: Collaboration for Child Care and Early Education Services* (New York: Teachers College Press, 1991).

[10] Cartsen Greve and Graeme A. Hodge, "Introduction: Public-Private Partnerships in Turbulent Times," in *Rethinking Public-Private Partnerships: Strategies for Turbulent Times*, eds. Cartsen Greve and Graeme A. Hodge, 1 (Abingdon: Routledge, 2013), 1–32.

[11] John Kania and Mark Kramer, "Collective Impact," *Stanford Social Innovation Review*, 2011.

[12] Sandra A. Waddock, "Building Successful Social Partnerships," *Sloan Management Review; Cambridge* 29, no. 4 (Summer 1988): 17.

[13] K. G. Provan and H. B. Milward, "A Preliminary Theory of Interorganizational Network Effectiveness: A Comparative Study of Four Community Mental Health Systems," *Administrative Science Quarterly* 40, no. 1 (1995): 1–33.

[14] Networks as an area that can represent a wide variety of relationships among organizations. In this text, we exclusively focus on collaborative and referral links.

[15] Guo and Acar, "Understanding Collaboration among Nonprofit Organizations."

[16] Austin, "Strategic Collaboration Between Nonprofits and Businesses"; Kagan, *United We Stand: Collaboration for Child Care and Early Education Services.*

[17] Beth Gazley and Chao Guo, "What Do We Know about Nonprofit Collaboration? A Comprehensive Systematic Review of the Literature," *Academy of Management Proceedings* 2015, no. 1 (January 1, 2015): 15409, https://doi.org/10.5465/ambpp.2015.303.

[18] Austin, "Strategic Collaboration Between Nonprofits and Businesses."

at the far end of the continuum, including mergers,[19] service integration,[20] and multifaceted collaborations that transform both organizations' core business practices.[21]

Throughout this book, we use the term network to describe various types of collaborations between organizations. Interorganizational networks are a system of "high interdependence among otherwise autonomous agencies."[22] As such, we mean more than casual acquaintances or groups that gather once a month for breakfast and "networking." Instead, these organizations coordinate their activities, collaborate on joint projects, or integrate their services on behalf of clients. However, we exclude mergers or conglomerates, or when organizations merge their structures and identities. Also, we exclude social movements. Social movements rely on individuals to collectively describe their grievances through coordinated action. These individuals may coordinate their responses through the work of organizations or via technology.[23] Relatedly we exclude networks that exist purely online. Individuals make up these communities. In this book, we instead focus on the interrelationships between organizations that seek to make concrete gains.

Interorganizational networks for social impact take different forms. What makes interorganizational networks different from other types of organizing, like hierarchies or markets? A good deal of network and organizational science research has tackled this topic,[24] and the answer boils down to two key features: autonomy and interdependence.

[19] David La Piana and Michaela Hayes, "M&A in the Nonprofit Sector: Managing Merger Negotiations and Integration," *Strategy & Leadership* 33, no. 2 (2005): 11–16.

[20] Kagan, *United We Stand: Collaboration for Child Care and Early Education Services*.

[21] James E. Austin and Maria May Seitanidi, "Collaborative Value Creation: A Review of Partnering Between Nonprofits and Businesses. Part 2: Partnership Processes and Outcomes," *Nonprofit and Voluntary Sector Quarterly* 41, no. 6 (December 1, 2012): 929–68, https://doi.org/10.1177/0899764012454685.

[22] Michael W. Lawless and Rita A. Moore, "Interorganizational Systems in Public Service Delivery: A New Application of the Dynamic Network Framework," *Human Relations* 42, no. 12 (1989): 1167.

[23] W. Lance Bennett and Alexandra Segerberg, *The Logic of Connective Action: Digital Media and the Personalization of Contentious Politics* (New York: Cambridge University Press, 2013); Doug McAdam, "Conceptual Origins, Current Problems, Future Directions," in *Comparative Perspectives on Social Movements: Political Opportunities, Mobilizing Structures, and Cultural Framings*, eds. Doug McAdam, John D. McCarthy, and Mayer N. Zald (New York: Cambridge University Press, 1996), 23–40; Sidney Tarrow, *Power in Movement: Social Movements in Contentious Politics* (Cambridge: Cambridge University Press, 1998); Manuel Castells, *Networks of Outrage and Hope: Social Movements in the Internet Age* (Hoboken, NJ: John Wiley & Sons, 2015); Mario Diani, "Networks and Social Movements," in *The Wiley-Blackwell Encyclopedia of Social and Political Movements*, American Cancer Society (Hoboken, NJ: Wiley-Blackwell, 2013), https://doi.org/10.1002/9780470674871.wbespm438.

[24] E.g., Ronald S. Burt, "The Network Structure of Social Capital," *Research in Organizational Behavior* 22 (2000): 345–423; W. W. Powell, "Neither Market nor Hierarchy: Network Forms of Organization," *Research in Organizational Behavior* 12 (1990): 105–24.

First, in networks, participating organizations maintain their *autonomy*. Organizations do not take orders from a lead organization or become a single new organization. Because network participants come as delegates for their organizations' decision-making authority,[25] organizational participation, program alterations, and resource allocation ultimately lie with the organizations that comprise the network. In contrast to hierarchies, this autonomy means that networks rely on different governance structures than command and control or directive leadership. In many networks, "authority is based on expertise and the ability to reach an agreement as a collective."[26] Network leaders must rely on distributive or collaborative leadership, agreed-upon decision-making processes, and the power of persuasion.[27]

Second, although organizations maintain their autonomy, they do not act independently. Instead, multiple relationships with other organizations impact and are impacted by their activities. These relationships create *interdependencies* across the field of organizations working together so that one organization's choices have ramifications for others in the network.

Using this broad definition of networks, we bring together research on serendipitous and goal-directed networks.[28] Serendipitous networks are created by the individual partnerships that organizations make with one another but are not centrally coordinated.[29] The ASPIRE network described at the beginning of this chapter is an orchestrated serendipitous network. A lead agency arranges the ties between companies; organizations register with the network to seek waste alternatives or seek new resource inputs. But partnerships are developed between the companies.

In goal-directed networks, organizations pool their efforts to achieve a common purpose or purposes. The AgeWell Pittsburgh, Chattanooga Museums Collaborative, and Chicago Benchmarking Collaborative, described at the beginning of this chapter, are goal-directed networks. In each case, the organizations, as a collective, make a social impact. In this book, we argue that goal-directed networks more frequently result in social impact than serendipitous

[25] Robert Agranoff, *Managing within Networks: Adding Value to Public Organizations* (Washington, DC: Georgetown University Press, 2007).

[26] Agranoff, *Managing within Networks*, pl 87.

[27] Robert Agranoff and Michael McGuire, "Big Questions in Public Network Management Research," *Journal of Public Administration Research and Theory* 11, no. 3 (July 1, 2001): 295–326, https://doi.org/10.1093/oxfordjournals.jpart.a003504; Chris Silvia, "Collaborative Governance Concepts for Successful Network Leadership," *State and Local Government Review* 43, no. 1 (2011): 66–71.

[28] Sherrie E. Human and Keith G. Provan, "Legitimacy Building in the Evolution of Small-Firm Multilateral Networks: A Comparative Study of Success and Demise," *Administrative Science Quarterly* 45, no. 2 (2000): 327–65; Martin Kilduff and Wenpin Tsai, *Social Networks and Organizations* (Thousand Oaks, CA: SAGE, 2003).

[29] E.g., Powell, "Neither Market nor Hierarchy: Network Forms of Organization."

networks. However, serendipitous networks are often the most appropriate choice to achieve organization-level outcomes (Chapter 2), when problems are chaotic (Chapter 2), and are necessary to develop the trust required for goal-directed networks (Chapter 7).

Research methods

In this book, we draw on both our research and studies conducted by scholars from various disciplines. In particular, we draw from several different types of research we have completed over the last several years to further the conversation and provide illustrations. This research includes the following:

- In-depth interviews with the leaders of nine collaborations that were finalists for or were awarded the Lodestar Collaboration Prize during the past decade. Also, we researched three additional partnerships to add diversity to the types of social impact that networks address. These interviews provide illustrations of the principles that we describe.
- Case studies we have written over the years. They include a case study of the Chicago Benchmarking Collaborative;[30] in-depth case studies of collective impact education initiatives;[31] the study of two networks addressing gender-based violence in Lusaka, Zambia;[32] and a case study of a healthcare collaborative in Canada.[33] Again, these cases bring color to the research we describe.
- Social network analyses focusing on NGO collaboration, including international development NGOs,[34] children's rights NGOs,[35] and a

[30] Michelle Shumate and Liz Livingston Howard, "Making the Most of the Chicago Benchmarking Collaborative," *Kellogg School of Management Cases*, accessed November 8, 2019, https://store.hbr.org/product/making-the-most-of-the-chicago-benchmarking-collaborative/KE1066.

[31] Katherine R. Cooper, "Nonprofit Participation in Collective Impact: A Comparative Case," *Community Development* 48, no. 4 (2017): 499–514, https://doi.org/10.1080/15575330.2017.1332654.

[32] Katherine R. Cooper and Michelle Shumate, "Interorganizational Collaboration Explored through the Bona Fide Network Perspective," *Management Communication Quarterly* 26, no. 4 (2012): 623–54.

[33] H. Brinton Milward, Katherine R. Cooper, and Michelle Shumate, "Who Says a Common Agenda Is Necessary for Collective Impact?," *Nonprofit Quarterly*, 2016, https://nonprofitquarterly.org/who-says-a-common-agenda-is-necessary-for-collective-impact/.

[34] Yannick Atouba and Michelle Shumate, "Interorganizational Networking Patterns Among Development Organizations," *Journal of Communication* 60, no. 2 (2010): 293–317, https://doi.org/10.1111/j.1460-2466.2010.01483.x; Yannick C. Atouba and Michelle Shumate, "International Nonprofit Collaboration Examining the Role of Homophily," *Nonprofit and Voluntary Sector Quarterly* 44, no. 3 (2015): 587–608.

[35] Nina F. O'Brien et al., "How Does NGO Partnering Change Over Time? A Longitudinal Examination of Factors That Influence NGO Partner Selection," *Nonprofit and Voluntary Sector Quarterly*, in press.

longitudinal study of HIV/AIDS international NGOs.[36] These network analyses provide insight into how networks of NGOs self-organize.

- A survey of 852 NGOs from 12 countries described their capacity and relationships with other NGOs, businesses, and government agencies.[37] We use this study to describe typical associations' patterns and the degree to which these differ based on geography, NGO type, and organizational size.
- Finally, we draw from a study of 26 networks in U.S. cities designed to impact youth's educational outcomes. Thirteen of these communities used highly planned, centralized strategies, and the other 13 used self-organizing methods. We compare their structure, processes, and social impact.

The dimensions of networks for social impact

To weave together research from across various academic disciplines, we offer a standard set of terms. Using these terms, we parse whether studies are applicable to all networks or just some types of networks. We use six dimensions to describe these networks: (1) organizational composition, (2) number of organizations, (3) relationship type, (4) network governance, (5) type of social impact, and (6) longevity.

Organizational composition

Organizational composition describes types of organizations in the network. In general, most research emphasizes sector, focusing on the role of NGOs, corporations, and governments in civil society.[38] Of these actors, NGOs and governments have received the most considerable attention. Both sectors

---

[36] Michelle Shumate, Janet Fulk, and Peter R. Monge, "Predictors of the International HIV/AIDS INGO Network over Time," *Human Communication Research* 31 (2005): 482–510, https://doi.org/10.1111/j.1468-2958.2005.tb00880.x.

[37] Michelle Shumate, Jiawei Sophia Fu, and Katherine R. Cooper, "Does Cross-Sector Collaboration Lead to Higher Nonprofit Capacity?," *Journal of Business Ethics* 150, no. 2 (June 1, 2018): 385–99, https://doi.org/10.1007/s10551-018-3856-8.

[38] E.g., Hildy Teegen, Jonathan P. Doh, and Sushil Vachani, "The Importance of Nongovernmental Organizations (NGOs) in Global Governance and Value Creation: An International Business Research Agenda," *Journal of International Business Studies* 35, no. 6 (November 1, 2004): 463–83, https://doi.org/10.1057/palgrave.jibs.8400112; Jens Steffek, "Explaining Cooperation between IGOs and NGOs—Push Factors, Pull Factors, and the Policy Cycle," *Review of International Studies* 39, no. 4 (October 2013): 993–1013, https://doi.org/10.1017/S0260210512000393.

have traditionally been viewed as responsible for the public good, but with different mandates. NGOs are located outside the government and generally do not distribute profits back to owners. In the United States and many European countries, they are governed by a board with fiduciary responsibilities, including responsibilities to fulfill a social mission. They are "owned" by the public.[39] However, NGOs' accountability depends upon the responsiveness of the board to the public.[40] Board members are not elected officials, and there are no mechanisms beyond regulation to influence their actions.[41] In contrast, governments respond to the public in the ways that their form of government dictates. For example, in democratic countries, elections serve as the primary way that the public enacts change.

Traditionally, corporations were not actors in civil society. Instead, in its original form in the 1920s and before,[42] corporate social responsibility focused on individual temperance, morality, and owner generosity. Increasingly corporate social responsibility is defined differently, as the expectations of the public and industry standards have evolved to bring the private sector to bear in civil society.[43] In response, corporate giving has become more focused on "impact," and corporate social responsibility has moved from mere philanthropy to transformative partnerships designed to change corporate operations and communities.[44]

Networks for social impact vary according to the involvement of actors from different sectors. Many networks include organizations from only one sector. These include NGO networks, interagency government networks, and business networks. AgeWell Pittsburgh and the Chicago Benchmarking Collaborative, described at the beginning of this chapter, are nonprofit networks. Both networks include only nonprofits and foundations.

The second type of organizational composition is cross-sector networks. These networks include research into public-private partnerships and

[39] P. Frumkin, *On Being Nonprofit* (Boston, MA: Harvard University Press, 2009).

[40] Anthony J. Spires, "Lessons from Abroad: Foreign Influences on China's Emerging Civil Society," *The China Journal*, no. 68 (2012): 125–46, https://doi.org/10.1086/666577; Patricia Dautel Nobbie and Jeffrey L. Brudney, "Testing the Implementation, Board Performance, and Organizational Effectiveness of the Policy Governance Model in Nonprofit Boards of Directors," *Nonprofit and Voluntary Sector Quarterly* 32, no. 4 (December 1, 2003): 571–95, https://doi.org/10.1177/0899764003257460.

[41] Frumkin, *On Being Nonprofit*.

[42] Morrell Heald, *The Social Responsibilities of Business: Company and Community 1900–1960* (Rutgers, NJ: Transaction Publishers, 1970).

[43] Archie B. Carroll, "The Pyramid of Corporate Social Responsibility: Toward the Moral Management of Organizational Stakeholders," *Business Horizons* 34, no. 4 (1991): 39–48.

[44] Austin and Seitanidi, "Collaborative Value Creation"; Michael E. Porter and Mark R. Kramer, "Philanthropy's New Agenda: Creating Value," *Harvard Business Review* 77, no. 6 (1999): 121–30.

NGO-corporate networks and increasingly networks with actors from all three sectors in complex, multiparty structures. Crescent Moon/Red Rock Crossing Recreation area provides an interesting example. The park is public and part of the U.S. Forest Service. However, the park is managed and run by Recreation Resource Management, a private firm, which returns profits to the U.S. Forest Service. The Chattanooga Museums Collaborative described at the beginning of this chapter provides a salient example of an NGO-government partnership. The joint capital campaign undertaken by the Chattanooga Museums Collaborative was matched by government funding as part of an effort to further develop the city.

In sum, different types of actors compose networks for social impact. Some are single-sector networks, like NGO-NGO partnerships or interagency government networks. Others are cross-sector networks that arise from new relationships between NGOs, government agencies, and businesses.

Number of organizations

One of the key elements differentiating networks is the number of organizations involved. Some network research, our own included, examines networks of organizations engaged in two-party partnerships.[45] Early research on cross-sector social partnerships also had a two-party bias.[46] A set of these partnerships, mapped out by a researcher, can be considered a network. For example, the collection of contracts made by companies using the ASPIRE system described at the beginning of the chapter could be viewed as a network, even though each deal was between two organizations.

Other research examines multiparty partnerships,[47] in which the relationship occurs among a group of organizations. In these partnerships, group dynamics play an essential role in the network processes. Indeed,

---

[45] Atouba and Shumate, "International Nonprofit Collaboration Examining the Role of Homophily"; Shumate, Fulk, and Monge, "Predictors of the International HIV/AIDS INGO Network over Time."

[46] J. W. Selsky, "Lessons in Community Development: An Activist Approach to Stimulating Interorganizational Collaboration," *The Journal of Applied Behavioral Science* 27, no. 1 (1991): 91–115, https://doi.org/10.1177/0021886391271005; Barbara Gray and Jenna Stites, "Sustainability through Partnerships: A Systematic Review" (Ontario, Canada: Network for Business Sustainability, 2013), https://nbs.net/p/sustainability-through-partnerships-a-systematic-revie-e39afcb5-1fe6-4644-90d1-992aaf0918b5.

[47] Gray and Purdy, *Collaborating for Our Future*; Jacqueline N. Hood, Jeanne M. Logsdon, and Judith Kenner Thompson, "Collaboration for Social Problem Solving: A Process Model," *Business & Society* 32, no. 1 (June 1, 1993): 1–17, https://doi.org/10.1177/000765039303200103; Keith G. Provan and Patrick Kenis, "Modes of Network Governance: Structure, Management, and Effectiveness," *Journal of Public Administration Research and Theory* 18, no. 2 (April 1, 2008): 229–52, https://doi.org/10.1093/jopart/mum015.

coalition effectiveness measures focus on things like the goal directedness of the group, the efficiency of meetings, the participation of all parties, and group cohesion.[48]

Relationship types

Relationship types describe the type of connections between organizations in the network. There are several typologies of such relationships. Different disciplines have created their distinct way of talking about the relationships between organizations within the same sector. For NGOs, Sharon Kagan, a professor of early childhood education and family policy, suggested a collaboration continuum.[49] At one end of the continuum, cooperation offers a looser form of partnership, followed by coordination and collaboration. Service integration is a more formalized approach at the other end of the continuum, necessitating a more significant commitment from partners. For governments, Bob Hudson and his colleagues in public policy[50] describe three broad options, ranging from a system of contacts with no clear expectations or commitments to the pooling of resources to serve a single set of objectives. For businesses, Walter Powell and colleagues[51] describe various types of contractual relationships that exist between firms. These include licensing, R&D, finance, and commercialization. Additionally, businesses come together to further their joint agenda, often in industry-based coalitions and standard-setting groups.

Cross-sector collaboration, too, has continuums of relationships. Robert Agranoff classifies public management networks as informational and development networks, outreach networks, and action networks.[52] The key differentiator among these types is the degree to which they engage in joint planning, joint program making, or how the organizations adjust their programs due to the network. James Austin and May Seitanidi, both business scholars,[53] describe different types of relationships between corporations and

---

[48] Valerie B. Shapiro et al., "Measuring Dimensions of Coalition Functioning for Effective and Participatory Community Practice," *Social Work Research* 37, no. 4 (December 2013): 349–59, https://doi.org/10.1093/swr/svt028.

[49] Kagan, *United We Stand: Collaboration for Child Care and Early Education Services.*

[50] Bob Hudson et al., "In Pursuit of Inter-Agency Collaboration in the Public Sector: What Is the Contribution of Theory and Research?," *Public Management (1461667X)* 1, no. 2 (1999): 235–60.

[51] Powell, "Neither Market nor Hierarchy: Network Forms of Organization."

[52] Agranoff, *Managing within Networks.*

[53] James E. Austin and Maria M. Seitanidi, "Collaborative Value Creation: A Review of Partnering between Nonprofits and Businesses: Part I. Value Creation Spectrum and Collaboration Stages," *Nonprofit and Voluntary Sector Quarterly* 41, no. 5 (2012): 726–58.

NGOs on a collaboration continuum that ranges from purely philanthropic to transformational relationships. Beth Gazley and Jeffrey Brudney, both public management scholars,[54] distinguish between government and NGO contracting relationships, informal collaboration, and formal collaboration relationships.

Network governance

Network governance describes how leaders ensure that "participants engage in collective and mutually supportive action, that conflict is addressed, and that network resources are acquired and utilized efficiently and effectively."[55] In Chapter 3, we describe network governance more fully. Here, suffice it to say that network governance has a different focus and forms than organizational governance (e.g., board of directors, the board of trustees). Network governance operates differently for three reasons. First, organizations remain autonomous in networks. Second, networks often have no legal entity for which a governing board would be a fiduciary. Finally, networks rely, at least to some extent, on cooperative behavior in the absence of a legal imperative.

Type of impact

Networks also differ in the type of impact they seek. In self-organized networks, organizations are often seeking individual, organizational benefits. However, in more planned networks, the social impact goals are more diverse.[56] Some networks focus on a single measurable goal related to advocacy, services to clients, or a mix. Alternatively, some are focused on multiple purposes that have varying degrees of relationship to one another. In Chapter 2, we describe some of these goals: organizational learning, innovation, better outcomes for clients, and advocacy.

[54] Beth Gazley and Jeffrey L. Brudney, "The Purpose (and Perils) of Government-Nonprofit Partnership," *Nonprofit and Voluntary Sector Quarterly* 36, no. 3 (September 1, 2007): 389–415, https://doi.org/10.1177/0899764006295997.

[55] Provan and Kenis, "Modes of Network Governance," 231.

[56] see Agranoff, *Managing within Networks*.

Longevity

Finally, networks differ based upon their longevity. Myrna Mandall and Toddi Steelman[57] describe various arrangements that range from intermittent coordination to more long-lasting types. Periodic coordination describes short-term, low-level flow, and low-risk methods, such as coordinating agencies in the case of a disaster (e.g., hurricane, earthquake) or emergent situation (e.g., a shooting in a neighborhood, a chemical spill). Similarly, task forces have limited interaction and are organized for short-term goals, often planning or making joint recommendations. In comparison, partnerships, coalitions, and networks are more enduring, require more generous resource sharing, and are more stable. For example, the Summit Education Initiative was founded nearly 20 years ago (see the case study in this chapter). Regardless of type, some networks are more stable than others.[58] Networks can change their membership, the types of relationships required, governance structures, and goals. The degree of this dynamism has necessary implications for the social impact the network makes.

As evident from the description above, networks can differ in several different ways. However, up to this point, we have not examined how these differences result in achieving social impact or not. Two groups of scholars have studied the compilation of these choices, which we describe in the next section. After we introduce the prior research on the topic, then we present our model of networks for social impact.

Configurational and process approaches to social impact

In this book, we build on the work of two groups of scholars who study networks for social impact, although coming from different fields. One group of scholars, mostly from the public management field, focus on what is known as configurational approaches.[59] The second group of scholars, mainly from

[57] Myrna P. Mandell and Toddi A. Steelman, "Understanding What Can Be Accomplished Through Interorganizational Innovations," *Public Management Review* 5, no. 2 (June 2003): 197–224, https://doi. org/10.1080/1461667032000066417.

[58] Laurie Lewis, "Collaborative Interaction: Review of Communication Scholarship and a Research Agenda," in *Communication Yearbook*, ed. Christina Beck, vol. 30 (Mahwah, NJ: Lawerence Erlbaum, 2006), 197–247.

[59] Weijie Wang, "Exploring the Determinants of Network Effectiveness: The Case of Neighborhood Governance Networks in Beijing," *Journal of Public Administration Research and Theory* 26, no. 2 (April 1, 2016): 375–88, https://doi.org/10.1093/jopart/muv017; Jörg Raab, Remco S. Mannak, and Bart Cambré,

business schools, rely on process[60] approaches to networks' study. These perspectives inform our model, which combines the two into a systems perspective.

Configurational approaches[61] suggest that multiple formulas achieve social impact. These scholars identify how different combinations of factors lead to social impact when they are present together. Notably, any one of these conditions (or the combination of a subset of these conditions) alone doesn't lead to social impact. In short, the whole is more than the sum of the parts.

Alex Turrini, a management professor, and colleagues'[62] systematic literature review provides a good overview of the factors that predict whether a network will make a social impact. In that work, they identify three types of characteristics: contextual, functioning, and structural. Contextual characteristics describe the environment in which the network operates. Factors, such as resource munificence, community support, and system stability, influence network outcomes, even though the network does not control them.[63] Functioning characteristics describe the influence of network processes, like managerial work and the steering network processes. These factors each influence the outcomes that networks are likely to achieve. Finally, structural characteristics describe the setup of the network. They include accountability, network centralization, network density, and formalization. The results of these factors are somewhat mixed.

From the configurational approaches, we gain insight into how combinations of factors influence networks' social impact. Moreover, we agree that there is more than one way to achieve social impact. However, the approach ignores that the choice of some configurations precludes the availability of others. In other words, the characteristics described in these models are

---

"Combining Structure, Governance, and Context: A Configurational Approach to Network Effectiveness," *Journal of Public Administration Research and Theory* 25, no. 2 (April 1, 2015): 479–511, https://doi.org/ 10.1093/jopart/mut039; Daniela Cristofoli and Josip Markovic, "How to Make Public Networks Really Work: A Qualitative Comparative Analysis," *Public Administration* 94, no. 1 (March 2016): 89–110, https:// doi.org/10.1111/padm.12192; Stefan Verweij et al., "What Makes Governance Networks Work? A Fuzzy Set Qualitative Comparative Analysis of 14 Dutch Spatial Planning Projects," *Public Administration* 91, no. 4 (2013): 1035–1055.

[60] Clarke and Fuller, "Collaborative Strategic Management."
[61] Alan D. Meyer, Anne S. Tsui, and C. R. Hinings, "Configurational Approaches to Organizational Analysis," *The Academy of Management Journal* 36, no. 6 (1993): 1175–95, https://doi.org/10.2307/ 256809.
[62] Alex Turrini et al., "Networking Literature About Determinants of Network Effectiveness," *Public Administration* 88, no. 2 (2010): 528–50, https://doi.org/10.1111/j.1467-9299.2009.01791.x.
[63] Some scholars suggest that contextual characteristics moderate the effect of functional and structural features (Provan and Milward, "A Preliminary Theory of Interorganizational Network Effectiveness: A Comparative Study of Four Community Mental Health Systems"); but other scholars describe the relationship as direct (i.e., Raab, Mannak, and Cambré, "Combining Structure, Governance, and Context: A Configurational Approach to Network Effectiveness").

interdependent. For example, the use of a network administrative organization to govern the network lends itself to network management as facilitation instead of directive leadership.[64]

In general, process models describe the stages or sequence of network activity. Most models begin by describing different stages in the network formation process and then proceed into describing network management work ending with some outcomes. These models then complicate matters by asserting that these sequences are not linear, but recursive. Networks may move back and forth along this sequence at different times.

Barbara Gray, an emeritus professor of organizational behavior, offers the most well-known of these models.[65] Her work on collaboration conceptualizes networks for social impact as formed through the process of negotiation. She states, "we view collaboration as the process of negotiating a common set of both norms and routines that will govern future interactions among the participating stakeholders but are subject to revision as stakeholders continually renegotiate their relationship over time."[66] As such, her model of collaboration suggests stages that focus on various agreements. She describes three phases in the collaboration process: problem-setting, direction-setting, and implementation. Problem-setting is a convening phase, where instigators identify stakeholders and resources and establish a standard definition of the problem, and parties commit to the collaboration. Direction-setting describes a set of agreements on how the partnership (or network) will function, including the ground rules, structures, and exploring agreements. The phase closes when participants "reach an agreement" and "close the deal." The implementation phase describes how the network leaders enact a deal and monitor compliance. A variety of stage models focusing similarly on the implementation of negotiated agreements are prominent[67] but do not differ significantly from Gray's model.

Process models offer three key insights that we pick up in this book. First, the design and management choices network leaders make are path dependent. In other words, choices become much more difficult or more likely once network leaders set off down a path. Second, not all options are available

---

[64] Cristofoli and Markovic, "How to Make Public Networks Really Work."

[65] Barbara Gray, *Collaborating: Finding Common Ground for Multiparty Problems* (San Francisco: Jossey-Bass, 1989).

[66] Gray *Collaborating*, 45.

[67] Austin and Seitanidi, "Collaborative Value Creation"; Maria May Seitanidi and Andrew Crane, "Implementing CSR through Partnerships: Understanding the Selection, Design and Institutionalisation of Nonprofit-Business Partnerships," *Journal of Business Ethics* 85 (2009): 413–29; Hood, Logsdon, and Thompson, "Collaboration for Social Problem Solving."

to all networks—the environment in which a network operates influences each step of the network formation and management process. Finally, network design alone does not determine success. Ultimately, a combination of environmental conditions and the theory of change does.

One contribution of this book is that it brings configurational approaches and process models together. Configurational approaches take a snapshot of networks' work, which is dynamic by its very nature. For example, steering processes and managerial work changes over time. Process models inherently address this dynamism. However, process models offer little prescription about the most effective way to organize a network. The models provide a general formulation for how networks unfold and a retrospective assessment of why they unfolded as they did, implicitly suggesting a singular, windy path to achieving social impact.

In *Networks for Social Impact*, we contend that there are multiple ways that networks can make a social impact. However, network design is the result of a dynamic process. Choices that network leaders make in the design and management of these networks depend on agreements made at the outset of a process. In bringing the two perspectives together in a systems approach to social impact, we address the limitations of the two approaches and shed new light into *how* networks can make a social impact.

Axioms of this book

We introduce a systems approach to integrate the configurational and the process approaches. A system comprises both actors and resources and the set of relationships between them.[68] However, the interactions among the elements in the system can combine in unexpected ways. In other words, the whole is more than the sum of the parts. Much like process models, a systems approach suggests that elements interact over time through feedback loops and are sensitive to their environment. With this as a grounding, we present the five axioms of our approach to networks for social impact (see Box 1.1).

---

[68] Pennie G. Foster-Fishman, Branda Nowell, and Huilan Yang, "Putting the System Back into Systems Change: A Framework for Understanding and Changing Organizational and Community Systems," *American Journal of Community Psychology* 39, no. 3–4 (June 1, 2007): 197–215, https://doi.org/10.1007/s10464-007-9109-0; Marshall Scott Poole, "Systems Theory," in *The SAGE Handbook of Organizational Communication: Advances in Theory, Research, and Methods*, eds. Linda L. Putnam and Dennis K. Mumby (Thousand Oaks, CA: SAGE, 2014), 49–74; Dale Ainsworth and Ann E. Feyerherm, "Higher Order Change: A Transorganizational System Diagnostic Model," *Journal of Organizational Change Management* 29, no. 5 (August 8, 2016): 769–81, https://doi.org/10.1108/JOCM-11-2015-0209.

Box 1.1 Axioms of Networks for Social Impact

1. Outcomes are interdependent.
2. Networks for social impact are sensitive to their environment.
3. Networks' dilemmas are never solved, just managed within constraints.
4. Not all networks organized for social impact achieve that impact.
5. There is more than one path to achieving social impact.

---

1. Outcomes are interdependent

Researchers readily acknowledge that networks result in outcomes at different levels[69] (more on these levels in Chapter 2). As we suggested in the previous section, networks for social impact typically experience outcomes at four levels (i.e., individual, organizational, network, and social impact). However, most network research usually ignores the extent to which these outcomes may affect one another. Consider, for instance, an organization that experiences benefits resulting from being in a network, such as a boost in reputation or funding. A bump in status might make an organization a more desirable partner, leading to network growth. Increased funding may allow an organization to dedicate more resources to the network and contribute to the network's survival. The longevity of the network may, in turn, enable partners to become more adept at responding to a social concern, resulting in social impact.

This hypothetical example illustrates a systems approach.[70] In a systems view, network interaction transforms inputs into outputs that occur at different levels. System components—the organizations in the network—are related to each other through *interdependencies*.

In axiom one, we suggest that outcomes are interdependent as well. Outcomes at the individual and organizational levels influence network-level outcomes. Outcomes at the network level can influence social impact. And social impact has implications for both network- and organization-level outcomes. We identify three ways that outcomes at different levels influence each other: competition, aggregation, and temporal asynchronicity.

Competition refers to when outcomes of one level reduce results at another level. For example, networks for social impact may balance a social impact

---

[69] J. K. Popp et al., "Inter-Organizational Networks," Collaboration across Boundaries Series (Washington, DC: IBM Center for the Business of Government, 2014).
[70] Ainsworth and Feyerherm, "Higher Order Change."

goal, such as reducing the high school dropout rate, with implicit goals of net-work survival. A network that emerges in response to a community crisis may adopt processes to meet its explicit goals of improving educational outcomes. However, this network is likely to utilize other methods that serve implicit purposes such as fundraising, appeasing key stakeholders or donors, or revamping the leadership structure to ensure sustainability. Often these goals compete for leaders' attention and resources.

Outcomes can also reinforce one another through *aggregation*. Aggregation describes when the accumulation of outcomes at one level results in benefits at a higher level. For example, many social impact networks use organizational learning as a lever to promote systems change. The logic model is aggrega-tion. If organizations learn to enact evidence-based practices as a group, those improved practices will result in better outcomes for an entire community.

Finally, outcomes influence one another through *temporal interdepend-ence*. It occurs when results at one level influence the pace of results at an-other level. For instance, a network may find that it needs to continue to enact a series of changes, in keeping with a model of continuous quality improve-ment. However, some organizational members may lack the capacity to make changes at the same rate as the network. Thus, organizational members' rates of change may slow the network's ability to make changes.

2. Networks for social impact are sensitive to their environment

Networks for social impact are continually learning from, adjusting to, and compensating for changes in their environment. *The environment* is vital in open-systems theories and refers to that which is outside the system's boundary but relevant to the system.[71] In particular, we draw attention to three ways that network organizing implicates the environment. First, networks often emerge from a problem identified in the environment, which we describe in Chapter 2 as a "wicked problem." Second, resources in the environment are crucial to de-termining what types of organizing are viable. Third and finally, as the environ-ment changes, so do social change networks embedded in them.

First, the environment may act as a catalyst for networks for social impact; for example, organizations may come together because of a perceived oppor-tunity for policy creation concerning a social issue or a particular crisis that

---

[71] Poole, "Systems Theory."

triggers a new way of thinking. We describe how social problems emerge further in Chapter 2.

Second, resources in the environment can enable or constrain social impact networks. These include financial resources, infrastructure (e.g., databases, reliable power), and public attention.[72] Janice Popp and colleagues'[73] review of research suggests the following preconditions for networks: the technological capacity to support organizations' coordinated efforts; public support or consensus on the social issue at hand; government support for collaboration; or sector-specific resources, such as policy frameworks or financial resources.[74] We'll talk more about the effect of resources in Chapter 4.

Third, social impact networks respond to changes in their environment. In Barbara Gray's more recent work with Jill Purdy,[75] she notes that the joint agreements that network leaders make are influenced by and influence the broader societal discourse about social issues. In the cases described in this book, policy decisions impact the network's activities, and changes in government dictate changes in the resources they have to do their work. Florence Young, the former director of the Westbrook Children's Project, pointed out that her state was cutting back on budgets for direct service organizations, Medicaid, and other projects designed to help people that the network serves. In Akron, leaders in the Summit Education Initiative noted that "the changing landscape in public education" was frustrating because the tests used to measure student outcomes were subject to constant change. In Racine, Higher Expectations leaders were trying to navigate a political climate in which suburban elected officials were considering splitting up the broader Racine Unified School District. Networks for social impact are continually in flux.

3. Network dilemmas are never solved, just managed within constraints

The concept of *process* is central to the idea of systems models. Process describes coordinated changes in the system that are causally or functionally

---

[72] Cooper and Shumate, "Interorganizational Collaboration Explored through the Bona Fide Network Perspective."

[73] Popp et al., "Inter-Organizational Networks."

[74] T. R. Rose, "Research Project Report: Evolution, Development, and Maintenance of the Southern Alberta Child and Youth Health Network," *Center for Health and Policy Studies at the University of Calgary,* 2004; Popp et al., "Inter-Organizational Networks."

[75] Gray and Purdy, *Collaborating for Our Future.*

linked,[76] system structure changes,[77] or systems and component change and development over time.[78] In Janice Popp and colleagues'[79] comprehensive review of networks, researchers identified several different network processes, including service implementation and delivery, diffusion of information, problem-solving, and community capacity-building.

In this book, we build upon the work of Professors Amelia Clarke and Mark Fuller. They offer a four-stage systems model. The stages are context/partnership formation, collaborative strategic plan formulation, deliberate and emergent strategy implementation, and realized strategic outcomes. Most importantly, for axiom three, the model includes multiple feedback loops. *Feedback loops*[80] refer to the idea that causes become effects or that variables in the loop impact other factors. In their model, Clarke and Fuller suggest that networks return to previous phases due to feedback.

We depart from their model by adding path dependence. Path dependence describes how the series of choices that actors make lock networks into a particular configuration and set of outcomes.[81] Lock-in occurs because past decisions condition the choices available to network leaders in the future and are self-reinforcing. We combine path dependence and feedback loops in our model.

We think of combining the two concepts in terms of an old Buddhist proverb, "one can never enter the same stream twice." Similarly, networks receive feedback on their processes, structures, and resource allocations. However, they do not get to redo those choices again based on that feedback. Instead, the "water" has continued to flow and the context for the new choice is fundamentally different. At that point, the options available to them and the potential outcomes of those choices differ from earlier stages.

Education for All provides a helpful illustration. Kate attended two years of meetings at a network we are calling Education for All (see also the case in Chapter 3). Local NGO leaders, having read the 2011 issue of the *Stanford Social Innovation Review* that introduced the term "collective impact," were

[76] Marshall Scott Poole, "On the Study of Process in Communication Research," *Annals of the International Communication Association* 36, no. 1 (2013): 371–409; Nicholas Rescher, *Process Metaphysics: An Introduction to Process Philosophy* (New York: SUNY Press, 1996).

[77] William P. Barnett, "The Dynamics of Competitive Intensity," *Administrative Science Quarterly* 42, no. 1 (1997), 128–60.

[78] Poole, "On the Study of Process in Communication Research."

[79] Popp et al., "Inter-Organizational Networks."

[80] Clarke and Fuller, "Collaborative Strategic Management"; Gray and Purdy, *Collaborating for Our Future.*

[81] Jean-Philippe Vergne and Rodolphe Durand, "The Missing Link Between the Theory and Empirics of Path Dependence: Conceptual Clarification, Testability Issue, and Methodological Implications," *Journal of Management Studies* 47, no. 4 (2010): 736–59, https://doi.org/10.1111/j.1467-6486.2009.00913.x.

interested in undertaking coordinated, cross-sector initiatives to achieve more significant outcomes. Around the same time, incidents of gun violence rocked the city. Local teenagers' deaths and an awareness of disparities in the opportunities for local youth unsettled community leaders. They were convinced that some sort of intervention was necessary, and the rising popularity of the collective impact model provided the vehicle for this change. To get buy-in from the community, they convened a council of leaders from the nonprofit sector, local school districts, and the city. Two years after the initial steering committee began meeting, leaders began to hold community meetings to form task groups. Under pressure to show some results for their work, the leaders decided that literacy would be the first issue they addressed.

At that point, leaders received feedback about their choice. The local school district produced a report that revealed racial disparities, and other community members *not* a part of Education for All rose in protest. At an Education for All meeting shortly after that, leaders acknowledged a need to revise their process, admitting that the activities they were doing—and the ways they were organizing these activities—weren't doing anything to address equity. Ultimately, they began to talk about ways of adjusting their process to invite diverse participants and include activities that championed equity, such as diversity training and book drives to reach underserved areas in the community. In making equity more of an explicit goal, Education for All alienated some existing network members. Recruiting new people interested in equity initiatives also proved challenging because of the impression that Education for All hadn't been involved in equity at its inception.[82]

Feedback loops prompted Education for All leaders to make adjustments that included the restructuring of their network. However, they couldn't go back to the beginning of their network formation. Instead, there were forces to navigate retrofitting the network for equity goals, alienating some members, and making the recruitment of others more difficult. In short, path dependence created a different place in a "stream." Although an equity goal at the outset might have been challenging, retrofitting equity as a goal produced a different set of challenges.

Network dilemmas illustrate axiom three well.[83] Network dilemmas are never wholly resolved because they require the management of tensions or the pull between two opposing values.[84] For example, in social impact networks,

[82] Katherine R. Cooper, "Disconnect, Collide, Diverge: Tracing Diversity Discourse in Community Collaboration" (National Communication Association (NCA) Conference, convened virtually, 2020).
[83] Popp et al., "Inter-Organizational Networks" for a review.
[84] Gail T. Fairhurst et al., "Diverging and Converging: Integrative Insights on a Paradox Meta-Perspective," *The Academy of Management Annals* 10, no. 1 (January 1, 2016): 173–82, https://doi.org/

leaders often wear two hats: one representing their home organization and another representing their work in the network.[85] Managing these dual loyalties represents a network dilemma. Managers cannot solve it once and for all. Instead, at different times, they must prioritize one value or the other. But, as network leaders repeatedly prioritize one side of the tension, the feedback builds up in the form of the opposite value needing a response. For example, network leaders that ask their members to spend a significant amount of time in network meetings can expect to receive pushback as organizational leaders try to reassert that their organization also requires their time and energy. Throughout the remainder of this book, we refer to these tensions as *network dilemmas.*[86]

4. Not all networks organized for social impact achieve that impact

Networks for social impact offer potential benefits as well as limitations. Networks have the potential to benefit communities and can result in real and lasting social change. Throughout this book, we profile some networks—such as AgeWell Pittsburgh, the Westside Infant-Family Network in Los Angeles (WIN), Graduate Philadelphia, and Multi-Agency Alliance for Children (MAAC)—that have demonstrated the difference that interorganizational collaboration makes. These networks have resulted in measurable health or educational outcomes for hundreds of thousands of people.

However, networks may fall short of their social impact aspirations for several reasons. For some networks, social impact is not the goal (see Chapter 2). In other cases, network leaders may in good faith peruse social impact, but fail to make any systemic difference in their social issues. Others may prematurely

10.1080/19416520.2016.1162423; Linda L. Putnam, Gail T. Fairhurst, and Scott Banghart, "Contradictions, Dialectics, and Paradoxes in Organizations: A Constitutive Approach," *The Academy of Management Annals* 10, no. 1 (January 1, 2016): 65–171, https://doi.org/10.1080/19416520.2016.1162421; Jonathan Schad et al., "Paradox Research in Management Science: Looking Back to Move Forward," *The Academy of Management Annals* 10, no. 1 (January 1, 2016): 5–64, https://doi.org/10.1080/19416520.2016.1162422.

[85] H. Brinton Milward and Keith G. Provan, *A Manager's Guide to Choosing and Using Collaborative Networks*, vol. 8 (Washington, DC: IBM Center for the Business of Government, 2006).

[86] Organizational paradox, tension, and dilemmas are related but distinct terms. All have been used in network and management research, and our usage of "dilemma" is different from some research that would suggest that dilemmas can be resolved. Throughout this text, we refer to "network dilemmas" because it suggests the managerial implications for network leaders, who must continually monitor and negotiate contradicting demands. Although the underlying contradictions may never be resolved, managers experience dilemmas as moments in which they must weigh their options and make choices. Putnam, Fairhurst, and Banghart, "Contradictions, Dialectics, and Paradoxes in Organizations."

claim that the network had affected community change when the outcome occurred at the organizational or network levels. And networks disband as a consequence of strategy or negligence.

Throughout this book, we'll identify ways that networks fall short of their social impact aspirations. We refer to these pitfalls as *dead ends*. In Chapter 8, we summarize the seven deadly ends on the road to social impact. These dead ends are an essential complement to axiom 5. In short, although there is more than one path to achieving social impact, all roads don't lead there.

5. There is more than one path to achieving social impact

Configurational approaches highlight there is often more than one formula for achieving social impact. This insight is crucial because not all networks have the same raw materials. Some networks have an inspirational leader who can cast a compelling vision for the network and navigates complicated inter-personal and organizational dynamics with ease. Indeed, such a leader would be instrumental in creating social impact. However, some networks do not have such a leader among their stakeholders. Are they without hope? The an-swer in this book is a resounding no. Yes, a charismatic leadership model, with the right other conditions, might yield social impact. But there are different paths to impact in the absence of such a leader.

We build on the work on configurational scholars who have investigated the alternative paths to social impact. One of the critical aspects of the con-figurational approach is that the combination of characteristics, not just a single component (i.e., an inspirational leader), influences social impact outcomes. For example, in their study of mental health delivery networks, Keith Provan and Brint Milward[87] found a highly centralized network with fewer ties between providers, direct state control, high resource munificence, and stable mechanisms for awarding funding each contributed to better client outcomes.[88] In this research, centralization alone did not explain why Providence's mental health network was more effective than Tucson's. Instead, a combination of these factors did.

Moreover, different combinations of factors can add up to social impact. For example, Jörg Raab, Remco Mannak, and Bart Cambré,[89] organizational

---

[87] Provan and Milward, "A Preliminary Theory of Interorganizational Network Effectiveness: A Comparative Study of Four Community Mental Health Systems."

[88] They hoped to include case managers' or therapists' views as well but found that these views dramati-cally diverged from family and client views of client outcomes.

[89] Raab, Mannak, and Cambré, "Combining Structure, Governance, and Context: A Configurational Approach to Network Effectiveness."

studies scholars from the Netherlands, examined 39 crime prevention networks' effectiveness. They measured social impact as a significant reduction of recidivism over two years. They identified two different combinations of factors that both led to social impact. In path one, networks had existed for three years, had higher integration, and had more significant resources. In path two, networks had existed for at least three years, had stable funding, and had a centralized governance structure. Both paths led to social impact.

Similarly, other scholars[90] have found that networks can alternatively take a network management approach, based on strong governance and leadership, or a formalized coordination mechanism approach, with formal contracts and procedures, to alternatively reach social impact.[91] The two configurations are substitutable formulas for achieving social impact. Weijie Wang's public policy dissertation research goes even further,[92] suggesting that some network configurations might be necessary for some communities but unnecessary in others.[93]

In sum, axiom five suggests that there is more than one way that networks can achieve social impact. There is no single factor that explains this impact, but instead, the combination of choices that networks make each influences its likelihood. The outcomes of particular configurations will depend upon the type of social impact that the network aims to make (Chapter 2), the environment it is embedded in (axiom two), and the sequence of those choices (axiom three).

The plan of the book

This book describes how interorganizational networks can make a significant social impact. We then take a deep dive into each design element, represent

---

[90] Cristofoli and Markovic, "How to Make Public Networks Really Work."

[91] Cristfoli and Makovic studied 12 Swiss home and social care service networks and found a different role for network administrative organization governance. They define network effectiveness as the ability of the network to serve as many patients with as many services at the lowest cost possible. They find two paths to network effectiveness. Both routes, in their research, include governance led by network administrative organizations and resource munificence. However, in the presence of both of these factors, a network could become effective by adopting one of two paths. They could take a network management approach where a distinct actor or set of actors engage in facilitating network activities, mediating conflict, and promoting a vision for the network that activates members, that centralized governance and stronger network management. In contrast, in the absence of such network management, they could adopt formalized coordination mechanisms, such as well-organized meetings, contractual arrangements, and formalized procedures.

[92] Wang, "Exploring the Determinants of Network Effectiveness."

[93] Wang's studied 22 neighborhood governance networks in Beijing. He defined network effectiveness as homeowner's ratings of neighborhood cleanliness, safety, and maintenance of neighborhood facilities. There were two ways that network governance networks became effective. They could have high resource munificence and network stability, defined as whether the network was planning on making any changes to the distribution of resources among members. Or, they could have a neighborhood with resource munificence, high average socioeconomic status of residence, and low network centralization.

the academic literature, and review our research on this topic. In Chapter 2, we investigate how instigators frame social problems. The frames influence whether the network will achieve social impact. We introduce the typology of social impact that disciplines our thinking about the network configurations that are both possible and preferable. We also note that there are many circumstances where social impact is not the network's goal, but positive individual, organizational, or network outcomes result.

In Chapter 3, we investigate the various elements of network assembly. We begin the chapter by describing the different roles that network instigators can take. We then demonstrate how decisions made earlier in the process influence multiple aspects of network design, including recruiting strategy, membership requirements, functions and governance structure, legitimacy building, and funding. Throughout this chapter, we highlight network design elements that are more likely and less likely to lead to social impact.

Next, we turn to the influence of funding and resources on networks' social impact. Networks are generally a more expensive way to coordinate organizational activity. Chapter 4 describes the different types of resources typically required to achieve social impact, including money, technology, and time. In particular, we acknowledge the significance of funders in recognizing and resourcing interorganizational networks. However, foundation funding can also hinder social impact by setting deadlines too early for the network to achieve social impact, encouraging networks to focus on short-term wins, and requiring sustainability plans in the early stages of network emergence. We conclude with recommendations for both funders and network leaders.

Chapter 5 presents one of the biggest challenges that network leaders face after establishing the network and securing funding: addressing power and conflict. Networks bring together organizations with different resources, which often have different amounts of power. These power differentials provide opportunities for exploitation and conflict. Also, by increasing the interaction and interdependency among organizations, networks can catalyze conflict between partners and undermine the efforts of small, grassroots organizations. Finally, networks can galvanize communities that disagree with their goals or how the network spends its resources. We conclude with recommendations for managing both organization-network and community-network conflict.

In Chapter 6, we explore one of the most challenging but essential elements necessary for producing social impact—using data effectively. The network context makes the challenges of collecting data for organizational use more complicated. Partners struggle to gather appropriate and comparable data, share data across various sectors and partners, and measure results of network interventions. In this chapter, networks that use different mechanisms to achieve social impact can use data to support their efforts.

Networks navigate changes in their environment as they respond to complex social problems. In Chapter 7, we argue that networks must remain agile and flexible to sustain their social impact. We focus on concepts from organizational learning and organizational systems, such as feedback loops, to demonstrate how successful networks pick up cues from their environment and adjust their activities. Furthermore, we describe crossroads moments, where a network must change or disband. Finally, we highlight examples of networks that have successfully adapted their network, overcoming the loss of partners or environmental changes.

Chapter 8 synthesizes the arguments from the book. We return to the axioms laid out in this chapter, demonstrating how concepts from the other chapters provide further context and grounding for each. We describe the implications for scholars, practitioners, and funders. We also review the dead ends, dilemmas, and pathways to social impact described throughout this book.

Networks for Social Impact is about the multiple ways that organizations and their leaders try, and sometimes do, achieve gains that would not be possible alone. We have written this book as a bridge between the network leaders we talk to every week and the academic researchers that study them. We hope that students will find inspiration in this book's pages as they take their place leading and participating in these networks.

Case study: Summit Education Initiative

In 1994, a group of philanthropic leaders and big business CEOs started the Summit Education Initiative. The initial vision was a socioeconomic one, to "increase the economic vitality of the community." To achieve this vision, they determined that the root cause of low economic development was a lack of higher education. Their logic model posits that more education will lead to higher wages and happier lives, and through this increased economic prosperity, the Akron, Ohio, community will become stronger.

However, in 2010, the network nearly shut its doors. The small programs they were operating were not scalable or creating systematic improvement. The board ended or transitioned all their programs, and the affiliated staff. According to Derran Wimer, when he began as the executive director of the Summit Education Initiative in 2011, there were a "lot of broken promises," and the relationship with the community was fractured. The first year, he began a "massive listening tour and environmental scan, understanding the landscape, challenges, issues, and then building this model out." He continues "then we started to build the organization back, and because we did it in that way, we're enjoying incredible confidence, and additional resources come our way that are unsolicited . . . it was a kind of a resurrection of the organization." Eventually, they joined the StriveTogether Network, an umbrella organization for cradle-to-career collective impact networks.

The Summit Education Initiative now boasts a membership of 327 businesses, schools, higher education institutions, nonprofits, out-of-school providers, healthcare organizations, and philanthropy organizations. They have an annual budget of $1.2 million. Just a few of their current initiatives include additional training for public school counselors, free practice ACTs and math prep courses for high school students, partnerships with out-of-school time partners to improve student grades (and share data), middle school math teachers' circles to share best practices, and distributing 3,000 success kits for parents of incoming kindergarteners each year.

They use a highly tractable approach to improve outcomes along the cradle-to-career pipeline. First, they use data to identify the issues that need addressing. For example, they collect data from every preschool student in the area before they begin kindergarten. They can use that data to identify preschools that are achieving more substantial results and preschools that need attention. Second, they mobilize their teams and align funding to address identified problems. Third, they use statistical models to identify leading indicators of success, including a B average or above in 9th grade, math proficiency in 8th grade, reading proficiency in 3rd grade, and developing emotional regulation skills in preschool. All of these indicators point to Summit's final goal, 48,000 new post-secondary degrees by 2025.

Questions to consider

1. What types of outcomes does the Summit network produce (e.g., individual, organizational, network, and social impact)? How are those outcomes interdependent?
2. How did Summit's early phase and near-death experiences create the circumstances for the current network?
3. As a network focusing on education, what environmental factors influence the Summit initiative?
4. What challenges do Summit leaders face in leading a large network?

Tools for network instigators

In almost all chapters of this book, we include a section entitled "Tools for network instigators." The purpose of these sections is to give practical guidance to individuals and institutions interested in starting, managing, or changing a network. These tools provide practical advice into how a network can make a social impact or scale their efforts to create an even larger one. For scholars and students reading this book, these sections also draw from the best wisdom we have gained over the years working with networks. They include tools that we have seen networks use successfully and may provide insight into issues that the academic literature neglects.

Chapter 1 introduces the cases that *Networks for Social Impact* uses to illustrate many of its points. We hope by describing these cases here, practitioners may find a few that closely resemble their networks or the one that they aspire to start. For scholars and students, these cases illustrate the breadth and diversity of the networks that aim to create social impact.

AgeWell Pittsburgh

https://agewellpgh.org/
Focus: Senior care
Type of Activity: Service provision and learning
Location: Pittsburgh, PA, USA

AgeWell Pittsburgh is a collaboration between the Jewish Association on Aging, Jewish Community Center of Greater Pittsburgh, Jewish Family and Children's Services in Pittsburgh, and the Jewish Federation of Greater Pittsburgh. The collaboration began in 2004 and won the 2017 Lodestar Collaboration Prize. The Jewish Federation of Greater Pittsburgh convened the partnership around a Naturally Occurring Retirement Communities (NORC) grant. The first collaboration was a social worker-centered model that helped seniors navigate the range of services available. However, after the NORC grant restructured, they found that the model to be too expensive. AgeWell Pittsburgh now serves as the gateway to coordinated programs and services across the three agencies. They use a standard set of outcomes to measure their successes. Their outcome data demonstrates that AgeWell Pittsburgh seniors have better results than Medicare recipients nationwide.

AmericaServes networks

https://americaserves.org/
Focus: Veterans services
Type of Activity: Integrated referral system
Location: 17 networks in the USA

AmericaServes is the United States' first coordinated system of public, private, and nonprofit organizations working together in communities to serve veterans, transitioning service members, and their families. They improve access to a full range of care and supportive services through systems change. The AmericaServes model promotes service accessibility through systems alignment—namely a shared referral system, which reduces the transaction costs of coordinating services and addresses co-occurring needs that span social, public health, and medical services. AmericaServes currently has 17 networks, each operating in a different city. They use a common technological and analytics platform but vary on a range of factors such as number and types of providers, stage of development, types of organizations coordinating the network, funding strategies, geographic coverage, and community context.

ASPIRE program

https://aspire.csiro.au/about
Focus: Reduction of waste to landfill, reduce business costs
Type of Activity: Online marketplace
Location: Melbourne, Australia

The Advisory System for Processing, Innovation and Resource Exchange (ASPIRE) is a business-to-business resource exchange network for small- to medium-sized enterprises begun in 2015. Their goal is to divert industrial waste from landfills by encouraging other businesses to use that waste as inputs in their business processes. Aligned with principles such as the circular economy and industrial symbiosis, the network uses a technology platform and ASPIRE staff's knowledge about industrial engineering, ecology, and operations to match businesses. More than 3,000 businesses are using ASPIRE. From the sample of case studies collected, businesses have saved $207,000 in material and waste disposal costs. Through reuse and waste diversion, the region benefits from reducing waste to landfill and CO_2 emissions.

Blue Ribbon Commission on the Prevention of Youth Violence (now Voyage)

http://voyagewilmington.org/
Focus: Education and violence prevention
Type of Activity: Mentorship, family-focused social work, and community engagement
Location: Wilmington, NC, USA

The Blue Ribbon Commission, now Voyage, was founded in 2008 in response to a surge in gun violence. The network was modeled on the Harlem Children's Zone model and focuses on a 140-square block area on the just-north side of downtown Wilmington. The network includes more than 35 organizations, including local businesses, nonprofits, schools, and government agencies. During their tenure, they have worked to reopen a middle school serving the community. In 2019, they expanded their focus to their community advocate model. In that program, an advocate helps families set goals and connect them to services. They have also expanded their summer youth employment program.

Chattanooga Museums Collaborative

http://www.huntermuseum.org/brookings-paper/
Focus: Community arts and education
Type of Activity: Various, including fundraising, joint programs
Location: Chattanooga, TN, USA

The Chattanooga Museums Collaborative is a partnership between the Creative Discovery Museum, the Hunter Museum of American Art, and the Tennessee Aquarium. The Creative Discovery Museum and the Tennessee Aquarium initiated their relationship in 1995, and the Hunter Museum of American Art joined in 2000. The three museums shared the back-office costs associated with human resource management, bookkeeping, human resources management, and information communication technology management. Over time, the collaboration grew to include the 21st Century Waterfront Plan. There was a fundraising effort initiated by Bob Corker, then-mayor of Chattanooga. Together with the city, the group jointly raised $120 million. One of the unique characteristics was a memorandum of understanding that stipulated that "they wouldn't allow donors to cherry-pick," meaning that the funds raised were budgeted together. The network was a 2009 finalist for the Lodestar Foundation Collaboration Prize.

Chicago Benchmarking Collaborative

https://christopherhouse.org/chicago-benchmarking-collaborative/
Focus: Education
Type of Activity: Benchmarking and learning
Location: Chicago, IL, USA

In 2008, Christopher House applied for a grant from the Chicago Community Trust for software that would enable them to better track their early childhood and adult education programs' performance. The Chicago Community Trust suggested their application would be far more successful if they joined other similar organizations to fund program improvement. From that request, the Chicago Benchmarking Collaborative was born. It is a network of six agencies. They conduct no shared programs but use a shared measurement system to track the outcomes of their programs. In doing so, they can benchmark their results, develop goals and plans for improving outcomes, and hold each other accountable for those efforts.

The Climate Accord

https://www.klimaatakkoord.nl/
Focus: Climate change
Type of Activity: Establish a legal agreement
Location: Hague, Netherlands

In the Netherlands, NGOs, government agencies, and businesses came together both in 2013 and 2018 to establish a climate agreement for the next five years. The current climate agreement's goal is to reduce CO_2 emissions by at least 49% by 2030. The climate accord has been developed through sector tables, where many organizational leaders, through consensus, came to agreements about particular areas. Organizations and companies are invited based on whether they can make "tangible contribution(s) to the changes that are necessary within the sector, can contribute knowledge about the sector, and (also) make agreements on behalf of others." Through this process, the Netherlands has developed one of the most ambitious laws for addressing climate change and sets a higher standard than the Paris Climate Accords.

Community Reach (pseudonym)

Focus: Education
Type of Activity: Collective impact
Location: Midwest, USA

In 2012, the Community Reach network began as a community economic development initiative. It was a network that brought together business leaders and educators to increase the percentage of residents in their region that had a post-secondary degree to 60%. The network has changed its goals many times during its seven years of existence.

Education for All (pseudonym)

Focus: Education
Type of Activity: Joint programs
Location: Midwest, USA

Founded in 2012, the Education for All network set out to be a collective impact network that prepared every child for post-secondary education or careers. It was initially convened by the local community foundation, in partnership with the high school superintendent and the head of the local YMCA. In 2018, it was a partnership of approximately 40 organizations and 150 community volunteers that focused on improving equitable educational outcomes for the community. The network continues to formulate its model for collaboration, incorporating elements of the collective impact framework with aspects of the asset-based community development approach.

Gender-Based Violence Coalitions Zambia (multiple)

Focus: Gender-based violence
Type of Activity: Joint programs and referrals
Location: Lusaka, Zambia

Gender-based violence is "any act of violence that results in, or is likely to result in physical, sexual or psychological harm or suffering to women, including threats of such acts, coercion, or arbitrary deprivations of liberty, occurring in public or private life."[94] In a comparative case study, we focus on two networks.[95] The first network, including 8 nonprofits and two government organizations, was convened by international development agencies and included international NGOs. The second network, created through grassroots organizing, had at least 15 organizations, though membership was more fluid than in the first network. The second network included many Zambian and African NGOs and fewer international NGOs.

The Graduate! Network/Graduate! Philadelphia

https://www.graduatephiladelphia.org/
Focus: Post-secondary education
Type of Activity: Joint programs and referrals
Location: Philadelphia, PA, USA

Economic development, workforce, and higher education leaders in Philadelphia recognized an opportunity in 2005; nearly 300,000 Philadelphians had started college but not completed it. Based on the recognition that this was not a single organization's problem, an ecosystem problem, a diverse set of stakeholders, was brought into the collaboration. These included college leaders, the United Way, an economic development agency, workforce investment boards, employers interested in expanding their workforce, the mayor's office, consumer credit counseling agencies, the library, and local nonprofits. The group worked in committees to establish services and coaching that enabled their participants to succeed. The program has been successful by many standards. In Philadelphia, it has served upward of 8,000 low-income individuals. There have been over 2,000 people who graduated from college. Of those who started the program, an astounding 80% remain continuously enrolled in post-secondary institutions, and 43% graduate in five years. And the program has been replicated by others around the country through the Graduate! Network, reaching over 80,000 comebackers. It was a 2011 Lodestar Collaboration Prize Finalist.

---

[94] United Nations, "Human Development Report 2003" (United Nations), 275, accessed November 23, 2019, http://hdr.undp.org/en/content/human-development-report-2003.
[95] Cooper and Shumate, "Interorganizational Collaboration Explored through the Bona Fide Network Perspective."

Higher Expectations for Racine County

https://www.higherexpectationsracinecounty.org/
Focus: Education and workforce development
Type of Activity: Systems alignment
Location: Racine, WI, USA

Higher Expectations for Racine County started in 2014. The mission of the network is to create a fully capable and employed workforce for Racine County. The network has 40 participating organizations, including several government agencies. These include the University of Wisconsin Parkside, Gateway Technical College, Racine Unified Public Schools, the public library, human services, workforce development, the police department, the Racine city government, and the health department. The initiative has many data-sharing agreements and takes a continuous quality improvement approach. A network administrative organization with six full-time staff and three part-time employees on loan from or shared with other organizations leads the network. It is part of the StriveTogether network.

LawHelp New York Consortium

https://www.lawhelpny.org/
Focus: Legal Aid
Type of Activity: Create common repository of information
Location: New York, USA

LawHelp was created in 2000, in the very early years of the internet, as an online legal information and referral platform for New York City initially and then New York State. It began as a collaboration among just a few legal services organizations—The City Bar Justice Center, the Legal Aid Society, Legal Services NYC, Pro Bono Net, and Volunteers of Legal Services—it grew by 2009 to include a dozen partners statewide. The organizations jointly fundraised to create the technology platform and to hire staff to collect and manage referral information and curate straightforward language legal rights information sourced from partner organizations across the state. In 2002, Pro Bono Net, a founding member specializing in developing technology services to improve access to justice, received grants that allowed them to replicate the platform in over 25 other U.S. states. The network has traditionally measured their success by examining website traffic but are now developing measures of how organizations and individuals use the information from the site to make a social impact. The program was a 2009 Lodestar Collaboration Prize finalist.

My Brother's Keeper, Mt. Vernon, NY

https://www.mtvernoncsd.org/Page/7444
Focus: Education
Type of Activity: Programs
Location: Mt. Vernon, NY

The My Brother's Keeper Alliance in Mt. Vernon's primary mission is to close the achievement gap that impacts young men of color. This network was founded in 2016 in Mt. Vernon, New York. In 2017, they had working groups that focus on grade-level outcomes, graduating from high school, entering the workforce, and living violence free. The superintendent's office, police department, United Way, and mayor's office are strong network supporters. They focus on engaging with parents through a parent university program, which emphasizes the importance of education. They also hosted a mental health summit that educates community members about the intersection of mental health and violence.

Multi-Agency Alliance for Children (MAAC)

http://www.maac4kids.org/
Focus: Child welfare system
Type of Activity: Referral network, joint training, and advocacy
Location: Atlanta, GA, USA

The Multi-Agency Alliance for Children strives to provide a seamless continuum of services and supports for young people in the foster care system. In 1996, the network began with 6 foster agencies. In 2018, that number expanded to 9 programs that serve 1,000 children each month. The program has a robust vetting process for potential members, and current members vote on whether new agencies are qualified to be a part of the network. MAAC places youth in foster homes and coordinates the additional services that they may require. In addition, it conducts joint training and advocates on behalf of children's welfare. Moreover, the agency uses a joint database system and monitors its programs' performance by examining critical indicators of success. MAAC was a 2017 Lodestar Collaboration Prize finalist.

NF Collective

http://nfcollective.org/
Focus: Health
Type of Activity: National database of healthcare providers
Location: USA

Developed in 2015, the NF Collective is a collaborative of seven nonprofit funders that focus on neurofibromatosis. Neurofibromatosis describes three conditions where tumors grow on the nervous system. The disease has no cure or known prevention. The network has developed a nationwide database of NF providers.

Power Scholars Academy

Focus: Education
Type of Activity: Summer learning program
Location: USA

Power Scholars Academy, a partnership between BellXcel and the YMCA USA, is a summer program that expands learning time to improve the academic achievements, self-confidence, and life trajectories for students performing below grade level in underserved communities. The organizations partnered on this collaboration, beginning with a pilot program in 2013 because of a shared goal to narrow the achievement gap and the opportunity to combine unique resources each organization could lend to the program to make it successful. What sets the collaboration apart from other programs is the systematic way that the partners have evidenced-based evaluation and implementation fidelity up front as they expanded the program to YMCAs nationwide. The program emphasized program evaluation at each site and offered technical assistance to local YMCAs. Power Scholars Academy was a 2017 Lodestar Collaboration Prize finalist.

Ready, Set, Parent!

Focus: Infant development
Type of Activity: Classes and individual parent visits
Location: Buffalo, NY, USA

Starting in 2005, Every Person Influences Children (EPIC), Baker Victory Services, and Catholic Health partnered to create a new program to support parents who had recently given birth to a baby and provided education for parents during the first few weeks of the child's life. Baker Victory Services provided the infrastructure to bill Blue Cross & Blue Shield for EPIC's parent education programs. EPIC hired the staff and ran the program. Fisher-Price sponsored the program and provided a toy to each newborn. However, changes in the average length of a hospital stay for new mothers and babies became shorter, averaging around 48 hours, causing program implementation challenges. Also, program funding shifted, as funders found other priorities. The collaboration came to an end in 2010, shortly after the partnership was a Lodestar Collaboration Prize finalist.

RE-AMP

https://www.reamp.org/
Focus: Climate change and energy policy
Type of Activity: Advocacy
Location: Midwest, USA

Founded in 2003 by the Garfield Foundation, today, RE-AMP is a network of over 130 member organizations from across the Midwest. Since their founding, they have contributed to several climate victories, including blocking new coal power plants' development in the Midwest, dismantling existing coal power plants, and legislation in several states. Over time, they have expanded their view of climate action as a problem, moving from a technical problem view to a more systemic view. As of 2018, their new goal is to equitably eliminate greenhouse gas emissions in the Midwest by 2050. This new focus on equity can transform the composition, structure, and activities of the network.

Summit Education Initiative

https://seisummit.org/
Focus: Education
Type of Activity: Collective impact network
Location: Akron, OH, USA

Founded in 1994, The Summit Education Initiative is recognized as one of the most successful collective impact networks for education reform in the United States. The original goal of the network was to improve reading scores in Akron Public Schools. Now the purpose of the collaborative is to create a robust data system to build predictive models of pathways to success from preschool through post-secondary completion. The network currently has 329 partners and is coordinated by a staff of 6. The network's most significant turning point occurred in 2010–2011; all programs were shut down, and they dismissed 11 staff. They rebooted the network by going on a listening tour and an environmental scan. From there, they re-created the model of the network, basically reinventing it from the ground up.

Westside Infant-Family Network in Los Angeles (WIN)

https://www.winla.org/
Focus: Early childhood mental health
Type of Activity: Joint case management
Location: Los Angeles, CA, USA

During a 2003 meeting with one of their funders, The Atlas Family Foundation, six agencies serving young children realized that all of their organizations saw evidence of early childhood mental health issues. With support from the foundation, these agencies' executive directors met for two years and developed the framework for the Westside Infant-Family Network (WIN) in Los Angeles. If infants and toddlers were traumatized during the most significant period for human brain development, lifetime outcomes, including health, mental health, and success in school, work, and life, could be significantly impacted. As early childhood mental health issues tend to be intergenerational, significant problems in the family had to be addressed, including parental depression, post-traumatic stress disorder, domestic violence/intimate partner violence, and housing security and childcare issues. In-home, child-parent mental health therapy, preceded by comprehensive case management to help families stabilize their homes, emerged as the ideal model. The program has won five national awards, including a Robert Wood Johnson Foundation local funding partnership, and has an ongoing collaboration with Harvard University Center on the Developing Child.

The Wisconsin Association of Independent Colleges and Universities

http://www.waicu.org/
Focus: Cost reduction
Type of Activity: 40 different collaborative efforts
Location: Wisconsin, USA

In 2002, Wisconsin Colleges and Universities joined together to reduce their costs. Between 2004 and 2016, the collaboration has saved over $136 million for the participating organization. Early efforts included a jointly administered self-funded health plan and purchased a standard enterprise resource planning system. Now there are over 40 different collaborations between the various colleges and universities, extended to a multi-employer retirement plan and training for department chairs. The partnership was a 2011 Lodestar Collaboration Prize Finalist.

Westbrook Children's Project

http://westbrookchildrensproject.org/
Focus: Education
Type of Activity: Collective impact
Location: Portland, Maine, USA

The United Way of Greater Portland convened the Westbrook Children's Project in 2009. It is a StriveTogether community. The project's goal is to ensure post-secondary readiness for all Westbrook children. Local businesses, elected officials, and school districts are significant players within the network. In 2017, the network had 22 organizations, including significant government representation. Local businesses provided the initial funding for the project, but more recently, the United Way has begun funding staffing, and they received a city grant. Most of their data is housed and managed by the school district. They have key indicators showing that they are achieving each of their pipeline goals and leverage existing assessments from the schools to measure those key performance indicators.

2

Is Social Impact the Goal?

When forming the RE-AMP network in 2003, nonprofit organizations and foundations focused their initial conversation around the development of clean energy in the midwestern United States. However, despite partner and funder interest, network leaders took time to articulate the goal of their partnership. The network eventually settled on reducing greenhouse gasses from the power sector by 80% by 2030. Many people thought the target was too idealistic. Gail Francis, the strategic director of RE-AMP, recalled that "Some people would actually get mad when they heard the goal because it just seemed so absurd." But that was not the only problem that RE-AMP members faced. As network members formed their working groups and began a systems analysis to further explore climate change—growing from 20 to over 130 organizations in the process—their understanding of the problem started to shift. According to Gail, as the network became more diverse, some of the original members came to understand that "climate change is not primarily a technical problem. There are important technical aspects to it. But it's primarily a social and political problem." As the network grew, members wrestled with this new understanding of the problem and how they would know if their efforts were making any difference. Initially, RE-AMP measured its efforts by tracking various energy use indicators, which had little to do with the social or political aspects of climate change. After meeting for several years, leaders within the network wondered how they could better address climate change in light of what they now understood, and whether they could evaluate their efforts in response to the problem.

The RE-AMP network is not alone in their struggle to understand the social problem they address. This chapter introduces a typology of social problems and distinguish social impact from other types of outcomes that the network seeks. We present this typology to demonstrate how and when networks are likely to make a social impact. We explore how networks confuse *impact* with *outcomes* or intentionally focus on outcomes instead of impact. Second, we argue that network approaches are appropriate to address some social issues, but not others. We conclude the chapter by

Networks for Social Impact. Michelle Shumate and Katherine R. Cooper, Oxford University Press. © Oxford University Press 2022.
DOI: 10.1093/oso/9780190091996.003.0002

describing dead ends unlikely to result in social impact, along with some pathways to social impact.

Defining social impact and network outcomes

Researchers and practitioners have championed interorganizational networks to effect social change in response to social problems. Often collaboration scholarship is normative, assuming that working together is "a goal in itself."[1] The prevalent assumption across disciplines is that networks offer an opportunity to succeed where organizations have failed.[2] In the introduction to their extensive review of network research, Janice Popp and her fellow researchers from across the United States and Canada[3] acknowledge a widespread, underlying rationale for networks is their ability to increase capacity in responding to complex social problems.[4] However, research on their ability to do so is mixed.

On the practitioner side, leaders regularly invoke the promise of "impact" as an incentive for partnering with others. For instance, consultants John Kania and Mark Kramer launched an international movement around "collective impact" through their article in *Stanford Social Innovation Review* (SSIR).[5] They call on organizations to avoid "isolated impacts" by focusing only on organizational and program outcomes; instead, they argue that organizations should coordinate and leverage their collective efforts and resources to achieve long-lasting change. They assert that independent organizational actions are insufficient for the kind of transformation needed in society. Only by working closely and intently with other organizations can organizations realize the social impact they seek to make.

[1] Beth Gazley and Jeffrey L. Brudney, "The Purpose (and Perils) of Government-Nonprofit Partnership," *Nonprofit and Voluntary Sector Quarterly* 36, no. 3 (September 1, 2007): 389–415, https://doi.org/10.1177/0899764006295997.

[2] John M. Bryson, Barbara C. Crosby, and Melissa Middleton Stone, "Designing and Implementing Cross-Sector Collaborations: Needed and Challenging," *Public Administration Review* 75, no. 5 (2015): 647–63, https://doi.org/10.1111/puar.12432; Barbara Gray, *Collaborating: Finding Common Ground for Multiparty Problems* (San Francisco: Jossey-Bass, 1989).

[3] J. K. Popp et al., "Inter-Organizational Networks," Collaboration across Boundaries Series (Washington, DC: IBM Center for the Business of Government, 2014).

[4] Alison Gilchrist, "Maintaining Relationships Is Critical in Network's Success," *HealthcarePapers* 7, no. 2 (November 2006): 28–31, https://doi.org/10.12927/hcpap.18553. Commentary; Susan Hoberecht et al., "Inter-Organizational Networks," *OD and Sustainability* 43, no. 4 (2011): 23–27; Karen Maas and Kellie Liket, "Social Impact Measurement: Classification of Methods," in *Environmental Management Accounting and Supply Chain Management*, eds. Roger Burritt et al. (Dordrecht: Springer Netherlands, 2011), 171–202, https://doi.org/10.1007/978-94-007-1390-1_8.

[5] John Kania and Mark Kramer, "Collective Impact," *Stanford Social Innovation Review* (Winter 2011): 36–41.

Despite these arguments, there is not widespread agreement as to what constitutes impact. Part of the confusion stems from the use of similar terms, including impact, output, effect, outcome, social return, and social value creation.[6] Another point of contention is the challenge of linking network activity to impact. Further, the type of social impact that networks seek to achieve is so diverse, many may wonder whether we are studying the same thing at all.

In Chapter 1, we defined social impact as how people or environments most affected by the problem experience change as a result of the network's work. To unpack this definition further, we distinguish social impact by the level of outcome and the degree to which networks contribute. Without both elements, there is no evidence of social impact.

First, social impact refers to a significant achievement on the level of whole communities or society.[7] The impact varies by context; it depends on the network's goals and the social issue's nature.[8] However, social impact is always at the community or society level. Social impact studied in previous research includes mental health outcomes for clients and their families;[9] satisfaction with the substantive outcomes of spatial planning networks;[10] reduction of crime and criminal recidivism;[11] serving more patients with a greater number of health services;[12] and neighborhood cleanliness, safety, and maintenance of facilities.[13]

Second, social impact results from network activity. In other words, the impact must be "above and beyond what would have happened anyway" without the network's activity.[14] Network social impact refers to outcomes experienced

---

[6] Maas and Liket, "Social Impact Measurement"; Karen E. H. Mass, "Social Impact Measurement: Towards a Guideline for Managers." In EMAN-EU 2008 Conference: Sustainability and Corporate responsibility accounting measuring and managing business benefits (October 2008): 75–78.

[7] Kellie C. Liket, Marta Rey-Garcia, and Karen E. H. Maas, "Why Aren't Evaluations Working and What to Do about It: A Framework for Negotiating Meaningful Evaluation in Nonprofits," *American Journal of Evaluation* 35, no. 2 (June 1, 2014): 171–88, https://doi.org/10.1177/1098214013517736.

[8] K. G. Provan and H. B. Milward, "A Preliminary Theory of Interorganizational Network Effectiveness: A Comparative Study of Four Community Mental Health Systems," *Administrative Science Quarterly* 40, no. 1 (1995): 1–33.

[9] Provan and Milward, "A Preliminary theory of Interorganizational Network Effectiveness."

[10] Stefan Verweij et al., "What Makes Governance Networks Work? A Fuzzy Set Qualitative Comparative Analysis of 14 Dutch Spatial Planning Projects," *Public Administration* 91, no. 4 (2013): 1035–55.

[11] Jörg Raab, Remco S. Mannak, and Bart Cambré, "Combining Structure, Governance, and Context: A Configurational Approach to Network Effectiveness," *Journal of Public Administration Research and Theory* 25, no. 2 (April 1, 2015): 479–511, https://doi.org/10.1093/jopart/mut039.

[12] Daniela Cristofoli and Josip Markovic, "How to Make Public Networks Really Work: A Qualitative Comparative Analysis," *Public Administration* 94, no. 1 (March 2016): 89–110, https://doi.org/10.1111/padm.12192.

[13] Weijie Wang, "Exploring the Determinants of Network Effectiveness: The Case of Neighborhood Governance Networks in Beijing," *Journal of Public Administration Research and Theory* 26, no. 2 (April 1, 2016): 375–88, https://doi.org/10.1093/jopart/muv017.

[14] Catherine Clark et al., "Assessing Social Impact in Double Bottom Line Ventures," Double Bottom Line Project (Rockefeller Foundation, 2004), https://centers.fuqua.duke.edu/case/wp-content/uploads/sites/7/2015/02/Report_Clark_DoubleBottomLineProjectReport_2004.pdf; Popp et al., "Inter-Organizational Networks."

by a community as a result of coordinated interorganizational activity. Here we include both social impact attributed to a network's activity and to which a network contributes. Notably, social impact is more easily attributable to the network's efforts regarding its clients. When network leaders define social impact as transforming an entire geographic community, the role of the network's activity is *one* contributing factor to community change instead of the *only* factor to attribute change.

Although these two elements distinguish social impact from many other types of outcomes, we recognize that social issues' diversity is a complicating factor when trying to determine impact. Indeed, much of the academic research on social impact focuses on one social issue, such as substance abuse or climate change. A typology of social impact is needed to discern when research about social impact applies to a network.

The character of social impact

Academic research before this book has tried to distinguish among the various approaches to social impact.[15] For example, Alex Turrini and colleagues[16] distinguish between two scales of social impact, affecting either clients or a geographic community. We've seen examples of both in our research; some social impact networks, like AgeWell Pittsburgh, only take responsibility for outcomes related to the clients that their network serves. There are advantages to this approach. In contrast, some networks measure their social impact against outcomes for a geographically bounded community. Summit Education Initiative, described in Chapter 1, is such a network. They measure the outcomes of their efforts against gains for all children in Akron, Ohio. When networks attempt social impact at this scale, they almost always involve government institutions that serve all citizens in a community or an entire geographic region (e.g., public schools).

We suggest that the character of social impact can differ according to *type*, *scale*, and *approach* (see Table 2.1). *Type* refers to the way that the network seeks to create a community-level or geographic-level improvement. *Scale* refers to whether the network aims to increase the number of people or communities served or improve the quality of those services.

---

[15] For example, Clarke and Fuller's (2010) typology refers to plan-centric, process-centric, partner-centric, outside stakeholder-centric, person-centric, or environmental centric outcomes of collaborative strategy management.

[16] Alex Turrini et al., "Networking Literature about Determinants of Network Effectiveness," *Public Administration* 88, no. 2 (2010): 528–50, https://doi.org/10.1111/j.1467-9299.2009.01791.x.

Table 2.1 The Character of Social Impact

Dimensions of Social Impact	Distinctions	Key Question
Focus	Client-focused versus geography-focused	Does the network seek to impact their clients/owned properties, or does it seek to impact an entire community or unowned geographic region?
Type	Project-based, service-based, or advocacy-based	Will the network create a new product/facility, provide continuous services, or achieve institutional change, such as legislation?
Scale	Scale up an intervention or improve an intervention	Are the interventions set or does the network seek to improve the interventions?
Approach	Prevention or remediation	Does the network seek to prevent the problem or remediate the problem?

Approach refers to whether the network seeks to remediate or prevent a social problem.

Types of social impact

The type of social impact refers to the kind of improvement that a network seeks to make. The type of social impact influences both the tasks that networks perform to achieve their goal and the necessary action's longevity. We distinguish between project-, service-, and advocacy-based social impact.[17]

Project-based social impact refers to a circumstance in which a network creates a physical resource for the community's benefit. For example, in Chicago, the Pritzker Traubert Family Foundation announced the Chicago Prize of $10 million to a Chicago-based collaboration between a community group, financing groups, developers, and a construction company to create a new development in neglected Chicago neighborhoods. In this example, the social impact is the new facility. Other projects focus on the creation of innovative products or services. When Greenpeace formed its partnership with German-based Foron in 1992, they worked together to create a new ozone-safe

---

[17] See Robert Agranoff, *Managing within Networks: Adding Value to Public Organizations* (Washington, DC: Georgetown University Press, 2007); Robert Agranoff, *Collaborating to Manage: A Primer for the Public Sector* (Washington, DC: Georgetown University Press, 2012) who also distinguished between these types of efforts.

hydrocarbon.[18] They created the partnership to bring a new, environmentally safe refrigerant to market that would replace the chlorofluorocarbon that was the standard in refrigerators at the time. The benefit is through the invention of a better product for both the environment and the corporation. This type of social impact, though requiring maintenance, typically assumes a start and an end date. Moreover, success is measured based on creating the asset and its effectiveness in building the infrastructure to address the social problem.

Service-based social impact describes the provision of care or benefits. In networks organized around service-based social impact, the network may coordinate its activities indefinitely. For example, mental health patients continue to receive high-quality care, or children continue to receive a high-quality education. Service-based social impact is the goal of referral networks, such as the AmericaServes networks. These long-term projects usually assess social impact in terms of improvement over the status quo and measure success in terms of continuous improvement, year over year.

Advocacy-based social impact refers to the creation of regulatory or institutional change. For example, the Climate Accord introduced in Chapter 1 is a legal agreement to reduce CO_2 emissions. Like project-based impact, these efforts may have an end date if they are time-sensitive (e.g., a campaign) or result in something tangible (e.g., new legislation). For example, the human rights language present in the first United Nations charter was the accomplishment of a dedicated group of international NGOs representing labor, places of worship, ethnic groups, and peace movements.[19]

The production of these social impact types is not mutually exclusive; some networks pursue multiple types of impact either by design or because, in pursuit of one kind of impact, another opportunity presents itself. In Zambia, for example, we studied a donor-driven coalition sponsored by international development agencies.[20] This coalition pursued project-based social impact through the development of new care centers and a gender-based violence hotline. Additionally, it sought advocacy-based social impact through a nationwide campaign to end gender-based violence.

---

[18] John Elkington, *Cannibals with Forks: Triple Bottom Line of 21st Century Business* (Oxford: John Wiley & Son Ltd, 1999).

[19] Margaret E. Keck and Kathryn Sikkink, "Transnational Advocacy Networks in International and Regional Politics," *International Social Science Journal* 51, no. 159 (1999): 89–101, https://doi.org/10.1111/1468-2451.00179.

[20] Katherine R. Cooper and Michelle Shumate, "Interorganizational Collaboration Explored through the Bona Fide Network Perspective," *Management Communication Quarterly* 26, no. 4 (2012): 623–54.

The scale of social impact

Social impact also differs based on the *scale of activities*; we distinguish between efforts to *scale up* an innovation or *improve* upon an innovation. Scaling up involves providing the same social innovation to many people or environmental regions. The Power Scholars Academy and LawHelp are both examples of networks scaling up innovations. The Power Scholars Academy began with a pilot program before being implemented across the country. LawHelp started with an online consumer legal information platform for low-income New Yorkers before replicating the platform in 25 other U.S. states.

In contrast, some initiatives make a social impact by providing better services to the same group of people or across the same region. These groups have learning and innovation baked into their logic model of how social impact works. They align services with combinatorial effects and engage in continuous quality improvement to identify underserved populations and ineffective programs. Examples include the Multi-Alliance Agency for Children (MAAC), which serves youth in foster care in Georgia; and Westside Infant-Family Network (WIN), which addresses whole-family mental health and serves Los Angeles-area families with children under five. Both networks are examples of partnerships organized around improving services to clients.

Approaches to social impact

Finally, social impact may require different *approaches*; some networks seek to *prevent* a social problem while others seek to *remediate* it. The prevention of a social problem is much more challenging to measure than the remediation of the same problem. For example, the number of people in recovery from substance abuse is more straightforward to measure than the number of people who never began abusing substances in the first place. However, some networks explicitly focus on the prevention of social problems. For example, the Communities That Care networks have demonstrated that their network approach effectively prevents youth from engaging in risky behaviors, including drug and alcohol use.[21] In contrast, the RE-AMP networks referenced at the beginning of this chapter advocate for programs to reduce carbon emissions to slow or reverse climate change. The response to a social problem may include implementing new interventions, or disinvestment, which refers to efforts to cut out ineffective or harmful practices.

---

[21] M. Lee Van Horn et al., "Effects of the Communities That Care System on Cross-Sectional Profiles of Adolescent Substance Use and Delinquency," *American Journal of Preventive Medicine* 47, no. 2 (August 1, 2014): 188–97, https://doi.org/10.1016/j.amepre.2014.04.004.

This typology clarifies many of the nuances and variations in social impact that networks achieve. In Chapter 3, we return to this typology and suggest that the character of the social impact that a network seeks to make determines its likely structure. However, not all networks achieve social impact (axiom four) or are *trying* to do so. Instead, some networks organize to achieve organizational or network outcomes.

Outcomes other than social impact

Some network designs benefit participating individuals and organizations. If networks ignore network outcomes, like survival and attracting network resources, they are unlikely to achieve any outcome at all. We use the term *outcome* to describe those changes at the level of individuals, organizations, or the network itself. Network leaders and organizational actors are right to seek these benefits[22] as they incentivize individuals and organizations to stay the course as they pursue social impact. A summary of the individual, organizational, network, and social outcomes are included in Table 2.2.

Individual outcomes

Despite the natural tendency to focus on organizations, network activity is initiated and sustained by individuals. Research points to multileveled participation in networks that entails coordination between individuals and organizations.[23] Individuals working within the network can benefit from learning new skills or learning from network activity.[24] Researchers James Austin and May Seitanidi[25] describe these outcomes as instrumental (e.g., new skills). Also, they note that individuals sometimes gain psychological or emotional benefits (e.g., new friendships or positive feelings about participation in the network). Participation conditions individual feelings[26] and instrumental gains, but organizational affiliations also influence these outcomes.

[22] Sandra A. Waddock, "A Typology of Social Partnership Organizations," *Administration & Society* 22, no. 4 (February 1, 1991): 480–515, https://doi.org/10.1177/009539979102200405.

[23] Shiv Ganesh and Cynthia Stohl, "Collective Action, Community Organizing and Social Movements," in *Sage Handbook of Organizational Communication*, 3rd ed., eds. D. K. Mumby and L. L. Putnam (Newbury Park, CA: Sage Publications, 2014), 743–65.

[24] John W. Selsky and Barbara Parker, "Platforms for Cross-Sector Social Partnerships: Prospective Sensemaking Devices for Social Benefit," *Journal of Business Ethics* 94, no. 1 (July 1, 2010): 21–37, https://doi.org/10.1007/s10551-011-0776-2.

[25] James E. Austin and Maria May Seitanidi, "Collaborative Value Creation: A Review of Partnering between Nonprofits and Businesses. Part 2: Partnership Processes and Outcomes," *Nonprofit and Voluntary Sector Quarterly* 41, no. 6 (2012): 929–68.

[26] Katherine R. Cooper, "Exploring Stakeholder Participation in Nonprofit Collaboration." Dissertation, University of Illinois at Urbana-Champaign, 2014, https://core.ac.uk/download/pdf/29152991.pdf.

Table 2.2 Evaluating the Work of Networks for Social Impact

Term	Definition	Examples
Activities	The processes that stakeholders engage in to support the network	• Sharing, interpreting, and making decisions based on data • Regular meetings • Allocation of network funding
Outputs	Programs or products resulting from network activity	• Adjustment of organizational activity in response to benchmarking data • New programs to meet client needs • Coordination of existing programs to better address client needs • Purchase of shared equipment • Creation of shared community report
Individual Outcomes	Outcomes experienced by individuals as a result of their network activity	• New skills • New relationships • Feelings of satisfaction with work
Organizational Outcomes	Outcomes experienced by individual organizations resulting from their network activity	• Organizational learning • Prestige • Survival/Resources
Network Outcomes	Outcomes experienced by the partnership as a result of network activity	• Continued funding • Network growth • New relationships between organizations
Social Impact	Outcomes experienced by the community attributable to network activity; may vary in terms of the scale, type, innovation, and approach	• Improved educational outcomes for youth • Reduction in seniors' emergency room visits • Policy change

Organizational outcomes

Organizational outcomes describe the benefits that member organizations experience as a result of their participation. Previous research identified three types of organizational outcomes: survival, legitimacy, and learning. Often, organizations that participate in social impact networks seek a combination of organizational outcomes and social impact.

First, many organizations operate in a turbulent environment due to financial uncertainty,[27] and organizations that join self-organizing networks face a greater likelihood of survival even in turbulent environments.[28] Network

[27] Douglas C. Eadie, *Changing by Design: A Practical Approach to Leading Innovation in Nonprofit Organizations* (San Francisco: Jossey-Bass, 1997).
[28] Joseph Galaskiewicz, Wolfgang Bielefeld, and Myron Dowell, "Networks and Organizational Growth: A Study of Community Based Nonprofits," *Administrative Science Quarterly* 51, no. 3 (September 1, 2006): 337–80, https://doi.org/10.2189/asqu.51.3.337; Mark A. Hager, Joseph Galaskiewicz, and Jeff A.

membership may provide better access to tangible and intangible resources needed for survival, as suggested by resource-based collaboration views.[29] The Chattanooga Museums Collaborative provides an example of organizations that were first motivated by these needs. Robert Kret, then executive director of Hunter Art Museum, first approached the Tennessee Aquarium to form what eventually became the Collaborative because of a "lack of infrastructure," including a computer network system, voicemail, and robust HR materials at Hunter. The first activities of the Museums Collaborative were to share the costs of back-office functions, such as finance, accounting, human resources, and information technology support.

Previous research suggests that organizations can increase or decrease their legitimacy as a result of their network affiliations. For example, organizations may experience a boost in legitimacy[30] or, as in our research on gender-based violence networks in Zambia, organizational referrals.[31] This "associational value" typically results in greater visibility or support for the organization.[32] However, relationships with organizations also carry reputational risks;[33] affiliations with other agencies can also reduce perceived legitimacy and lead to adverse outcomes.[34] For example, when Susan G. Komen's decision to discontinue funding Planned Parenthood

Larson, "Structural Embeddedness and the Liability of Newness among Nonprofit Organizations," *Public Management Review* 6, no. 2 (2004): 159–88.

[29] Amelia Clarke and Adriane MacDonald, "Outcomes to Partners in Multi-Stakeholder Cross-Sector Partnerships: A Resource-Based View," *Business & Society* 58, no. 2 (2019): 298–332, https://doi.org / 10.1177/0007650316660534; Gazley and Brudney, "The Purpose (and Perils) of Government-Nonprofit Partnership"; Jeffrey Pfeffer and R. Gerald Salancik, *The External Control of Organizations: A Resource Dependence Perspective* (New York: Harper & Row, 1978); Lester M. Salamon and Helmut K. Anheier, "Social Origins of Civil Society: Explaining the Nonprofit Sector Cross-Nationally," *Voluntas: International Journal of Voluntary and Nonprofit Organizations* 9, no. 3 (September 1, 1998): 213–48, https://doi.org/ 10.1023/A:1022058200985.
[30] Lewis Faulk et al., "Network Connections and Competitively Awarded Funding: The Impacts of Board Network Structures and Status Interlocks on Nonprofit Organizations' Foundation Grant Acquisition," *Public Management Review* 18, no. 10 (November 25, 2016): 1425–55, https://doi.org/10.1080/ 14719037.2015.1112421.
[31] Cooper and Shumate, "Interorganizational Collaboration Explored through the Bona Fide Network Perspective."
[32] James E. Austin and Maria M. Seitanidi, "Collaborative Value Creation: A Review of Partnering between Nonprofits and Businesses: Part I. Value Creation Spectrum and Collaboration Stages," *Nonprofit and Voluntary Sector Quarterly* 41, no. 5 (2012): 726–58.
[33] Michelle Shumate and Amy O'Connor, "The Symbiotic Sustainability Model: Conceptualizing NGO-Corporate Alliance Communication," *Journal of Communication* 63 (2010): 577–609, https://doi.org/ 10.1111/j.1460-2466.2010.01498.x.
[34] Heidi Herlin, "Better Safe Than Sorry: Nonprofit Organizational Legitimacy and Cross-Sector Partnerships," *Business & Society* 54, no. 6 (November 1, 2015): 822–58, https://doi.org/10.1177/ 0007650312472609; Michelle Shumate and Amy O'Connor, "Corporate Reporting of Cross-Sector Alliances: The Portfolio of NGO Partners Communicated on Corporate Websites," *Communication Monographs* 77 (2010): 238–61, https://doi.org/10.1080/03637751003758201.

became a controversy, businesses that partnered with Susan G. Komen also experienced a backlash.[35]

Third, organizations can *learn* from their network partners. Moreover, through partnering, they can create new knowledge;[36] some scholars describe such outcomes as interaction value or synergistic value.[37] The Chicago Benchmarking Collaborative, for instance, began as a means of sharing data across organizations. By accessing other organizations' data, members of the collaborative had benchmarks to evaluate their organizational data and an opportunity to ask other partners what worked—and what did not—within their programs. When no agencies performed well on a metric, they could engage in joint training, creating new knowledge of what worked together.

Organizational survival, legitimacy, and learning are three crucial benefits of networks. In some theories of change (see Chapter 3), they are a precondition for social impact. In all cases, these organization-level outcomes are intertwined with social impact (see axiom 1).

Network outcomes

Network-level outcomes are also related to social impact. For instance, networks must continue to operate long enough to accomplish their focal activity to make a social impact. Previous network research suggests factors that lead to network failure[38] or sustainability,[39] but many networks struggle to survive the turbulent environments in which they operate. When we conducted interviews with winners and finalists of the Lodestar Collaboration Prize, leaders told us time and time again that the network's survival amidst so much change was in and of itself an accomplishment. For instance, the Multi-Agency Alliance for Children (MAAC) began in 1996 and is still going strong several decades later. The network experienced threats to funding, leadership changes, and multiple network transitions, yet the partnership survived and continued to serve children in foster care.

---

[35] Laura Winig, "Social Media and the Planned Parenthood/Susan G. Komen for the Cure Controversy," *Harvard Kennedy School of Government Case Number* 1975.0 (2012), https://case.hks.harvard.edu/social-media-and-the-planned-parenthood-susan-g-komen-for-the-cure-controversy/.

[36] Austin and Seitanidi, "Collaborative Value Creation";Edward J. Zajac and Cyrus P. Olsen, "From Transaction Cost to Transactional Value Analysis: Implications for the Study of Interorganizational Strategies*," *Journal of Management Studies* 30, no. 1 (1993): 131–45, https://doi.org/10.1111/j.1467-6486.1993.tb00298.x.

[37] Austin and Seitanidi, "Collaborative Value Creation."

[38] Keith G. Provan, Amy Fish, and Joerg Sydow, "Interorganizational Networks at the Network Level: A Review of the Empirical Literature on Whole Networks," *Journal of Management* 33, no. 3 (June 1, 2007): 479–516, https://doi.org/10.1177/0149206307302554.

[39] Keith G. Provan and Kun Huang, "Resource Tangibility and the Evolution of a Publicly Funded Health and Human Services Network," *Public Administration Review* 72, no. 3 (2012): 366–75, https://doi.org/10.1111/j.1540-6210.2011.02504.x.

Another outcome is improved *network capacity*. One typical example of this is the use of referral networks to serve large populations with complex needs. MAAC relied on its network of partners to provide a broad set of services for children's adoption or reunification with their family (i.e., housing, therapy, trauma-informed care). The AmericaServes networks focus on developing and refining veterans' access community services, including housing, health, education, and workforce development.

The *creation of social capital* is another network benefit.[40] Social capital refers to benefits resulting from the trust, reciprocity, information, and cooperation present in social networks.[41] A network's presence enables connections between its members or between the network and members. Relationship strength within the network and member commitment to the network are possible network outcomes.[42] A study of coalitions working on prevention initiatives to improve youth's behavioral health finds that the coalition's capacity to establish relationships with community organizations is one of the factors that ultimately enable prevention, suggesting linkages between network outcomes and social impact.[43]

The promise of individual, organizational, or network outcomes may be enough to compel participation in a network. Indeed, some social impact organizations form networks for these outcomes alone, like the Chattanooga Museums Collaborative's early stages. One reason that networks fail to achieve social impact is that they prioritize these outcomes at its expense, as suggested in axiom four. However, there are other reasons that a network may not achieve social impact. Specifically, we draw on our research to explore whether communities that fail to achieve social impact have focused on the wrong problem—or ineffectively framed the right one.

What kind of problem is the network trying to solve?

Over the years, researchers, practitioners, and policymakers have developed various terms to describe complex social problems typically beyond

[40] L. David Brown and Darcy Ashman, "Participation, Social Capital, and Intersectoral Problem Solving: African and Asian Cases," *World Development*, Implementing Policy Change, 24, no. 9 (September 1, 1996): 1467–79, https://doi.org/10.1016/0305-750X(96)00053-8.

[41] James S. Coleman, "Social Capital in the Creation of Human Capital," *American Journal of Sociology* 94 (January 1, 1988): S95–120, https://doi.org/10.1086/228943.

[42] Popp et al., "Inter-Organizational Networks."

[43] Valerie B. Shapiro et al., "Measuring Dimensions of Coalition Functioning for Effective and Participatory Community Practice," *Social Work Research* 37, no. 4 (December 2013): 349–59, https://doi.org/10.1093/swr/svt028.

any organization or sector's reach. Scholars describe these problems as metaproblems,[44] wicked problems,[45] indivisible problems,[46] nettlesome problems,[47] or simply as messes.[48] Although these definitions vary slightly, they typically refer to challenging problems to diagnose and difficult—or perhaps impossible—to resolve.

Wicked problems

Like many of our colleagues in research and practice, we have relied upon the wicked problem terminology. Admittedly, wicked sounds like a pseudonym for *evil*, though the intention is not to assign morality to the problem. Instead, this term refers to the intractability of the problem itself and the varying stakeholders involved.[49] Wicked problems have three significant characteristics; they are *unstructured, cross-cutting,* and *relentless.*[50] They are unstructured because there is little consensus in identifying either the problem or solution—or sorting out the cause and effect. They are *cross-cutting* in that the problem involves diverse and overlapping stakeholders with different perspectives. Because the issue is impossible to solve once and for all, wicked problems are *relentless.*

Such problems are typically beyond individual organizations' reach because of the resources they require and the increasingly blurred boundaries between sectors.[51] Such complex social problems are not the exclusive domain of nonprofit, government, or business stakeholders; instead, they demand organizational actors' attention from across sectors. Many of the education-focused networks we studied are aware that they are facing a wicked problem. For example, leaders in Education for All described their efforts using the term when relating the contributing factors to the educational disparities within

---

[44] M. Chevalier, "A Wider Range of Perspectives in the Bureaucratic Structure" (Ottawa, Ontario, Canada: Commission on Bilingualism and Biculturalism, 1966).

[45] Horst W. J. Rittel and Melvin M. Webber, "Dilemmas in a General Theory of Planning," *Policy Sciences* 4, no. 2 (1973): 155–69.

[46] Howard E. Aldrich, "Visionaries and Villains: The Politics of Designing Interorganizational Relations," *Organization and Administrative Science* 8, no. 1 (1977): 23–40.

[47] Robert Agranoff, *Intergovernmental Management: Human Services Problem-Solving in Six Metropolitan Areas* (New York: SUNY Press, 1986).

[48] Russell Ackoff, *Redesigning the Future* (New York: Wiley, 1975).

[49] Rittel and Webber, "Dilemmas in a General Theory of Planning."

[50] Brian W. Head, "Wicked Problems in Public Policy," *Public Policy* 3, no. 2 (2008): 101–18; Edward P. Weber and Anne M. Khademian, "Wicked Problems, Knowledge Challenges, and Collaborative Capacity Builders in Network Settings," *Public Administration Review* 68, no. 2 (2008): 334–49, https://doi.org/10.1111/j.1540-6210.2007.00866.x; Joop Koppenjan and Erik-Hans Klijn, *Managing Uncertainties in Networks. A Network Approach to Problem Solving and Decision Making* (London: Routledge, 2004).

[51] Selsky and Parker, "Platforms for Cross-Sector Social Partnerships."

their community. They noted that many stakeholders, including educators, administrators, students, and families, are implicated and that an effective response should be multifaceted.

Although wicked problems provide a helpful frame for how and why partners come together, the term is often used as a catch-all for any social problem and any coordinated, interorganizational response to that problem. But not every social issue is wicked. Social problems vary in their severity, complexity, and resource availability,[52] and we suggest that organizations may rush to form networks even if a network response is not necessary. We turn to the Cynefin framework to differentiate social problems and suggest how networks might coordinate in response to these problems.

Simple, complicated, complex, and chaotic problems

David Snowden and Mary Boone, both consultants, introduced the Cynefin framework to describe the contexts in which leaders make decisions.[53] The framework suggests that problems, including social problems, are simple,[54] complicated, complex, or chaotic.[55] We draw upon this typology to indicate which types of problems warrant a network response, and the type of network best suited to these problems.

In simple problems, the cause and effect are relatively straightforward and distinct. Consequently, leaders know how to respond. They are aided by past precedent or best practices to guide their decision-making. A single organization may readily solve such problems or, if an interorganizational response is needed, a network may form to complete a project and then disband relatively quickly. For example, the Chattanooga Museums Collaborative sponsored a joint capital campaign intended to benefit the participating museums in an example of project-based impact. Although this campaign served to raise money that would support community resources and education through these museums, the partnership was a response to a relatively specific organizational need—the need for money. In such cases, the network participants

---

[52] Jacqueline N. Hood, Jeanne M. Logsdon, and Judith Kenner Thompson, "Collaboration for Social Problem Solving: A Process Model," *Business & Society* 32, no. 1 (June 1, 1993): 1–17, https://doi.org/10.1177/000765039303200103.

[53] David J. Snowden and Mary E. Boone, "A Leader's Framework for Decision Making," *Harvard Business Review*, PMID 18159787, November 2007, 69–76.

[54] Sometimes simple problems are referred to as obvious problems in the literature. We've kept them simple throughout for consistency.

[55] Rob Van Tulder and Nienke Keen, "Capturing Collaborative Challenges: Designing Complexity-Sensitive Theories of Change for Cross-Sector Partnerships," *Journal of Business Ethics* 150, no. 2 (2018): 315–32; Snowden and Boone, "A Leader's Framework for Decision Making."

often represent the same sector. Many networks formed in response to a simple problem pursue organizational outcomes as opposed to social impact.

In *complicated* problems, a cause-effect relationship exists but may not be readily apparent to leaders; in this scenario, the problem requires analysis and expert input. A more coordinated network response is useful, particularly one focused on organizational learning. In such networks, organizations learn new things through their involvement in the network and form new connections; these connections provide additional resources if the problem is persistent or recurring. Many networks respond to complicated problems by seeking service-based social impact. For example, Communities That Care networks focus on learning and new connections among organizations to reduce youth violence, substance abuse, and delinquency.[56] Networks for continuous quality improvement or service networks created to exchange organizational referrals are also good responses to a complicated problem.

Complex problems are a step beyond complicated problems. These problems are often prone to change and require trial and error as leaders figure out their response. More unknowns also characterize complex problems, and the root causes of a problem (see "Tools for network instigators" at the end of this chapter) are challenging to isolate. Networks that form in response to complex problems are best served by taking a systems' view and focusing on the alignment of organizational resources and approaches. Networks formed in response to complex problems also require some room to innovate because so much in a complex problem is unknown. These networks do best when they have time and resources to try different approaches. Communities working on improving educational outcomes, in which partners from various sectors address the many factors that contribute to disparities in education, address a complex problem. Similarly, networks that pursue geography-bounded social impact are often addressing a complex problem.

In Snowden and Boone's typology, chaotic problems are turbulent. The relationships between cause and effect are unknown and are changing. No logic model would work. In chaotic problems, serendipitous networks provide a better response than goal-directed ones. Recall from Chapter 1 that serendipitous networks are woven through organizations forming partnerships that are not centrally controlled or managed. Serendipitous networks are

---

[56] M. Lee Van Horn et al., "Effects of the Communities That Care System on Cross-Sectional Profiles of Adolescent Substance Use and Delinquency," *American Journal of Preventive Medicine* 47, no. 2 (August 1, 2014): 188–97, https://doi.org/10.1016/j.amepre.2014.04.004; Valerie B. Shapiro, Sabrina Oesterle, and J. David Hawkins, "Relating Coalition Capacity to the Adoption of Science-Based Prevention in Communities: Evidence from a Randomized Trial of Communities That Care," *American Journal of Community Psychology* 55, no. 1 (March 1, 2015): 1–12, https://doi.org/10.1007/s10464-014-9684-9.

unlikely to make a social impact, but they are the most responsive network form. This responsiveness stems from a lack of unified coordination. But what serendipitous networks lack in coordination, they make up for in nimble innovation. As an example, serendipitous networks often emerge to address natural disasters.[57] In such circumstances, the goal is to provide responsive relief, not development. In short, these networks provide whatever good they can to meet the needs they see, but do not aim to make gains on a social issue (i.e., social impact).

The problems that networks should address

Complicated or complex problems provide an opportunity for most networks described in this book; these problems are multifaceted and necessitate the involvement of different stakeholders to assess the problem. These problems are also uncertain, in that it is difficult to discern a single clear path forward. Research suggests that networks work best as a strategy in which partners have an opportunity to innovate,[58] and complicated or complex problems allow for innovation.

In contrast, simple and chaotic problems are not contexts where network approaches effectively make a social impact. Networks mobilized in response to simple problems are more likely to result in outcomes as opposed to impact. Serendipitous networks formed in response to chaotic problems may provide relief and do good, but they cannot make a sustainable social impact. In both simple and chaotic problems, *networks fail to achieve social impact because they are organized in response to the wrong problem.*

Leaders may be unsure which type of problem that they are facing[59] or become more aware of a problem in phases. Networks typically spend time analyzing the problem and trying out different tactics, reminiscent of Gail Francis's observations of the RE-AMP network shared at the beginning of this chapter. Network leaders began by focusing on a technical problem before realizing that climate change is also a political and social problem. This realization prompted them to revisit their reasons for coming together in the

---

[57] *See* Naim Kapucu, "Interagency Communication Networks During Emergencies: Boundary Spanners in Multiagency Coordination," *The American Review of Public Administration* 36, no. 2 (June 1, 2006): 207–25, https://doi.org/10.1177/0275074005280605.

[58] June Holley, *Network Weaver Handbook: A Guide to Transformational Networks* (Athens, Ontario, Canada: Network Weaver Publishing, 2012).

[59] Snowden and Boone's Cynefin framework uses the term *disorder* to describe circumstances in which leaders cannot determine which of the other contexts apply.

first place. Ultimately, they chose to frame the problem differently, focusing on the social aspects of the problem, and declared a goal "to equitably eliminate greenhouse gas emissions from the Midwest by 2050."

In many ways, RE-AMP is a fitting example for this chapter on social impact and problem type. Although climate change's technical problem is sufficiently complicated, the network's challenge grew considerably when the network members reframed climate change as both political and social—that is, a complex problem. In revising their goal, the network has changed its means of tracking their success, struggling with distinguishing between organizational outcomes, network outcomes, and impact in the process. Francis further acknowledges that RE-AMP's decision to revisit the problem of climate change has been frustrating to some members and funders because the process requires network members to "go back to the beginning" by redoing the analysis that they had initially conducted when they formed the network.

Dead ends to social impact

In this chapter, we indicated a few reasons that networks do not achieve social impact. At the end of each chapter, we describe these situations as dead ends. Dead ends are network decisions that are unlikely to result in social impact.

Networks prioritize organizational or network outcomes over social impact

Although all networks seek individual, organizational, or network outcomes in addition to social impact, some networks exclusively pursue organizational or network outcomes. A primary reason that these networks fail to achieve social impact is that they have not prioritized it as the goal. Instead, participants try to achieve goals for their organizations or for the network itself. The pursuit of individual and organizational outcomes is not a wrong choice for networks, and network participants might expect both individual and organizational outcomes in addition to social impact. Moreover, networks need to survive and attract resources to make a social impact. Network outcomes, thus, are a necessary but not sufficient condition for social impact. However, networks can focus exclusively on outcomes such as the number of member organizations added, fundraising success, or media mentions. The excessive pursuit of individual, organizational, or network outcomes precludes networks from achieving social impact.

Networks fail to address root problems

In coming together in response to a problem, network partners may have difficulty distinguishing the problem's cause from its symptoms. This difficulty is typical of wicked problems[60] but presents a challenge for networks. Uncovering root causes typically involves more time and partner input (see "Tools for network instigators" in this chapter). Instead of addressing root causes, networks may be tempted to launch programs that address symptoms of the problem itself. Such efforts may be more indicative of outputs or outcomes as opposed to impact.

Networks form in response to either simple or chaotic problems

This chapter explored the nuances of social problems and suggested that networks may be unnecessary or insufficient to address these problems. Specifically, a single organization or a more loosely coordinated network can address simple or obvious problems. These problems may lend themselves to organizational or network outcomes as opposed to social impact. Goal-directed networks require time and are a poor fit for chaotic problems, as leaders are typically acting to minimize damage, not achieve social impact.

Pathways to social impact

Pathways to social impact reflect axiom five; there is more than one approach to achieving social impact. The social impact typology and types of social problems described in this chapter point to two pathways to impact. Specifically, networks can achieve social impact by adhering to the following pathways.

Network leaders articulate social impact in terms of focus, type, innovation, and approach of the network

The social impact typology introduced in this chapter suggests several critical choices for network leaders. Although network leaders may find that their choices are constrained by resources (as we'll discuss in Chapter 4) and that

---

[60] Rittel and Webber, "Dilemmas in a General Theory of Planning."

they have implications for other stages of the network (as suggested by axiom 3), each of these social impact choices represents a potential pathway to success. Network leaders can carve that path by articulating their focus on community or clients. They can determine the type of work their network will do in terms of projects, services, or advocacy. By delineating the scale of work in terms of increasing or improving interventions and their work approach, as expressed in terms of prevention or remediation, leaders better articulate their theory of change. When leaders specify the nature of social impact, they empower their networks because stakeholders know how to focus their energy and resources. We describe the implications of these choices for network design in Chapter 3.

Networks form in response to complicated or complex problems

Simple or chaotic problems are dead ends to impact because a coordinated network response is unwarranted or insufficient. Alternatively, complicated or complex problems provide pathways to social impact. In these cases, the complexity of a problem necessitates an interorganizational response and suggests room to try something new. Specifically, complicated problems may be responsive to organizational learning networks. Networks focusing on systems alignment may be an appropriate strategy for complex problems. We further unpack these design choices in Chapter 3.

Conclusion

In this chapter, we introduced a typology of social impact and a framework for social problems that warrant a network response. Despite the potential for networks to achieve more than individual organizations, networks are not a solution to every problem. Specifically, some problems are better suited to organizational or network outcomes than social impact. The typology we introduced in this chapter offers freedom for network partners to focus their efforts and suggests that leaders make some choices concerning the type of social impact they seek—a concept we will return to throughout the book.

Not all networks are worth the effort. Networks work best when there is room to innovate and try new things; for those complicated-enough problems to warrant a network response, it may take several attempts for networks to land on a pathway that leads to impact. By focusing on nuances in network goals and social problems, leaders have taken the first step in setting up a network.

Case study: The Wisconsin Association for Independent Colleges and Universities

The Wisconsin Association for Independent Colleges and Universities (WAICU) began in 1961, primarily to do government relations for its member universities. However, over the years, as funding to higher education dwindled, the universities faced the difficult but all too common options for controlling costs: cut programs, raise tuition, or raise more money. But the network, led by Dr. Rolf Wegenke since 1992, was beginning to explore other financial options for WAICU members.

"Collaborating on various functions seems a no-brainer," said Wegenke, "though it didn't happen right away." The presidents of the universities participating in WAICU were interested in working together to reduce their costs, and WAICU launched a feasibility study to further explore the possibility. The WAICU started with a few collaborative offerings to build success; one of the first joint projects was a group life and disability insurance program. Nearly 20 years after launching the program, Wegenke reported that there had been no premium increases, and there had been three premium reductions—a rarity, as he notes, in insurance. The WAICU built on these successes with the addition of other programs, both small—for example, buying office supplies together—and large, such as a jointly administered self-funded health plan and the purchase and implementation of a common administrative system. The WAICU now offers more than 40 collaborative projects that enable its member universities to save on expenses. Between 2004 and 2016, the network saved over $136 million for the members. At that time, the average savings per member was $835,267.

Additionally, WAICU offers cost-saving programs intended to strengthen each university. These include workshops open to incoming department chairs from any WAICU members, or environmental health and safety audits. WAICU trains representatives from one campus to conduct an independent audit of environmental health and safety issues at another participating WAICU campus. "It's sometimes hard to say how much [money] you saved if you prevented trouble, prevented future accidents or spills or misuse of chemicals," Wegenke admits. But there is a sense that universities benefit from these collaborative projects and the joint ventures intended to cut costs. He points out the example of the WAICU partner who reported that their participation in the WAICU environmental health and safety peer audit program changed their own campus culture.

Although WAICU offers dozens of collaborative projects, Wegenke says that no individual project has 100% participation for all WAICU members.

Instead, universities within the network choose the programs in which they want to participate. The network employs staff to administer these programs and ensure that members know the offerings available to them. If a program fails to catch on, Wegenke's team has a process in place to evaluate and fine-tune the program and to close out the project if it's no longer serving members. Overall, WAICU's trend is to adjust existing programs and add new ones. Wegenke gives credit to the university presidents who choose to collaborate. "When I was hired," Wegenke says, "they said to me: *Make something out of this organization.* . . . They were taking a huge risk. At that time, I didn't know of anyone else who was doing this sort of thing. We started small . . . and we took it from there, sort of a step-in-time. It's been building over these last several years."

WAICU leaders are continually looking to brainstorm new ways to save members money. When asked about his WAICU colleagues view their joint efforts, Wegenke says that collaboration "is now so much a part of the culture . . . and partners want more."

Questions to consider

1. How would you characterize the problem WAICU addresses?
2. Who benefits from involvement in WAICU? What are these benefits?
3. How does WAICU coordinate network activity in response to the network's stated problem? How do these activities result in benefits for members?
4. Do WAICU's actions result in social impact?

Tools for network instigators

Root cause analysis

One of the reasons organizations and networks have trouble setting goals and determining how to set up their networks is that they haven't defined the problem. One helpful tool in determining the problem, instead of the causes or symptoms, is root cause analysis. By way of analogy, consider a doctor's visit. The patient may report a variety of symptoms, such as headaches, weight gain, and lethargy. Rather than addressing each symptom, a good doctor addresses the underlying disease. Root cause analysis is like that. Social impact organizations and networks can manage the problem's symptoms, like students not having school supplies or low vaccination rates. But, if they are going to move the needle on social issues, they need to address these symptoms' underlying causes.

Step 1: A situational analysis

First, a group of stakeholders comes together to investigate their local problem context, review relevant data, and then prioritize the most critical issues that they see. For example, a group of stakeholders might address educational outcomes, affordable housing, or substance abuse in a community. Ideally, there would be either technical reports or presentations that the group would review about the problem, presented from multiple stakeholders' viewpoints, in advance of their brainstorming session. Then stakeholders would jointly brainstorm about the most pressing problems they see evidence of in their community.

Step 2: Prioritizing the issues

Often communities come up with too many issues to trace for a root cause analysis effectively. The next step is to cluster the problems into groups. These groups might come together because the issues are related. Alternatively, stakeholders might group them because they jointly affect the same area or group of people. Once they have a group of issues, the nascent partnership can evaluate if they can address all of the issues in a root cause analysis or if they need to choose one issue. If issues groups are quite distinct, meaning the problems seem unrelated, they might rank them or vote.

Step 3: Choose the appropriate tool to conduct a root cause analysis

There are many tools available for root cause analysis.[61] We review three of the most common tools in application to social issue analysis. For each of these tools, leaders must identify evidence that establishes the relationship between each cause and its effect. Speculative maps, based on intuition alone, can provide a faulty foundation for further action.

The five whys

The five whys tool[62] is best for complicated problems and only one group of issues to address. The process begins by defining the problem from the group of issues created in step 2. Often a single sentence or two is sufficient. Then the group asks itself, *why is it happening?* This answer is the surface cause. Once a group identifies a surface cause, they ask, *why is the surface cause happening?* The answer often reveals a possible root cause. Then the group asks itself, *why is the possible root cause happening?*

Because the five whys is the simplest of the methods provided, only one possible solution per why is identified. For problems with a relatively narrow scope, this may be sufficient. However, it is insufficient for multifaceted problems.

Fishbone diagrams

Fishbone diagrams[63] sometimes help groups that prefer a more visual approach and are best suited for complex wicked problems, where the causes are not readily knowable. In this tool, the effect or the identified overarching social issue is in the right box. Then categories of causes are placed as lines off a diagonal, like the dorsal fins of a fish. Under each category, groups identify multiple underlying causes. They may also put secondary causes or underlying causes of causes in the lines off of the first-order causes.

Figure 2.1 provides a sample Fishbone diagram for childhood obesity. Typically, there are more fins or categories in Fishbone diagrams, but in this

[61] Bjørn Andersen and Tom Fagerhaug, *Root Cause Analysis: Simplified Tools and Techniques* (Milwaukee, WI: ASQ Quality Press, 2006); The Compass for SBC, "How to Conduct a Root Cause Analysis," accessed October 15, 2019, https://www.thecompassforsbc.org/how-to-guides/how-conduct-root-cause-analysis.

[62] The Compass for SBC, "5 Whys Template," accessed October 15, 2019, https://www.thecompassforsbc.org/sbcc-tools/5-whys-template.

[63] The Compass For SBC, "Fishbone Diagram Template," accessed October 15, 2019, https://www.thecompassforsbc.org/sbcc-tools/fishbone-diagram-template; The American Institutes for Research, "Center on Great Teachers & Leaders," Webpage, Center on Great Teachers & Leaders, accessed October 15, 2019, https://www.gtlcenter.org/.

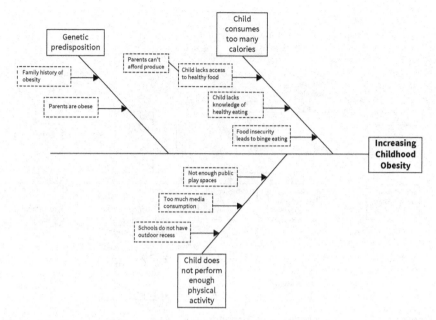

Figure 2.1. Example fishbone diagram for childhood obesity.

case, evidence supports three categories of causes. Fishbone diagrams identify more possible causes than the five whys' tool, but the analysis stops at surface causes or possible root causes. For problems where more research on causes exists (i.e., more is known about the underlying causes and possible solutions), Fishbone diagrams are unsuitable for finding the real root causes. However, in the case of complex problems, where there is not yet research available on the problem's nature, they are the most appropriate tool.

Root cause tree

Root cause trees[64] are best when the problem is multifaceted, has persisted for a long time, and has generated significant research interest. In root cause trees, a group identifies the overarching apparent problem with several symptoms. Then the apparent root causes of each of the symptoms are identified.

Figure 2.2 provides a sample root cause tree for childhood obesity. Here, not only are surface causes identified, but also several layers of root causes. Sometimes root cause trees arrive at only a few underlying problems. However, in this case, there are several root causes.

---

[64] The Compass for SBC, "Root Cause Tree Template," accessed October 15, 2019, https://www.thecompassforsbc.org/sbcc-tools/root-cause-tree-template.

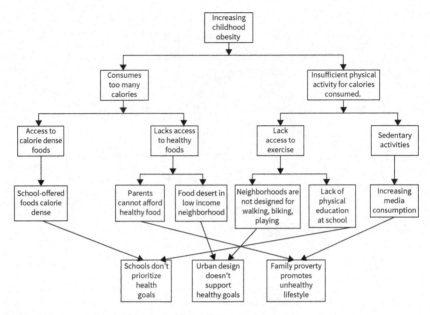

Figure 2.2. Example root cause tree for childhood obesity.

Step 4: What kind of problem is it?

The final step in root cause analysis is determining what kind of problem it is. Network instigators may need to experiment with different methods to determine the true nature of the problem. Some social problems present at first as technical problems, like RE-AMP's initial focus on decarbonization. However, upon further research, they may be more complicated or complex than they first appeared.

Depending on the type of social problem identified, a network solution may not be appropriate at all. Networks are too costly to use unless the social problem demands a network solution. Networked solutions are most appropriate in the case of complex or complicated wicked problems. Suppose the problem is simple (i.e., the solution is easily identifiable and actionable by one organization), and there are sufficient resources to address it. In that case, there is no need for a networked solution. If the problem is chaotic (i.e., the landscape is changing so fast around the issue that any action would quickly be out of date), root cause analysis would be complicated indeed. If a group has trouble putting anything into the root cause map definitively, then it indicates that the problem is chaotic. In such circumstances, a network solution is unlikely to be successful, no matter how effective the network is.

However, if the problem is complicated or complex, then a network solution may be helpful. Complicated wicked problems often have multiple known solutions, but the challenge is either implementing solutions or determining which one is best. In these cases, learning networks are often the right solution, where organizations maintain their interdependence but improve their capacity to address the social issue. In complex problems, where the answers are unknown, networks may be a good solution for another reason; the interdependencies between the problems require interdependent solutions. The problem demands more complex networks that alignment multiple organizations' efforts across domains.

3

Setting Up the Network

In August 2017, Michelle walked into a familiar scene. A former student and a United Way board member had asked her to lunch. The topic was setting up an education-focused collective impact network in their community. Both had recently attended a training Michelle had conducted on collective impact, and the United Way had indicated there could be start-up funding for the network. As the conversation turned to business, they both had the same question. "We believe that a network approach is the best way to achieve social impact. How do we get started?"

The topic of this chapter is how organizational leaders might set up a network. We draw from both the process[1] and configurational[2] approaches to describe the decisions network instigators and leaders must make. In keeping with the model presented in this book, we argue that the combination of elements and processes in establishing the network determines whether or not the network will achieve social impact.

Setting up a network is an entrepreneurial process. Many actions are similar to starting a new business or nonprofit organization, like establishing a mission, developing an organizational structure, finding funding, and gaining legitimacy. However, because networks are about coordinating existing organizations, there are some additional layers of complication. For starters, people often convene networks while acting as a member of an organization. Moreover, organizations in the network maintain their autonomy (see Chapter 1).

We describe network creation in a step-by-step sequence of decision-making. These steps include deciding what role the network instigator will play, recruiting network participants, establishing decision-making processes, setting the network's goal(s), developing external legitimacy, and getting funding. Throughout the chapter, we emphasize axiom five—there is more than one way to set up a network to achieve social impact.

---

[1] Amelia Clarke and Mark Fuller, "Collaborative Strategic Management: Strategy Formulation and Implementation by Multi-Organizational Cross-Sector Social Partnerships," *Journal of Business Ethics* 94, no. 1 (July 1, 2010): 85–101, https://doi.org/10.1007/s10551-011-0781-5.

[2] Alex Turrini et al., "Networking Literature about Determinants of Network Effectiveness," *Public Administration* 88, no. 2 (2010): 528–50, https://doi.org/10.1111/j.1467-9299.2009.01791.x.

Networks for Social Impact. Michelle Shumate and Katherine R. Cooper, Oxford University Press. © Oxford University Press 2022.
DOI: 10.1093/oso/9780190091996.003.0003

Network instigators

Before establishing the mission, before identifying organizations to recruit and developing a recruitment strategy, the instigator must determine their position. Individuals who want a network must decide what role they will play in making that happen. The instigators' roles must come first because some choices imply relinquishing the control of mission and recruitment to network participants or other groups. There are several possible choices, each with its strengths and liabilities: network host, opinion leader, network convener, and network orchestrator. In this chapter, when we describe positions that instigators may take, we almost always refer to organizations' roles.

Network hosts

Network hosts are the least prescriptive network instigator. The goal of network hosts is to maximize the serendipitous relationships that should develop among a field of organizations. Hosts hold meetings or events that have the goal of "networking" existing organizations and, in doing so, facilitate the development of network ties. Network hosts often have no prescribed plan for these interactions but instead seek to generate social impact through innovation. The host is the lowest cost role and empowers the network organizations to make their own choices.

Research[3] finds that most participants follow up with contacts to exchange resources after capacity building and networking events. Although these participants make new acquaintances, collaboration most frequently occurs after an event for participants who already knew each other. These results suggest that events more often build strong relationships from existing contacts rather than create new ties. Indeed, a two-day workshop often does not provide the necessary time or sufficient information about the other party for new partnerships to emerge. However, meetings can also have negative consequences for networks.

In Michelle's work on HIV/AIDS international NGO (INGO) networks,[4] the initial convening that the World Health Organization's Global AIDS

[3] Jennifer Ihm and Elizabeth A. Castillo, "Development and Transformation of Collaborative Networks in Events," *Journal of Convention & Event Tourism* 18, no. 3 (July 3, 2017): 205–24, https://doi.org/10.1080/15470148.2017.1322021.

[4] Michelle Shumate, Janet Fulk, and Peter R. Monge, "Predictors of the International HIV/AIDS INGO Network over Time," *Human Communication Research* 31 (2005): 482–510, https://doi.org/10.1111/j.1468-2958.2005.tb00880.x.

Programme held for HIV/AIDS INGOs and intergovernmental organizations was an important configuring event. Through the conference, various INGOs became aware of one another. These interactions laid the framework for the development of a set of relationships among those organizations. Events like this one can lead to cooperation, but it can also lead to conflict. In the 1990 conference in Paris, the International Coalition of AIDS Service Organizations' emergence created controversy because they neglected to consult the African AIDS Service Organizations in its founding. The result was a series of votes that excluded groups from different caucuses. The Africans voted the Europeans out. The women's caucus voted out the men, and the homosexual caucus (as it was named at the time) voted out the organizations with a human rights perspective on AIDS. These fractures could not have happened without the global meeting. Without the worldwide gathering, the coalition would have been more difficult to propose, and excluded participants would not have become aware of the process. Moreover, it would have been more difficult to exclude other participants if they were not at the same meeting.

Additionally, as we have shown in our research,[5] serendipitous ties are more likely among organizations that are similar to one another. In this context, this meant that HIV/AIDS INGOs from the same region or with similar views of the disease were more likely to form partnerships than organizations with different perspectives or addressing the illness in other continents. What resulted was a geographically fragmented network that further marginalized INGOs that were working in the Global South.

Opinion leaders

Opinion leaders differ from hosts in their efforts to start the network. Instigators sometimes become opinion leaders[6] when they are passionate about the potential of a network approach. Still, they realize that they are not the right person or organization to create the network. Opinion leaders are often well regarded by potential network members. They tend to carry

[5] Shumate, Fulk, and Monge, "Predictors of the International HIV/AIDS INGO Network over Time"; Yannick C. Atouba and Michelle Shumate, "Interorganizational Networking Patterns Among Development Organizations," *Journal of Communication* 60, no. 2 (2010): 293–317, https://doi.org/10.1111/j.1460-2466.2010.01483.x; Yannick C. Atouba and Michelle Shumate, "International Nonprofit Collaboration Examining the Role of Homophily," *Nonprofit and Voluntary Sector Quarterly* 44, no. 3 (2015): 587–608.
[6] Everett M. Rogers and David G. Cartano, "Methods of Measuring Opinion Leadership," *The Public Opinion Quarterly* 26, no. 3 (1962): 435–41.

new information to the group and have a high social status in the community. However, they may lack the organizational resources or access to the populations of interest. Rather than try to convene the network on their own, these leaders solicit the early support of other influential leaders. Although a convener or orchestrator may step into their role, opinion leaders often remain the network's champions.

ROC the Future, a collective impact education network in Rochester, NY, USA, provides an example of this role. Nancy Zimpher, the former chancellor of the State University of New York, served as the network's opinion leader. She was not from Rochester but engaged with the community as part of her effort to build a statewide coalition of networks. She encouraged Monroe Community College, the local community college in Rochester, to step up as the first network convener and lead agency. In many ways, Zimpher provides an emblematic example of the opinion leader's role. She brought new information to the community, and her role as chancellor gave her high status, even though she was not a resident of Rochester. However, as an outsider, she was not the right leader to coordinate the network.

Network conveners

Network conveners are organizations that "identify and bring all the legitimate stakeholders to the table."[7] These organizations play a more prescriptive role than either the network hosts or opinion leaders. They ideally have convening power, legitimacy among stakeholders, appear unbiased, have facilitation skills, and can identify all the relevant stakeholders.[8] Network conveners are often but not always funders (more on funders in Chapter 4). They have the power to call organizations to the table and encourage them to form a network. One example from our case research is the RE-AMP network. The Garfield Foundation acted as a convener in that it brought together about 20 energy sector organizations in the Midwest to work on reducing climate emissions. They funded their initial conversations and were the first funder of the network. Garfield encouraged RE-AMP's formation. But they allowed the organizations to set the goals and develop their strategy for how to work together. The foundation got the ball rolling but didn't determine its trajectory.

[7] Barbara Gray, *Collaborating: Finding Common Ground for Multiparty Problems* (San Francisco: Jossey-Bass, 1989), 71.
[8] Gray, *Collaborating*.

The network convener role is not available to all organizations. Organizations must have both the resources and the legitimacy (ideally both) to fulfill the role.[9] Also, conveners typically choose which organizations should be a part of the network, at least initially. Some conveners have a better knowledge of the organizational landscape than others.

However, we note that conveners with legitimacy, resources, and power may still not be the right candidate. In particular, foundations and other funders may undermine equitable approaches to social solutions unless they are careful because of their relative power. Michelle was facilitating an early meeting of the network begun by the United Way board member and a former student mentioned at the beginning of this chapter. They convened a meeting of key stakeholders, including the school superintendents, all the United Way education grantees in the area, a staff member in charge of neighborhood networks from the United Way, and the local police chief. She had to kick the United Way staff member out of the room because everyone who spoke stared at her face, trying to judge her reaction. Sometimes the real work and issues can get hampered by the desire for grantees to manage impressions.

Conveners influence networks in a variety of ways.[10] They respond to the requests of stakeholders for their leadership. Informally, they do this by facilitation, where they help stakeholders negotiate a common goal and understanding of the problem domain. Formally, they respond to stakeholders by granting the new network legitimacy, lending their formal authority to the new collaboration. Conveners also have a proactive role. Informally, and especially when the convener lacks formal authority, they use persuasion to convince stakeholders to participate. When the convener has official authority, they can mandate participation in the network.

Our research on conveners' activities,[11] based on 28 education-reform network case studies, found that conveners often play different roles in the network before launch and after launch. Before formation, they recruit members, host meetings, communicate the work to the public and collect and analyze data. After the network emerges, if they continue in a leadership role, network conveners mitigated confusion among stakeholders, managed rotating leadership in organizational members, dealt with differing organizational needs, and made sense of programs with different goals.

---

[9] Gray, *Collaborating*.

[10] Donna J. Wood and Barbara Gray, "Toward a Comprehensive Theory of Collaboration," *Journal of Applied Behavioral Science* 27 (1991): 139–62, https://doi.org/10.1177/0021886391272001.

[11] Katherine R. Cooper et al., "The Role of Conveners in Cross-Sector Collaborative Governance" (Association for Research on Nonprofit Organizations and Voluntary Associations, San Diego, CA, 2019).

Network orchestrators

The final role is the most prescriptive of the four, that of the network orchestrators. Network orchestrators "recruit organizational members and shape their interactions."[12] They are sometimes, but not always, founded as part of creating the network. Whether they were established for the purpose or not, network orchestrators remain central in the continued management and governance of the network going forward.[13] They often determine the answers to all of the questions in setting up the network themselves, whereas the other roles delegate the decisions to at least some others in the group.

Network orchestrators play different roles in goal-directed and serendipitous networks. In goal-directed networks, network orchestrators help to manage the network as an entity moving forward. They continue to recruit members, manage projects, secure and allocate resources (see Chapter 4); address conflict (see Chapter 5); address network data needs (see Chapter 6); and manage network change (see Chapter 7). They often facilitate working groups of various types. For example, Christopher House played this role for the Chicago Benchmarking Collaborative. They initiated the network, recruited the participants, and managed the network and its resources.

In contrast, in serendipitous networks, orchestrators help to arrange marriages among partners. Research[14] on the National Industrial Symbiosis Network in the United Kingdom provides a useful example of network orchestration. The United Kingdom formed the network to create joint environmental and economic benefits by matchmaking industrial and government organizations. They develop projects, for example, to divert landfill waste and reduce energy consumption. The National Industrial Symbiosis Network, as a matchmaker for these projects, served as a network orchestrator. They recruited organizations into the network, held events for them to meet, made strategic introductions, and encouraged the replications of projects. They continued to shape the network and its activities long after there was a network.

---

[12] Raymond L. Paquin and Jennifer Howard-Grenville, "Blind Dates and Arranged Marriages: Longitudinal Processes of Network Orchestration," *Organization Studies* 34, no. 11 (November 1, 2013): 1624, https://doi.org/10.1177/0170840612470230.

[13] Giovanni Battista Dagnino, Gabriella Levanti, and Arabella Mocciaro Li Destri, "Structural Dynamics and Intentional Governance in Strategic Interorganizational Network Evolution: A Multilevel Approach," *Organization Studies* 37, no. 3 (March 1, 2016): 349–73, https://doi.org/10.1177/0170840615625706.

[14] Paquin and Howard-Grenville, "Blind Dates and Arranged Marriages."

Recruiting network participants

The next step in setting up the network is recruiting organizations. In keeping with axiom three, the instigator's role influences the type of network recruiting possible, locking them into particular choices. Network instigators' roles imply different tasks and options.

Using events

Network hosts, for example, market events for participants to attend. All of the principles of good event marketing apply, including identifying a target market, creating a communication campaign, employing multiple channels to enact that campaign, and evaluating the strategy's success compared to goals. They rely on market demands to determine which organizations constitute the network. Prior research[15] makes three recommendations for event organizers as they recruit participants to their events. First, invite organizations with similar goals. Attendees from organizations with similar social goals are more likely to form collaborative ties than attendees from organizations with different social purposes. Second, prime organizations to think strategically about the connections they want to make through the marketing leading up to the event. Finally, network hosts use events to bring together organizations that are aware of one another but do not have an existing collaboration. Creating an actor map of existing partnerships can help identify opportunities for collaboration (see "Tools for network instigators" at the end of this chapter).

Snowball recruiting

In contrast, *opinion leaders* must first recruit prominent individuals that they think are essential to the network's functioning. Often this process involves shuttle diplomacy between influential community leaders. During these meetings, opinion leaders press the importance of the social issue and how a single organization alone cannot solve it. They describe the benefits that different types of relationships between organizations might garner, and they cast a vision of the social impact they seek to make. Network opinion

---

[15] Ihm and Castillo, "Development and Transformation of Collaborative Networks in Events."

leaders may operate alone, use a bottom-up approach to influence organizations to join the network, or find a powerful organization to serve as network instigator.

Bottom-up recruiting

A bottom-up strategy uses meetings and persuasion to entice organizations to join the network of their own volition. Like event-based recruiting, the bottom-up approach relies on market demand to determine the composition of the network. Brian Christens and Paul Speer's[16] work on community organizing participation has implications for recruiting and retaining members using a bottom-up strategy. They studied meeting attendance for 115 community-based organizations for five years. They found that over half of participants only attend one meeting, suggesting that recruitment does not stop when organizations show up. They investigated what factors led people to keep attending meetings and found that individual factors like demographics and motivation had little to do with it. Instead, it was the meeting that they attended. One type of meeting that increased the likelihood of future attendance emphasized training members on the importance of relationships and building those relationships. The other kind of meetings that worked were small research action gatherings, where participants had a role and were making sense of the data together. Participation at large event meetings decreased the likelihood that attendees would show up again.

The concept of path dependence from axiom three is evident. Network hosts and network opinion leaders rarely can engage in a top-down recruitment strategy, demanding that participants attend and form a network. And because participants have a choice, critical organizations in the network may choose not to attend or participate in the network. Failure to attract particular organizations may hamper the social impact of the network.

In bottom-up approaches, two key factors influence the composition and size of the final network (see the network typology in Chapter 1). The first is the *frame* that network opinion leaders, conveners, and orchestrators use to describe the problem. Framing means to select some aspects of a problem and make them more salient through communication as a way to "promote a particular problem definition, moral evaluation, or treatment

---

[16] Brian D. Christens and Paul W. Speer, "Contextual Influences on Participation in Community Organizing: A Multilevel Longitudinal Study," *American Journal of Community Psychology* 47, nos. 3–4 (2011): 253–63.

recommendation."[17] Frames fix ideas about the roots of the social problems and which organizations activities most concretely address that issue. For example, in Community Reach, leaders initially framed the educational outcomes they hoped to achieve in economic development terms. Their primary concerns were the movement of talented young people to larger cities and that employers would not have enough talent to stay in their communities. Kate's interviews[18] demonstrated that businesses and economic development leaders were highly engaged in the network, but educators were not. The economic development frame attracted some organizations and not others.

The second factor is the existing *network relationships*. Networks often form based on the remnants of previous networks (Chapter 7 includes more information about this process, including network reincarnations).[19] Consistent with axiom three, these latent ties can be a resource, building on the trust established in other circumstances. And they can constrain network formation since previously established patterns of relationships are more straightforward to reactivate than new ones.

However, network opinion leaders have a way out of this bottom-up recruiting lock-in effect. They can recruit influential organizations to act as network conveners or orchestrators. And organizations in these roles have a wider variety of options when recruiting other organizations.

Top-down and hybrid recruiting strategies

Network conveners and orchestrators can recruit using a bottom-up, top-down, or hybrid strategy. Some network conveners and orchestrators have the power and opt to use a top-down strategy; that is, they demand that organizations that they fund or over which they have regulatory authority form a network. When top-down methods are employed, supply-side factors, such as the number of organizations in a funder's portfolio, drive the network's composition. Sometimes a hybrid approach is attempted, where instigators mandate that some organizations join the network and invite others. Research[20]

[17] Robert M. Entman, "Framing: Toward Clarification of a Fractured Paradigm," *Journal of Communication* 43, no. 4 (1993): 52, https://doi.org/10.1111/j.1460-2466.1993.tb01304.x.

[18] Katherine R. Cooper, "Exploring Stakeholder Participation in Nonprofit Collaboration" (Dissertation, University of Illinois at Urbana-Champaign, 2014), https://core.ac.uk/download/pdf/29152991.pdf.

[19] DaJung Woo, "Exit Strategies in Interorganizational Collaboration: Setting the Stage for Re-Entry," *Communication Research*, June 4, 2019, 0093650219851418, https://doi.org/10.1177/0093650219851418.

[20] Keith G. Provan, Jonathan E. Beagles, and Scott J. Leischow, "Network Formation, Governance, and Evolution in Public Health: The North American Quitline Consortium Case," *Health Care Management Review* 36, no. 4 (2011): 315–26, https://doi.org/10.1097/HMR.0b013e31820e1124.

on the North American Quitline Consortium provides a helpful example that illustrates the hybrid approach. The North American Quitline Consortium is a network of Quitline providers that served all 50 U.S. states, 10 Canadian provinces, and 3 Canadian territories at the time of the research. Health Canada and the U.S. Department of Health and Human Services used top-down strategies to recruit members. They provided funding to encourage member organizations to create a network, supported local promotions through grants and contribution agreements, funded a national mass media campaign and a national study of quitlines, and consolidated funding from the Centers for Disease Control. The former executive director of the Center for Tobacco Cessation took a bottom-up tact, consistent with how members made decisions. She held discussions, solicited feedback, and sought to persuade quitline organizations that the network was in their interest (or better than allowing the federal government to consolidate quitlines into a national-level organization). Both strategies, in tandem, helped shape the final form and goals of the consortium.

In our research on gender-based violence organizations in Zambia,[21] we investigated two networks that used different recruitment strategies. One network operated using a bottom-up approach. The other had been convened by a dominant funder who mandated specific organizations' participation as a condition of funding (i.e., a top-down strategy). We found that the network that used the bottom-up approach had a vibrant and multiplex network, where organizations found many ways to offer services to shared clients and sometimes share scarce resources. In contrast, the top-down network had relationships that operated precisely as the grant specified—no additional serendipitous ties formed between the network members. Although we wouldn't generalize to all networks from this example, research does suggest that a bottom-up strategy makes serendipitous relationships between organizations more likely than a top-down approach.

Managing network membership

Once they begin recruiting, network leaders need to make decisions about how organizations and individuals can become a part of the network. First, will people participate in the network as individuals or organizational representatives? Most network hosts recruit individuals rather than organizations

---

[21] Katherine R. Cooper and Michelle Shumate, "Interorganizational Collaboration Explored through the Bona Fide Network Perspective," *Management Communication Quarterly* 26, no. 4 (2012): 623–54.

to participate in network events and hope that they will go back to their organizations and catalyze a relationship at the organizational level. If an instigator chooses only to recruit organizational representatives, the consequence of that choice is both positive and negative. On the positive side, individuals with the resources to make decisions on behalf of their organizations are present. As such, decisions can be much faster, and the scale of impact can often be substantial. However, because members of marginalized communities are less likely to be leaders of such organizations, these approaches further exacerbate inequality in communities. The decision locks instigators into one of these two paths (see axiom three).

Network instigators, even when they focus on organizational representatives, must also make choices about how inclusive to be in creating their network. Organizations that operate using the same values, address similar social issues, and have a similar operating strategy have an easier time working together than organizations from different social sectors.[22] Organizations with varying levels of legitimacy and resources often find it challenging to work together.[23] However, many social issues are complex and require a strategy and resources that cross sectors. An approach that relies only on one type of organization is likely insufficient to address unrelenting complex problems (see Chapter 2 for types of wicked problems).

Further, network instigators must decide the number of individuals or organizations that will participate in the network. Larger networks have more resources available to address social problems but require more complex governance structures to operate effectively. For example, the Dutch Climate Accord,[24] introduced in 2019, aims to reduce the Netherlands' carbon emissions by 49% by 2030. Hundreds of groups, including government, nongovernmental, and business organizations, developed the accord. Leadership grouped the organizations into five sector tables, with the oversight of a sixth

---

[22] Atouba and Shumate, "Interorganizational Networking Patterns Among Development Organizations"; Atouba and Shumate, "International Nonprofit Collaboration Examining the Role of Homophily"; Steve Waddell, "Complementary Resources: The Win-Win Rationale for Partnership with NGOs," in *Terms of Endearment: Business, NGOs and Sustainable Development*, ed. Jem Bendell (Sheffield, UK: Greenleaf Publishing, 2000), 193–206.

[23] Yannick C. Atouba, "Let's Start from the Beginning: Examining the Connections between Partner Selection, Trust, and Communicative Effectiveness in Voluntary Partnerships among Human Services Nonprofits," *Communication Research*, February 3, 2016, 0093650215626982, https://doi.org/10.1177/0093650215626982. Yannick C. Atouba, "Let's Start from the Beginning: Examining the Connections between Partner Selection, Trust, and Communicative Effectiveness in Voluntary Partnerships among Human Services Nonprofits," *Communication Research*, February 3, 2016, 0093650215626982, https://doi.org/10.1177/0093650215626982.

[24] Ministerie van Economische Zaken en Klimaat, "Over het Klimaatakkoord - Klimaatakkoord," *Webpage*, February 19, 2019, https://www.klimaatakkoord.nl/klimaatakkoord. Ministerie van Economische Zaken en Klimaat, "Over het Klimaatakkoord - Klimaatakkoord," *Webpage*, February 19, 2019, https://www.klimaatakkoord.nl/klimaatakkoord.

table. Each sector table was responsible for an area of concern: electricity, built environment, industry, agriculture, land use, and mobility. Organizations that could make concrete contributions to change, have vital knowledge, and make agreements on behalf of others were invited to participate at the appropriate table. A chairperson leads each sector table, and it includes several working groups and a coordinating masterplan working group. Also, there are three separate task forces for critical issues that touch each sector table, including the labor market and training, funding, and innovation. The network structure is so complex that they developed an organization chart listing tables, task forces, sub-tables, and working groups.[25] In short, having a large number of diverse participants requires more structures than a smaller number of organizations.

Finally, network instigators must decide how individuals or organizations join or leave the network. Some networks, especially those organized by network hosts, have few requirements to enter or exit. The advantage is that individuals and organizations can participate as they are able. However, this "network churn" makes it more difficult to achieve social impact. For example, the grassroots network we studied that addressed gender-based violence in Zambia had few membership requirements. This structure made it easier for organizations with little capacity, including local Zambian organizations, to participate as they were able. However, there were few network-level goals. Instead, organizations generally sought to help each other.

Alternatively, some networks, especially those created by funders, specify what roles each organization will play in the network as a grant-funding condition. In doing so, they set the exact terms of engagement and fix the boundaries of the network. The convener-led network we studied in Zambia operated in this fashion. The local chapter of a large, international development organization convened a relatively small group of organizations' work on projects funded by the United Nations and international development agencies of several Global North countries. They chose organizations for their specific skills and only recruited other international organizations, with local chapters, to participate in the network. When we asked why the coalition did not invite specific African or Zambian organizations, the partners stated that those organizations did not have the capacity to participate in these projects.

One of the most innovative membership rules we have encountered is used by the Multi-Agency Alliance for Children (MAAC), located in Atlanta,

[25] Ministerie van Economische Zaken en Klimaat, "Organisatie—Over het Klimaatakkoord—Klimaatakkoord," *Webpage*, April 18, 2018, https://www.klimaatakkoord.nl/klimaatakkoord/organisatie; Ministerie van Economische Zaken en Klimaat, "Organisatie—Over het Klimaatakkoord—Klimaatakkoord," *Webpage*, April 18, 2018, https://www.klimaatakkoord.nl/klimaatakkoord/organisatie.

Georgia, USA. Once potential members complete a rigorous vetting process, including examining the quality of their programs and services, current members vote on whether the agency is qualified to be in the network. Periodically, the network reviews current members and, if they fail to meet network standards based on a vote of existing members, dismiss them.

Once network hosts assemble the stakeholders of the network, they have few decisions left. As a weak instigator, they do not set the agenda for partnerships. Instead, they continue to host events, hoping to promote innovation and adaptation by organizations. However, other types of network instigators have several other decisions to manage, often with other organization leaders' input.

Decision-making processes

Network governance describes the ways that "participants engage in collective and mutually supportive action, that conflict is addressed, and that network resources are acquired and utilized efficiently and effectively."[26] Previous research suggests that network leaders may enact four types of network governance, three of which are addressed by Keith Provan and Patrick Kenis[27] in their foundational work on the subject. Provan and Kenis do not address serendipitous networks, which we submit are governed by concertive control. They address network governance for goal-directed networks and identify distributed, lead agency, and network administrative organization-governed networks as the three potential forms.

First, networks governed by *concertive control*[28] do not appear to have any governance at all. Instead, each organization seeks its partnerships for the benefit of the organization and its clients. However, research into these self-organizing networks demonstrates that there are mechanisms that partners use to control opportunistic behavior, including the repetition of previous partnerships[29] and partnering with partners of existing partners (i.e., triadic

[26] Keith G. Provan and Patrick Kenis, "Modes of Network Governance: Structure, Management, and Effectiveness," *Journal of Public Administration Research and Theory* 18, no. 2 (April 1, 2008): 231, https://doi.org/10.1093/jopart/mum015.

[27] Provan and Kenis, "Modes of Network Governance."

[28] Concertive control comes from the work of James Barker (J. R. Barker, "Tightening the Iron Cage—Concertive Control in Self-Managing Teams," *Administrative Science Quarterly* 38, no. 3 (September 1993): 408–37.) who describes how self-managing teams regulate the behavior of the members. Although Barker didn't apply this term to network governance, we argue that it provides a helpful analogy to the type of governance that happens in serendipitous networks.

[29] Shumate, Fulk, and Monge, "Predictors of the International HIV/AIDS INGO Network over Time."

closure).[30] These mechanisms ensure that there are consequences for opportunistic behavior and are a type of network governance. Through their application, organizations that do not keep their commitments or are harmful to their partners are organized out of the network.

Distributed governance operates differently because the network has a shared identity and seeks to optimize joint outcomes.[31] The governance strategy adopted here can be more or less structured. Sometimes, the network operates with a collective identity, but governance works much like that of a self-organizing network where each organization decides how it wants to participate. Social network research[32] on distributed-governance networks demonstrates some benefits of this option; namely, it allows human service organizations in the study to better integrate their services and become more responsive to the target population's complex needs. The Wisconsin Association for Independent Colleges and Universities Collaboration Project operates in this manner. Rolf Wegenke, president and CEO of the project, describes it this way: "Whether or not to participate and the nature of the participation, whether or not to proceed, is always made by the president of the individual institution, not by my board." Some distributed-governance networks operate using consensus-based or majority-based decision-making, where all the organizations (and sometimes citizens) in the network decide together. For example, the Chattanooga Museums Collaborative agreed to budget the funds raised in their joint capital campaign together. They mutually agreed on how to distribute all funds from the $120 million-dollar campaign. In other cases, networks create a board or executive committee, or leadership council structure. In these cases, representatives from some organizations in the network meet and make decisions for the organization.

In both lead agency and network administrative organization-governed networks, a single organization provides leadership and direction for the network. In *lead agency networks*, that organization is one of the members of the network. For example, Christopher House, a participating organization in the Chicago Benchmarking Collaborative, serves as the lead agency

---

[30] Nina F. O'Brien et al., "How Does NGO Partnering Change Over Time? A Longitudinal Examination of Factors That Influence NGO Partner Selection," *Nonprofit and Voluntary Sector Quarterly* 48, no. 6 (December 2019): 1229–49.

[31] Provan and Kenis, "Modes of Network Governance."

[32] Peter Raeymaeckers, "From a Bird's Eye View? A Comparative Analysis of Governance and Network Integration among Human Service Organizations," *Journal of Social Service Research* 39, no. 3 (2013): 416–31; see also Peter Raeymaeckers and Patrick Kenis, "The Influence of Shared Participant Governance on the Integration of Service Networks: A Comparative Social Network Analysis," *International Public Management Journal* 19, no. 3 (2016): 397–426.

coordinating the network, providing resources, and holding other network agencies accountable. In *network administrative organization*-governed networks, leaders establish a new entity that coordinates the network's activities. For example, the Westside Infant-Family Network of Los Angeles uses a network administrative organization model. The network is a legal entity with a governing board (see case study in Chapter 7).

In our work with Rong Wang on community-based networks,[33] we have found that governance through a single organization leans toward facilitation or direction. When the network governance leans toward facilitation, the governing organization views its role as enacting the members' wishes. Often agencies that lean in this direction manage multiple goals, corresponding to the many organizations that are a part of the network. For example, the Blue Ribbon Commission on the Prevention of Youth Violence in New Hanover County, North Carolina, USA, describes its network administrative organization as a "connector." In the early days of the network, action teams focused on different aspects of youth violence and each action team set its own goals.

In contrast, some lead agencies and network administrative organizations take a more directive role. They set the agenda for their network, often distribute resources to the member organizations, and hold members accountable for results. The Summit Education Initiative (see case study in Chapter 1), for example, distributes funds from its endowment and sets the direction of the network.

Governance has significant implications for achieving social impact. Research and theory demonstrate that networks with a lead agency or network administrative organization are more effective at achieving social impact than networks that operate using distributed governance in the areas of mental health and crime prevention.[34] In Chapter 2, we described this type of social impact as service-based improvement interventions. Also, both mental health and crime prevention are complicated wicked problems, where a great deal is known about the issue, and there are evidence-based interventions with a proven track record. In short, these are areas where there are standard and unchanging measures of success.

---

[33] Rong Wang, Katherine R. Cooper, and Michelle Shumate, "Alternatives to Collective Impact: The Community Systems Solutions Framework," *Stanford Social Innovation Review*, Winter 2020, https://ssir.org/articles/entry/community_system_solutions_framework_offers_an_alternative_to_collective_impact_model.

[34] Jörg Raab, Remco S. Mannak, and Bart Cambré, "Combining Structure, Governance, and Context: A Configurational Approach to Network Effectiveness," *Journal of Public Administration Research and Theory* 25, no. 2 (April 1, 2015): 479–511, https://doi.org/10.1093/jopart/mut039.

In contrast, Weijie Wang[35] finds that dense networks that connect many organizations or very stable networks are a more effective form of governance. He focused on Chinese neighborhood associations, which are small networks that are mostly self-governing. In circumstances where stable leadership is not possible, and the network is small, more dense ties are another route that enables networks to achieve social impact.

Furthermore, our research suggests that distributed-governance networks are more likely to be inclusive of community members.[36] In cases where the goal is to empower the community to address their goals, distributed-governance networks offer a better chance at success. Moreover, in such circumstances, network administrative or lead agency governance is likely to exacerbate rather than improve social inequality.

Setting the goal or goals of the network

The next step for network instigators is to determine the stated goal or goals of the network. In this step, decisions made earlier in setting up the network have a profound effect, further illustrating axiom three. Networks that are created, or catalyzed, through network hosts do not typically have an overarching goal. Instead, each organization that participates in these serendipitous networks sets their own goals, or organizations work together to set goals for dyadic or triadic partnerships.

For goal-directed networks, the process of goal setting depends on the network governance structure. Some network orchestrators who become the lead agency determine the purpose of the network at the outset. As a network instigator, they might even describe the goal before recruiting participants to the network.

Other network governance structures require participants to agree on the goal or goals of the network. As described in the "Tools for network instigators" section at the end of this chapter, many active networks use consensus-based decision-making to determine their goal. The advantage is that all network members agree to the goal, and organizations are less likely to leave the network due to goal setting. The disadvantage is that decision-making through consensus tends to be more tepid than goals set

---

[35] "Exploring the Determinants of Network Effectiveness: The Case of Neighborhood Governance Networks in Beijing," *Journal of Public Administration Research and Theory* 26, no. 2 (April 1, 2016): 375–88, https://doi.org/10.1093/jopart/muv017.

[36] Wang, Cooper, and Shumate, "Alternatives to Collective Impact: The Community Systems Solutions Framework."

independently.[37] Also, consensus-based decision-making takes a long time, which can be discouraging to network members. Our experience is that multiple goals are more likely to emerge out of the process of consensus-based decision-making, especially in larger and more diverse networks, to appease the desires of subgroups.

Some networks opt to use voting to determine their goal or goals. They solicit network members' opinions and can make decisions quickly. The downside is that network members can vote with their feet—that is, they can leave—if the group does not select their goal. Also, networks that have many small organizations and a few larger organizations face an additional challenge. Does every organization get a vote? For example, does it make sense that a nonprofit with three staff should get the same vote as the hospital that serves the entire community? A related problem is meeting attendance. Research suggests that meeting attendance in many networks is dynamic. The organizational representative may not be present to discuss goals or the vote on which goals to enact. Should attendance influence whether or not they get a vote? Here, following axiom five, we note that there are several ways to solve these issues, but networks need to be cognizant and make decisions about them in advance of a contentious vote.

Recruiting has implications for goal setting. Grassroots recruiting relies on framing the social issue to get participants to the table. Broader frames make goal setting more challenging. For example, in our study of education-focused collective impact networks across the country, some networks framed the problem primarily in terms of academic outcomes. These communities set a singular goal around post-secondary attainment or improving graduation rates.

In contrast, networks that framed the issue in terms of whole-child wellness often have multiple purposes. For instance, the Coalition for New Britain's Youth set goals around early learning, youth and workforce development, health and wellness, and family connections. Their vision is that "New Britain's youth, birth through age 24, will have the skills necessary to be successful in school, career, and life."

The research on goal setting indicates that some practices make a social impact more likely than others. First, over 35 years of research in goal-setting theory suggests that both difficult and specific goals are more likely to result in high performance.[38] The more concrete and measurable a goal is, the more

---

[37] Norbert L. Kerr and R. Scott Tindale, "Group Performance and Decision Making," *Annual Review of Psychology* 55, no. 1 (January 12, 2004): 623–55, https://doi.org/10.1146/annurev.psych.55.090902.142009.

[38] Edwin A. Locke and Gary P. Latham, "Building a Practically Useful Theory of Goal Setting and Task Motivation: A 35-Year Odyssey," *American Psychologist* 57, no. 9 (September 2002): 705–17, https://doi.org/10.1037/0003-066X.57.9.705.

likely that organizations and by extension networks are to make progress toward that goal. As a comparison, consider the difference between the network goal of Community Reach and Education for All. Community Reach's goal was to "increase the percentage of adults with high-quality degrees and credentials to 60% by 2025." Education for All's goal was to "improve the future for all of All's youth. Together." Where Community Reach had a clear, and somewhat narrow, benchmark against which to gauge their progress, Education for All did not. Instead, it was difficult to know if the network was making any progress. Moreover, by making goals very concrete and specific, groups can provide detailed feedback to members. Such feedback enhances performance.[39]

However, concrete goals are not always possible, depending on the type of social impact. Networks that seek to make advocacy-based social impact set specific policy goals, but in democratic societies, the final legislation always reflects some aspects of compromise. Similarly, networks that address complex social problems, by definition, do not have the solutions in hand that will remedy or prevent the social ill. In such networks, concrete goals are an illusion, like predicting when a scientist or inventor will make a great discovery.

Finally, the research on nonprofit effectiveness and goal setting provides some helpful guidance. The goal-attainment approach[40] generally viewed a nonprofit and, by extension, a network, as effective when it achieved its goals. However, there are several flaws with the approach that resonates with network goal setting: (1) differences in ambition and (2) goal displacement. First, some networks may have different levels of ambition when they set their goals. Consider a hypothetical example of two networks addressing the same social issue in an identical environment. Network A may set a 3% gain toward an outcome as their goal, and network B may set a 10% gain toward the same outcome as their goal. If both networks achieve a 5% gain, network A would be viewed as successful and network B as a failure. But both made the same gain. So, goal achievement is not necessarily a good indicator of the relative success of the networks. Instead, goal setting is a good motivator for network action.

Second, networks often face a problem of goal displacement,[41] where different constituencies' requirements and desires compete for attention with

[39] Edwin A. Locke and Gary P. Latham, "New Directions in Goal-Setting Theory," *Current Directions in Psychological Science* 15, no. 5 (October 1, 2006): 265–68, https://doi.org/10.1111/j.1467-8721.2006.00449.x.

[40] Daniel P. Forbes, "Measuring the Unmeasurable: Empirical Studies of Nonprofit Organization Effectiveness from 1977 to 1997," *Nonprofit and Voluntary Sector Quarterly* 27, no. 2 (June 1, 1998): 183–202, https://doi.org/10.1177/0899764098272005.

[41] Melissa M. Stone and Susan Cutcher-Fershenfeld, "Challenge of Measuring Performance in Nonprofit Organizations," in *Measuring the Impact of the Nonprofit Sector*, eds. Patrice Flynn and Virginia A. Hodgkinson (New York: Kluwer Academic/ Plenum Publishers, 2001), 33–57.

the stated system-level goal. Goal displacement is increasingly likely when networks are organized for long-term systems change. Goals about the long-term outcomes of the network are often productively paired with shorter term goals and leading indicators of success. These goals should be attainable and are often best set by organizations and professionals closest to the problem. For example, The Coalition for New Britain's Youth, in part, focuses on the mental health of children, youth, and young adults. The goal, appropriately, aims to have all children, youth, and young adults achieving "social and emotional well-being." Every two years, the working group, made up of professionals and organizations working on the issue, set up key indicators that would need to change to reach their goal. For example, a decrease in risky behaviors among middle schoolers is a leading indicator of mental health. In the short term, they set a goal of "decreased participation by 5% in risky behavior as reported by middle and high school students by 2017." Then, they created and refined programs that targeted that behavior.

Defining structures and roles

The next step in setting up a network is beginning to develop the organizational structure and roles. When networks first form, there is a great deal of ambiguity in membership status, representativeness, and structures.[42] Membership ambiguity occurs when people are not sure who is in the network and who is not. Depending on the formality of network recruitment, this may remain a challenge to identify. In informal networks and serendipitous networks, boundaries can be blurry.[43] Second, there is often early confusion on how much individuals who attend meetings for the network represent their organizations or just themselves. This problem can be especially challenging when citizens and organizational representatives are both included in the network. Finally, network structures themselves may be confusing to network members, especially if they are quite complicated.

Networks can take dramatically different forms (see Figure 3.1). At one end of the continuum is what network scholars call the hub and spoke network.[44] This structure occurs when a network administrative organization or lead

---

[42] Chris Huxham and Siv Vangen, "Ambiguity, Complexity and Dynamics in the Membership of Collaboration," *Human Relations* 53, no. 6 (2000): 771–806.

[43] Cooper and Shumate, "Interorganizational Collaboration Explored through the Bona Fide Network Perspective."

[44] Malcolm Alexander, "Big Business and Directorship Networks: The Centralisation of Economic Power in Australia," *Journal of Sociology* 34, no. 2 (1998): 107–22.

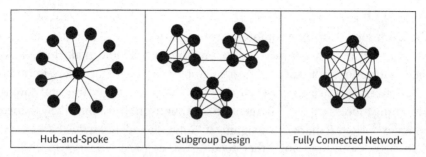

| Hub-and-Spoke | Subgroup Design | Fully Connected Network |

Figure 3.1. Idealized types of network designs.

agency acts as the central coordinator for a network, and all of the coordination occurs through their activities. For example, in our research in Zambia among organizations combating gender-based violence,[45] one organization dominated the goal-oriented coalition. They coordinated the meetings, kept all the notes, acted as the project manager for the grant, and distributed funds to the other organizations.

In contrast, at the other end of the spectrum is the fully connected network. Connected networks, in their pure form, have every organization linked to every other organization. In reality, these are densely connected networks, meaning that there are many connections compared to the possible number of connections.

In between these structures are networks that have densely connected subgroups. These subgroups are often conditioned either by homophily[46] or by network design. Homophily refers to the tendency for organizations that are similar to group together. It is the most consistent findings about why serendipitous networks have the patterns that they do. Without design intervention, subgroup networks consist of strong connections among similar organizations with bridging ties to other subgroups or network leaders.

In goal-directed networks, network design also conditions the formation of subgroups. Network design, where groups purposefully structure the subgroups to achieve some goal, operates by different terms. Examples of the designed subgroups from our research include executive committees, elected boards, steering committees, leadership tables, funder tables, action teams, working groups, and task forces. The type of common goal that organizations seek and the network's size and age influence network structure.[47]

[45] Cooper and Shumate, "Interorganizational Collaboration Explored through the Bona Fide Network Perspective."

[46] Atouba and Shumate, "International Nonprofit Collaboration Examining the Role of Homophily."

[47] Darcy Ashman and Carmen Luca Sugawara, "Civil Society Networks: Options for Network Design," *Nonprofit Management and Leadership* 23, no. 3 (2013): 389–406, https://doi.org/10.1002/nml.21062.

Networks that have a simple shared purpose, namely those that seek to exchange information or promote learning, rarely have a complex network structure. Instead, structures tend to remain relatively informal. However, as the organization's goals become more complex (e.g., joint advocacy, joint service delivery, service alignment), network structures begin to trend toward becoming more complex.[48] Larger and older networks are more likely to form complex designs if there is any significant interdependence involved.

Perhaps more than any other section, we emphasize axiom three here. Network managers continually face dilemmas brought on by the contradicting demands of the network. Their social issue framing (see Chapter 2), governance, size, membership requirements, and recruiting choices influence the eventual network structure.

Theory of change and network structure

Earlier choices made about social issue framing impact the configuration of the network. The mechanism that the network enacts to achieve social impact influences network design; put another way, task design influences network structure.[49] Here we return to the dimensions of social impact, described in Chapter 2. The social impact differs depending on the focus, type, scale, and approach. Here we introduce the theory of change that networks use—their model of how the network's activities result in social impact (see Table 3.1).

There are three corresponding mechanisms for complicated social issues, depending on the social impact the network desires to make. *Project-based mechanisms* focus on creating and delivering a new program or product from the network's joint activity. For instance, Ready, Set, Parent! created a new parent education program delivered in local hospitals and supported by health insurers and businesses. The success of that program determined their social impact. Project-based mechanisms generally require fewer organizations and, in our experience, tend to be more fully connected as a result.

Learning-based mechanisms focus on improving the quality of services that organizations already employ. Communities that Care coalitions, for example, utilize this approach. They train network members, including government agencies, on evidence-based practices that reduce youth substance abuse and

---

[48] Patrick Kenis and Jörg Raab, "Back to the Future: Using Organization Design Theory for Effective Organizational Networks Introduction: The Discovery and Study of Organizational Networks," *Perspectives on Public Management and Governance* 3, no. 2 (2020): 109–23.

[49] Kenis and Raab, "Back to the Future."

Table 3.1 Network Theories of Change

Theory of Change	Type of Problem	Dimensions	Examples
Project	Complicated or Simple (but lacks resources)	Type: Project-based	Chattanooga Museums Collaborative; Ready, Set, Parent!; MAAC
Learning	Complicated	Type: Service-based	Chicago Benchmarking Collaborative; Communities that Care coalitions
Policy	Complicated	Type: Advocacy-based	RE-AMP; Climate Action Accord;
Catalyst	Complicated	Scale: Scale an intervention	ASPIRE; Graduate! Network;
Systems Alignment	Complex	Scale: Improve an intervention	WINLA; Summit Education Initiative

other associated behaviors. The degree to which the members learn and adopt those evidence-based practices determines the outcomes of the network. In our experience, learning mechanisms tend to be associated with hub and spoke networks if they are smaller and less diverse and associated with more subgroups designs as the network grows and becomes more diverse.

Policy-based mechanisms focus on whether governments change policy as a result of the efforts of the network. A social impact results from the creation of new policies or the enforcement of existing policies. For instance, the Dutch Climate Action Accord presented its recommendations to the government. If the government enacts the recommendations, then we would expect a social impact. Depending on the breadth of the advocacy and network size, policy-based mechanisms condition the network toward a fully connected or subgroup design.

When they want to scale their impact, networks often act as a *catalyst* for partnerships or networks. They might, as in the case of ASPIRE, catalyze partnerships between organizations in their network. Alternatively, like Graduate! Network, AmericaServes, and LawHelp, they may act as catalysts for other networks in different geographies. Either way, the network holds a known solution that it seeks to scale up. As a result, the network tends toward a hub and spoke design.

In contrast, some networks do not have the benefit of a proven solution. In the face of a complex, wicked problem, *systems alignment* represents the best mechanism available for networked social impact. In it, diverse network members coordinate their joint services to explore service gaps and where earlier gains are lost. Cases reviewed earlier in this book, including WIN and the Summit Education Initiative, focus on systems alignment. Systems alignment, unless the network is small, is associated with a subgroup design.

Additionally, network design depends on the type of governance enacted and relatedly the size of the network. Distributed-governance networks tend to be more fully connected. Network administrative or lead agency networks, by in large, tend to operate in between the hub and spoke and subgroup design.

Similarly, the larger that a network becomes, the less likely that fully connected networks will emerge. A large number of organizations would make a fully connected network untenable. However, for very small networks, like the Chattanooga Museums Collaborative, this structure is quite common. In their network of three museums, everyone sat at the table as equal partners. In networks of this size, centralized and more complex network structures are both unnecessary and unlikely.

Membership requirements also shape the network structure that is likely to emerge. In some networks, only organizational representatives are allowed to participate. In others, interested citizens are also involved in network decision-making. In the networks that we have recently studied,[50] individual representatives appear to invoke more complex network structures. Often individuals will participate in action teams or working groups, not as representatives of any organization, but as interested citizens. Networks that include individual citizens are more likely to use subgroup designs.

Finally, the diversity of organizations influences network structure. In networks with diverse participation, some organizations will have missions more aligned to the common agenda than others. In other words, for some groups, the goal of the network will be central to their organization's mission and core competencies. In contrast, other organizations will have a program or service that is related. However, their mission is not. Given these different participation types, there are at least two ways that we have seen networks try to manage these apparent differences. Network leaders can create subgoals that focus on every organization's mission that they recruit to the network, thereby ensuring that everyone has a working group or task force to belong to. As discussed in the goal-setting section earlier, this reduces the potential social impact of the network.

In contrast, some networks acknowledge the difference between the two groups explicitly and define different roles for these organizations. In

---

[50] Wang, Cooper, and Shumate, "Alternatives to Collective Impact."

our article with Brint Milward,[51] we describe the Southern Alberta Child and Youth Network's strategy. They created two tables, one for the network members in the healthcare arena and one for members interested in education. They acknowledged that healthcare organizations shared a common agenda with the network. In contrast, those in the education table only partially shared the common agenda and had other more central plans for their organizations.

In later stages of the network, additional factors such as power, organizational capacity, and group processes influence the network's configuration. We dedicate Chapter 5 to discussing these dynamics. However, in the earliest stages, the network structure describes the idealized plan for operating.

Developing external legitimacy

The next step after creating roles and structures in the networks is to generate external legitimacy. Legitimacy refers to the recognition that the network is a real entity and that the networks' activities are appropriate.[52] Some serendipitous networks never seek or achieve external legitimacy because they are challenging to recognize as an entity. Instead, the network is an aggregation of each organization's partnerships. In contrast, goal-directed networks require three forms of external legitimacy: form, entity, and interaction.[53]

First, network ways of organizing, while more common now than perhaps ever before, are not as well-known and appreciated as top-down hierarchies and organizations working in relative isolation. Part of building legitimacy is to convince various stakeholders that the network's way of organizing is acceptable, and indeed, preferable.

Second, the network as an entity means that members and outsiders can perceive a network's presence. Often, this means creating a name for the network, creating marketing materials and a website, and holding meetings describing the network. Through the creation of these materials and discussion, the network becomes a reified thing.[54]

---

[51] H. Brinton Milward, Katherine R. Cooper, and Michelle Shumate, "Who Says a Common Agenda Is Necessary for Collective Impact?," *Nonprofit Quarterly*, 2016, https://nonprofitquarterly.org/who-says-a-common-agenda-is-necessary-for-collective-impact/.

[52] Sherrie E. Human and Keith G. Provan, "Legitimacy Building in the Evolution of Small-Firm Multilateral Networks: A Comparative Study of Success and Demise," *Administrative Science Quarterly* 45, no. 2 (2000): 327–65.

[53] Human and Provan, "Legitimacy Building in the Evolution of Small-Firm Multilateral Frameworks."

[54] Matthew A. Koschmann, Timothy R. Kuhn, and Michael D. Pfarrer, "A Communicative Framework of the Value of Cross-Sector Partnerships," *The Academy of Management Review* 37, no. 3 (2012): 332–54.

Third, the legitimacy for networks as interaction describes the acceptance by network members that cooperating would benefit their organizations. Network representatives often have to convince their boards, funders, and key external stakeholders that this type of interaction is valuable. They may have to overcome arguments that the network decreases their organization's unique value, competitiveness, or that network interaction is wasting time.

Legitimacy, in all its forms, is a prerequisite to social impact. Without legitimacy, it's difficult to hold the network together and maintain participation. Furthermore, legitimacy allows the network to seek external support.

Getting funding

Once the members have named the network and described its purpose, the next task is for network leaders to obtain resources (see Chapter 5 for more about network resources). Networks are not free—there are costs in coordination, technical expertise, data systems, and new collaborations to consider. The most consistent finding from configurational research is that networks require significant resources to achieve social impact.[55] In our experience and keeping with axiom five, there are at least two paths to funding.

The first is that the network members, in whole or in part, self-fund the network. The most common self-funding occurs when funders or corporate leaders are part of the network's early development. For example, when the Summit Education Initiative was founded, corporate leaders and philanthropists set up an endowment to support its work. Education for All adopted a more unusual self-funding strategy; each network member is required to donate toward the network's work on a sliding scale based upon revenues. This strategy may introduce a barrier to new organizations entering or staying in the network and ensures that all organizations have a stake. Finally, some network orchestrators or conveners have the funding to set up the network themselves. For example, the Dutch government provides funding for the Climate Action Accord.

---

[55] Raab, Mannak, and Cambré, "Combining Structure, Governance, and Context: A Configurational Approach to Network Effectiveness"; Daniela Cristofoli and Laura Macciò, "To Wind a Skein into a Ball: Exploring the Concept and Measures of Public Network Performance," *Public Management Review* 20, no. 6 (June 2018): 896–922, https://doi.org/10.1080/14719037.2017.1363904; Wang, "Exploring the Determinants of Network Effectiveness"; Provan and Milward, "A Preliminary Theory of Interorganizational Network Effectiveness."

The second path to funding is through external grant writing. Almost all of the networks we have interviewed have sought and received grants throughout their lifetime. However, some networks were founded using grant funding. For example, in part, AgeWell Pittsburgh was started to take advantage of the Nationally Occurring Retirement Communities funding that was available. These funds made it possible to create the first version of their network, where they created care teams across the participating organizations. Social workers or program coordinators went into seniors' homes and assessed the community-based services they needed to maintain their independence. Then the care team worked together to create a joint plan for each senior. This type of collaboration was only possible because of the funding available. Indeed, when AgeWell Pittsburgh lost their grant, they had to restructure how they collaborated (more on this example in Chapter 7).

Network reincarnations

Before we discuss the implications of all of these choices, we would be remiss not to mention one crucial factor influencing it all. Sometimes networks do not form out of raw organizational and community resources. Instead, some networks emerge out of other networks.

The most common way that networks emerge out of other networks is through network reincarnation. In reincarnation, a network forms out of the trace material from a dissolved network. Past relationships between organizations create the resource of latent ties.[56] Latent ties describe strong relationships where interaction is suspended or postponed. The advantage of latent ties is that organizations have worked together in the past and that history can increase trust and effectiveness in partnerships.[57] The disadvantage occurs when network instigators hope to set up the network differently than in the past. Network inertia describes a circumstance where the output of the collaboration becomes negligible and very little gets done.[58] Consistent with axiom three, latent ties can create a type of inertia where participants use

[56] Francesca Mariotti and Rick Delbridge, "Overcoming Network Overload and Redundancy in Interorganizational Networks: The Roles of Potential and Latent Ties," *Organization Science* 23, no. 2 (April 2012): 511–28, https://doi.org/10.1287/orsc.1100.0634.
[57] Atouba, "Let's Start from the Beginning."
[58] Chris Huxham and Siv Vangen, "Doing Things Collaboratively: Realising the Advantage or Succumbing to Inertia?," in *Collaborative Governance—A New Era of Public Policy in Australia?*, eds. Janine O'Flynn et al. (Australia: The Australian National University, 2009), 29–44, http://epress.anu.edu.au/anzsog/collab_gov/pdf/ch04.pdf.

their prior working relationships, rather than new network structures and plans, as guides.

Once the network has recruited members, created decision-making and network structure, set a goal or goals, and obtained resources, a network is born. The decisions that network instigators make throughout the process shape the network. Those choices have implications for the social impact that the network will make.

Dead ends in network emergence

Axioms three, four, and five, combined, guide the outcomes of network emergence. Axiom four reminds us that not all options will result in social impact. Indeed, most networks fail to launch.

Networks never get off the ground

Just like many entrepreneurs fail to launch an organization, many networks fail after an initial set of meetings. There are many reasons why network instigators abandon their plans to form a network. Sometimes they are unable to attract the necessary resources. Sometimes they had not considered their role as network instigators and how it might detract from their organization's mission and activities. With no network, organizations make their impact, which may be preferable in some cases. When networks fail to achieve impacts beyond what the organizations could have accomplished independently, they reduce the social impact that these organizations could have made. Our research[59] on 452 nonprofit organizations found that partnerships, including cross-sector partnerships, did not increase capacity. The implication is that collaborations do not usually make organizations better at what they do. Therefore, we echo Huxham and Vangen's[60] advice that partnerships and by extension networks are not worth the cost unless necessary to achieve the social impact sought and organized well.

[59] Michelle Shumate, Jiawei Sophia Fu, and Katherine R. Cooper, "Does Cross-Sector Collaboration Lead to Higher Nonprofit Capacity?," *Journal of Business Ethics* 150, no. 2 (June 1, 2018): 385–99, https://doi.org/10.1007/s10551-018-3856-8.

[60] Huxham and Vangen, "Doing Things Collaboratively."

Network instigators choose to become hosts

Additionally, when network instigators choose to act as network hosts, they reduce the likelihood that their network will make a social impact. Network hosts create lovely events and networking opportunities. However, at best, serendipitous networks are strengthened as a result. Serendipitous networks increase innovation,[61] and, in some cases, they may create programs, services, or products that benefit the constituencies of organizations involved. Moreover, they are often the basis for future goal-directed networks and are the most appropriate response to chaotic problems. However, large-scale social impact rarely results from serendipitous networks.

Network dilemmas in emergence

In setting up a network, instigators must navigate a variety of dilemmas. These tensions are not solved when the network is set up but continue as the network progresses. They demonstrate that some contradicting demands in networks are never resolved; they are simply managed. In this section, we highlight four ongoing contradictions that present managerial dilemmas in networks.

Efficiency and inclusivity

One of the first choices network instigators face is their recruitment strategy. Network instigators must choose whether they will recruit individuals or only organizational representatives and use grassroots or top-down recruiting, or a hybrid thereof. Networks that choose organizational representatives and top-down recruiting tend to have challenges addressing social and racial equity. In contrast, networks that allow for an unlimited number of individual members, in addition to organizational representatives, and use grassroots recruitment, will struggle to move forward toward achieving their goals efficiently. Similarly, networks manage the inclusion/efficiency dilemma[62]

---

[61] Walter W. Powell, K. W. Koput, and L. SmithDoerr, "Interorganizational Collaboration and the Locus of Innovation: Networks of Learning in Biotechnology," *Administrative Science Quarterly* 41, no. 1 (March 1996): 116–45.

[62] Provan and Kenis, "Modes of Network Governance"; J. K. Popp et al., "Inter-Organizational Networks," Collaboration across Boundaries Series (Washington, DC: IBM Center for the Business of Government, 2014).

when making choices about their network's decision-making process and the number of goals they will have.

Ambiguity and specificity in social issue framing

The broader the frame, the greater the potential for diverse organizations to participate in the network. However, a too-broad frame confuses potential participants about what the network will do and what their role might be in it. Most successful network instigators who use the bottom-up recruiting choose one of two strategies. They either opt for a highly concrete frame because they want a homogenous set of actors to accomplish a very particular task (often framed as a technical problem), or they operate using the principle of strategic ambiguity. Strategic ambiguity describes "an ambiguous statement of core values" that allows people to maintain different interpretations but perceive that they are in unity with others.[63] For example, consider the difference between a network that aims to reduce the opportunity gap in third grade reading with a network that seeks to promote the well-being and lifelong success of elementary-age youth. The latter aim employs strategic ambiguity that would allow both a literacy program and a mental health agency to see their interpretation of the social problem. Even though they may have very different definitions of "well-being and lifelong success," they can perceive themselves as united in their efforts to address this social issue. Through strategic ambiguity, various potential participants may interpret the complicated or complex problem differently and find a way to see themselves as a part of the solution.

Constant frame versus a dynamic frame

All of the social problems we refer to in this book—climate change, education, and child welfare, to name a few—are dynamic social issues that scholars and practitioners continue to learn about. With that said, network actors may choose to emphasize—or downplay this dynamism. Some networks may opt for constancy, framing a social problem over time. That does not mean that the network is unresponsive to its environment. Instead, it focuses on a long-term need or a population whose needs remain constant. For example,

[63] Eric M. Eisenberg, "Ambiguity as Strategy in Organizational Communication," *Communication Monographs* 51, no. 3 (September 1, 1984): 231, https://doi.org/10.1080/03637758409390197.

MAAC has existed for decades to fill service gaps for youth and families in the child welfare system. In these cases where there are ongoing needs and clientele already subject to turbulence, the use of a constant frame helps retain partners who remain fixated on the goal and helps funders identify a strong track record of success for the network.

In contrast, other networks find that a more dynamic frame allows them to be more responsive. Following the leadership of environmental justice organizations, RE-AMP reframed its goals to focus on equitable decarbonization. By doing so, they became more mutually relevant to a broader set of participants interested in the ways that climate change disproportionately affects individuals from historically marginalized populations.

Bottom-up or top-down framing

Who frames the social problem is potentially one of the most contentious debates in academic scholarship on networks.[64] When network researchers talk about framing, they typically describe it as a network manager or funders' function.[65] For example, WIN was formed after a funder provided money for nonprofits to focus on early childhood mental health. Leaders often choose top-down framing because of financial resources. However, top-down framing has the potential to alienate community members and undermine their support. To alleviate this concern, some networks invite community input in framing the problem. In doing so, the network addresses marginalized groups' disempowerment and integrates the communities' lived experience of the problem as essential to resolving it.[66] However, a bottom-up process tends to emphasize several different facets to the problem, which may not be easy to package for funders. For example, My Brother's Keeper Network in Mt. Vernon, New York, USA, used a bottom-up approach to frame opportunity gaps for Black men. The community identified six aspects of the problem: getting to school, ready to learn, reading by third grade, graduating from high school, entering the workforce, and living violence-free. However, they struggled to align these goals into a single overarching framework.

[64] Renee Guarriello Heath and Matthew G. Isbell, *Interorganizational Collaboration: Complexity, Ethics, and Communication* (Long Grove, IL: Waveland Press, 2017).

[65] Michael McGuire and Robert Agranoff, "The Limitations of Public Management Networks," *Public Administration* 89, no. 2 (2011): 265–84.

[66] Brian D. Christens, *Community Power and Empowerment* (New York: Oxford University Press, 2019); Marc A. Zimmerman, "Empowerment Theory," in *Handbook of Community Psychology*, eds. Julian Rappaport and Edward Seidman (Boston, MA: Springer, 2000), 43–63.

Pathways to social impact from network emergence

Finally, several different paths may lead to social impact (axiom five). The choice of pathway typically reflects the resources available (see Chapter 4), the mechanisms for social impact, and partnering history.

Goal-directedness, orchestration, and external legitimacy

The two essential elements that networks require, regardless of their context, are goal-directedness and external legitimacy. Serendipitous networks result in important organization- and network-level outcomes (see Chapter 2). Some orchestrated serendipitous networks, like ASPIRE, achieve social impact through the aggregation of organizational outcomes. However, most networks that make a social impact are goal-directed. Goal-directed networks have a common purpose or purposes.[67] Organizations act in coordinated ways to affect social issues. And because goal-directedness allows networks to become recognized as an entity, they are more likely to accrue external legitimacy.

External legitimacy[68] is a necessary, but not sufficient, condition for social impact. Without legitimacy, networks will struggle to get buy-in for their activities. And perhaps most importantly, with external legitimacy, networks can attract necessary resources. And research[69] suggests that networks require resources to make a social impact. It's a nonnegotiable.

The choices networks make work together

Beyond external legitimacy and goal-directedness, the combination of choices that network instigators make influences the likelihood of social impact. For instance, governance structure alone does not determine social impact.[70] Instead, governance choices should align with the network's size and the mechanism for social impact pursued. Distributive governance is often appropriate in small networks. Larger networks usually require network

---

[67] Human and Provan, "Legitimacy Building in the Evolution of Small-Firm Multilateral Networks."

[68] Human and Provan, "Legitimacy Building in the Evolution of Small-Firm Multilateral Networks."

[69] Wang, "Exploring the Determinants of Network Effectiveness"; Steffie Lucidarme, Greet Cardon, and Annick Willem, "A Comparative Study of Health Promotion Networks: Configurations of Determinants for Network Effectiveness," *Public Management Review* 18, no. 8 (September 2016): 1163–217, https://doi.org/10.1080/14719037.2015.1088567; Raab, Mannak, and Cambré, "Combining Structure, Governance, and Context."

[70] Turrini et al., "Networking Literature about Determinants of Network Effectiveness."

administrative organizations or lead agencies with significant capacity for the role. Networks hoping to make a catalyst social impact rely on network administrative organizations or lead agencies. Distributed governance, where each organization interprets the innovation in its own ways, would undermine fidelity. Similarly, systems alignment requires a lead organization or a network administrative organization because of the coordination tasks' complexity. However, networks that make project-based or policy-based social impact can often function using distributed-governance mechanisms, as long as they are relatively small.

The key to social impact is making the right combination of choices for the network's context and purpose. In Chapter 1, we described our approach as a systems approach. When the elements of a network design work together, the whole is more than the sum of the parts. When they do not align, networks are like a bicycle with a dropped chain. The parts no longer work together.

Conclusion

There were many more lunches with the former student and the United Way board member introduced at the beginning of this chapter. Over time, the conversation moved from starting their network to managing it. The next two chapters address the most pressing challenges that networks face after emergence: acquiring resources and dealing with conflict.

Case study: Education for All

The CEO and COO of the All Community Foundation, Eliza and Jane, were optimistic about their medium-sized organization's future. The United Way had consolidated in their area and moved its funding to other suburbs with greater need. Thus, the All Community Foundation became the largest non-profit providing grants in town. Most of its board members thought that the community foundation should continue their tradition of funding diverse projects that would make their suburb a vibrant place to live. Moreover, a large foundation had selected All Community Foundation to be part of a cohort of funders from across the United States. Their selection demonstrated that they were a national leader among community foundations.

The funding from that award allowed Eliza and Jane to attend conferences and participate in a monthly conference call with leaders from nearly 20 other community foundations. During those meetings, they had become convinced that their organization needed a signature issue, and that issue should be education. A signature issue would allow the All Community Foundation to stand out in a competitive donor marketplace and better position them for grant funding. Moreover, they had already established a group for early childhood educators that met quarterly, so they were already working in education. At a recent conference, they had heard about a new model of doing business called collective impact. It called for organizations across the cradle-to-career pipeline to work together to move the needle for youth in their community. The results that other communities reported were inspiring.

Just last week, at a community panel on education at their local high school, they heard the superintendent of schools say that about 100 students entering the high school each year were not prepared to do high school-level work. In another meeting, Jane had heard an early childhood nonprofit say that about 100 students entered kindergarten unprepared each year because they either didn't attend preschool or attended a poorly performing one. Jane wondered aloud to Eliza whether these were the same kids. Eliza, convinced they were, replied: "This is the reason we have to start a collective impact network here."

Questions to consider

1. What are the opportunities and challenges that Jane and Eliza face as they develop a collective impact network for their suburb?
2. What should Jane and Eliza say to their board members about the potential benefits of forming a network?
3. Assuming they are successful at convincing their board, what type of network instigator should Jane and Eliza be?

Tools for network instigators

The choices that network instigators make in setting up a network have significant consequences for the types of outcomes that the network is likely to achieve.
We have found two practices immensely helpful when setting up networks: creating actor maps[71] and consensus-based decision-making.[72] Both tools are essential for setting up a robust and productive network, but for different reasons.

Actor mapping

Actor maps are a form of environmental scan. They help the network instigator understand who should be in the network and to capitalize on existing
collaborations among actors. Without doing this activity, a nascent network runs
the risk of duplicating services (and therefore competing) with existing actors.

Moreover, key network actors can be overlooked or invited late to network
meetings. For example, in the Education for All network, a key political leader in
the town wasn't identified as an important actor until the group had nearly reached
consensus on its common goal. The late addition of this actor derailed their movement because that leader, a representative of the minority community in town,
noted that the process neglected her constituents and ignored the historical racism
that persisted in the city. An actor map can help prevent this circumstance.

The process of developing an actor map often takes two or three meetings of
at least two hours. It can take substantially longer as the number of actors the
network instigator hopes to recruit increases. Box 1 describes how to make an
actor map and Figure 3.2 is an example of one.

Once the map is created, there are several possible choices that network
instigators might make. They can use this information to begin to develop
collaborations for their organization. Alternatively, they might choose to
focus only on one segment of the map at first, defining the problem more
narrowly. They might try to recruit actors toward the center of the map, creating a network of the most influential players. Or they might identify existing
networks that could be expanded by including unconnected players. In each
case, network instigators will be more informed about the actors they might
want to bring to the table or potential partners.

---

[71] "Guide to Actor Mapping," *FSG*, December 1, 2015, https://www.fsg.org/tools-and-resources/
guide-actor-mapping.
[72] "Consensus Decision Making," *Seeds for Change*, accessed June 24, 2019, http://www.seedsforchange.
org.uk/consensus.

Box 3.1 Creating an Actor Map (step by step)

1. Draw a large circle. Define the central social problem that is the basis for the collaboration. It might be slowing climate change or improving the care of veterans. Put that in a smaller circle at the center of a large circle.

2. Consider the significant dimensions of the problem that would need to be included to create social change. Each of those dimensions should form slices of pie in the big circle, radiating out from the smaller circle. For example, an actor map that focuses on improving the lives of children might have slices for family, school, health and safety, social services and supports, and others.

3. Identify all of the roles, settings, and organizational actors that are influential. Put each of these on a sticky note. Place the sticky notes in the slices where they belong. Put entities that are more influential closer to the center of the circle and entities that are less influential closer to the edge of the ring.

4. Draw lines between the entities based on existing collaboration focusing on the central issues that were defined.

5. Identify groups of actors that form commonly understood areas of influence. A climate action network, for instance, might draw circles around energy companies as a set of actors and conservation nonprofits as a separate set of actors.

6. Step back and evaluate the map.

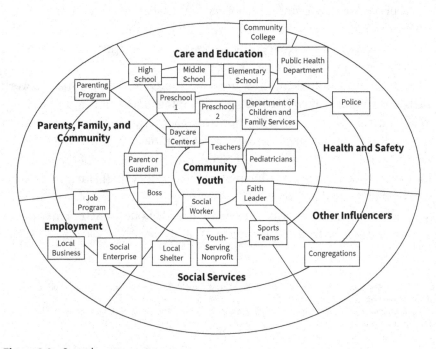

Figure 3.2. Sample actor system map.

Consensus-based decision-making

The second process that helps set up networks, not organized by network orchestrators or top-down conveners, is to develop consensus-based decision-making rules. Unless a powerful actor is compelling an organizational leader to be a part of the network, participants who disagree with the network's direction will either stop participating or seek to undermine the network. Voting often results in a core set of similar actors being a part of the network, and all that would stand in their way exiting. In some of the worst circumstances, we've seen disaffected members set up an alternative network of their own.

Consensus-based decision-making is a formal process. It often takes longer, but it doesn't mean that members of the potential network talk about the decision forever. There are several variants possible with larger groups, but the basic model formalizes the decision-making process. First, everyone needs to understand the decision to be made and why it's important. Then, a group that has the greatest or a significant stake in the decision raises a proposal. Next, the facilitator asks the group if there are any "blocks." Blocks mean that a person or group cannot live with the proposal, as stated. The group or person that blocks must offer a counterproposal. That process continues until there are no blocks. In the case of a real deadlock, actors involved in multiple rounds of blocks and counterproposals negotiate in others' presence. They are encouraged to listen carefully to the others' concerns and work creatively to find a solution that will benefit all involved.

When there are no blocks, the facilitator asks the group if there are any stand-asides, meaning they don't see their stake in the issue, or friendly amendments, which are small changes or additions that do not change the core of the proposal offered. The group that proposed is allowed to agree to or reject the friendly amendments. Once the group makes all the modifications, then they have an agreement.

We teach consensus-based decision-making to emerging networks because it forces networks to do the hard work of really listening to all the members and finding ways to meet everyone's needs. A transparent decision-making process that respects all of those with a stake in the issue goes a long way to building trust.

4

The Influence of Funders and Resources

The Ready, Set, Parent! program was created in Buffalo, NY, USA to promote parental education and involvement in babies' developmental growth. The partners developed a multi-pronged approach to helping parents, consisting of an in-room visit to the new family, the option of a newborn care class before leaving the hospital, and a series of workshops available to parents in the weeks and months following the arrival of their baby. Every Person Influences Children (EPIC) was smaller than its partner organizations, but it provided the program's educational materials, and a larger partner provided the connections to local hospitals. Shelley Richards of EPIC described their partnership as "a nice marriage in that way."

The foundations of participating hospitals, insurers, and even a corporate sponsorship funded the Ready, Set, Parent! collaboration. It was a finalist for the 2009 Lodestar Collaboration Prize. However, despite these successes, the program ended. And although the partnership had a good model in that partners contributed different resources (e.g., the money to implement the program, staff labor to make hospital visits or bill the insurers), the partners ultimately came up against the limitations of their most precious resource: time. As new parents and their babies spent less time in the hospital, there was no longer enough time to implement the program in its current form.

As illustrated in the EPIC case, the process of amassing and exchanging resources is fundamental to creating and sustaining networks. Organizations form networks to access unique resources that individual partners possess or to generate resources collectively. Often, the presence—or absence—of resources is the main reason why organizations collaborate at all.

However, much of what we understand from research and practice focuses on the availability of financial resources instead of knowledge, relationships, technology, and time. Although networks for social impact require extensive resources, the availability of resources does not guarantee results. Too often, networks focus their efforts on obtaining or maintaining financial resources, sometimes at the expense of cultivating other resources required to achieve impact.

Networks for Social Impact. Michelle Shumate and Katherine R. Cooper, Oxford University Press. © Oxford University Press 2022.
DOI: 10.1093/oso/9780190091996.003.0004

This chapter explores financial resources and the network's relationship with the funders that provide those resources. We also describe other types of relationships and resources that influence a network's ability to achieve impact. To that end, we start with the premise that all networks need resources and review types of resources required to achieve an impact. Next, we explore the resource-related challenges that can inhibit a network's ability to reach impact. Finally, we suggest how networks can overcome these challenges by offering additional pathways to social impact.

The resources that bring social impact networks together

Axiom two states that networks are sensitive to their environment. The presence of resources in an environment determines what kind of network arrangements are possible (see Chapter 3). In many cases, organizations are motivated to come together to access or share resources. Other organizations in the partnership[1] hold both tangible and intangible resources.[2] For example, when EPIC partnered with the local hospital, they gained access to tangible resources—like the hospital's funding and staff. Corporate partners also stand to benefit; in this case, Fisher-Price, the corporate sponsor, could receive intangible benefits by promoting its work with the community.[3] In serendipitous networks, organizations seek out partners with assets that complement those that they already possess.[4] For example, in ASPIRE, paired companies created new arrangements in which one company's industrial waste served as the input for another company's production. In goal-directed networks, both member organizations and the new network entity seek out resources. Goal-directed networks are costly activities, and they may compete with organizations for scarce resources (see axiom 1).

[1] Jeffrey Pfeffer and R. Gerald Salancik, *The External Control of Organizations: A Resource Dependence Perspective* (New York: Harper & Row, 1978).

[2] Birger Wernerfelt, "A Resource-Based View of the Firm," *Strategic Management Journal* 5, no. 2 (1984): 171–80, https://doi.org/10.1002/smj.4250050207.

[3] Michelle Shumate, Yuli Patrick Hsieh, and Amy O'Connor, "A Nonprofit Perspective on Business–Nonprofit Partnerships: Extending the Symbiotic Sustainability Model," *Business & Society* 57, no. 7 (September 1, 2018): 1337–73, https://doi.org/10.1177/0007650316645051; James E. Austin and Maria May Seitanidi, "Collaborative Value Creation: A Review of Partnering between Nonprofits and Businesses. Part 2: Partnership Processes and Outcomes," *Nonprofit and Voluntary Sector Quarterly* 41, no. 6 (2012): 929–68.

[4] Stuart L. Hart, "A Natural-Resource-Based View of the Firm," *Academy of Management Review* 20, no. 4 (October 1, 1995): 986–1014, https://doi.org/10.5465/amr.1995.9512280033.

Networks can also generate resources through interaction among partners.[5] When networks focus more on the exchange of resources than creating resources to make a social impact—that is, when networks are more focused on exchanging what they already have instead of securing or developing more resources together—they undermine the network's potential.[6] When organizational participants are more fixated on their interests than the social problem that unites partners, they remain relatively autonomous. In these circumstances, partner interaction tends to be transactional and, consequently, partnerships may not be long-lasting.

Transactional interactions are common when businesses participate in networks for social impact. James Austin, a management scholar, has criticized business-nonprofit relationships as too philanthropic (i.e., transactional) and failing to realize more significant interaction benefits. His initial collaboration continuum[7] described three types of collaboration.[8] In philanthropic partnerships, organizations act as a donor-recipient. Resources flow one way from the business to the nonprofit or social impact network. Philanthropic partnerships are the most common type.

In contrast, transactional partnerships are two-way resource exchanges. In this partnership, the social impact network received benefits, but the business benefits as well. Cause-marketing campaigns are emblematic of this type of relationship.

Integrative arrangements involve more interaction and the creation of a "mutual mission relationship."[9] For example, in Community Reach, local businesses were committed to the mission of the network. They were highly engaged in its work, attending meetings, contributing resources, and offering employee time. In integrative partnerships, the interaction among partners creates new resources.

In sum, when organizations focus on exchanging resources instead of creating resources, they miss a valuable opportunity. Some resource exchange is necessary. Indeed, businesses and foundations still contribute

---

[5] Edward J. Zajac and Cyrus P. Olsen, "From Transaction Cost to Transactional Value Analysis: Implications for the Study of Interorganizational Strategies*," *Journal of Management Studies* 30, no. 1 (1993): 131–45, https://doi.org/10.1111/j.1467-6486.1993.tb00298.x.

[6] John W. Selsky and Barbara Parker, "Platforms for Cross-Sector Social Partnerships: Prospective Sensemaking Devices for Social Benefit," *Journal of Business Ethics* 94, no. 1 (July 1, 2010): 21–37, https://doi.org/10.1007/s10551-011-0776-2; James E. Austin and Maria M. Seitanidi, "Collaborative Value Creation: A Review of Partnering between Nonprofits and Businesses: Part I. Value Creation Spectrum and Collaboration Stages," *Nonprofit and Voluntary Sector Quarterly* 41, no. 5 (2012): 726–58.

[7] James E. Austin, "Strategic Collaboration Between Nonprofits and Businesses," *Nonprofit and Voluntary Sector Quarterly* 29, no. 1_suppl (March 1, 2000): 69–97, https://doi.org/10.1177/0899764000291S004.

[8] See also Austin and Seitanidi, "Collaborative Value Creation."

[9] Austin, "Strategic Collaboration Between Nonprofits and Businesses," 75.

to financial and human resources in integrative arrangements. But, to make the most of these relationships, partners require more significant interaction.

One of the reasons why funders and businesses may be hesitant to move beyond philanthropic relations is power. When one or two organizations in a network possess resources that are not easily acquired, these resource-holding organizations have power.[10] They can then use that power to demand compliance from other organizations, especially if they do not depend on other organizations' resources in return. These differences may be particularly evident in networks where organizations represent different sectors, sizes, or cultures. For instance, in our research in Zambia, some locally operated coalitions were funded by international agencies, further highlighting this disparity. In contrast, when funders and businesses become involved in integrative partnerships with the network, the network's power disparities are less pronounced (see Chapter 5 for more about power disparities). Instead, all partners must rely on the intangible and tangible resources that different organizations possess.

What resources are needed to achieve social impact?

Both tangible and intangible resources are needed to achieve social impact.[11] Tangible resources include money, land, facilities, machinery, supplies, structures, and natural resources. Intangible resources include knowledge, capabilities, management practices, and skills. Although money—a tangible resource—tends to dominate the conversation, intangible resources (e.g., knowledge, relationships) may be more valuable because they are more difficult for other partners to replicate.[12]

Resources are properties that might be possessed, acquired, or manipulated by network members or actors in a network's environment (e.g., funders). We focus on those that tend to be most pertinent in the networks we have studied and those required to achieve social impact. Most networks for social impact typically mobilize around financial resources, human resources, technology, and time.

---

[10] Pfeffer and Salancik, *The External Control of Organizations: A Resource Dependence Perspective.*
[11] Austin and Seitanidi, "Collaborative Value Creation," 933.
[12] Hart, "A Natural-Resource-Based View of the Firm."

Financial resources

Some research considers financial resources part of a broader category of physical resources.[13] However, the hunt for financial resources takes up so much of network members' time and energy—not to mention that money is the most frequently mentioned resource within network and collaboration research—that we think it merits its own discussion.

Networks are expensive undertakings. Within research, the term "resource munificence" refers to the availability of financial resources and is a precondition for network effectiveness.[14] A major grant (e.g., AgeWell's Naturally Occurring Retirement Communities grant) helped launch many of the networks we studied. Partners find that their expenses add up very quickly, especially as the network has some early successes and begins to scale up their work. For example, in the Summit Education Initiative, leaders pointed out that their budget has increased from $300,000 to $1.5 million in its first six years of operation.

Axiom three suggests that some network management challenges are never-ending. One of those never-ending challenges is that of fundraising for the network while still responding to organizational needs. Nonprofit organizations are familiar with this practice, in general. However, there is an additional challenge for those raising funds for the network and their respective organizations. Heather Rowles of MAAC points out that not all network members like to fundraise. It's necessary, she says, because "if I'm fundraising, I can help the other agencies and the kids [we serve]." However, she acknowledged that some partners feel that fundraising on behalf of the network takes away time from their agency work supporting children.

Network members also find themselves pursuing resources for the network that would benefit individual organizations, an organization-network conflict discussed in Chapter 5. Alexis Mancuso of AgeWell Pittsburgh describes the shift from thinking about organizational resources to network resources in these terms: "If one of us sees a grant opportunity, we don't say ah, for [my organization], I can go do all of these great things for older adults. It's always in conversation with AgeWell partners about who's the right person to ask for the dollars at the lead agency."

Network members find innovative ways of responding to this challenge. Education for All requires partners to make a financial contribution to the

[13] Hart, "A Natural-Resource-Based View of the Firm."

[14] K. G. Provan and H. B. Milward, "A Preliminary Theory of Interorganizational Network Effectiveness: A Comparative Study of Four Community Mental Health Systems," *Administrative Science Quarterly* 40, no. 1 (1995): 161–190.

network so that partners "have skin in the game" instead of relying exclusively on external funding. Some networks use a fiscal sponsorship (see "Tools for network instigators" in this chapter for more about fiscal sponsorship). Hadass Sheffer of The Graduate! Network said that her team "always advocated that each local affiliate not be its own [organization] that then has to deal with issues of funding itself." Other networks become their own entity. MAAC ultimately changed its structure to become a 501(c)3, a legal designation for nonprofits in the United States. Heather Rowles of MAAC acknowledges that there can be competition between the network and the agencies for funds. But the "tremendous opportunities" provided by having this status has "allowed us to grow and serve more youth and also qualify for grants to help and sustain us and do new programming."

Although financial resources are essential to a network, they are not the only resources needed. Many network stories begin with a grant or financial gift of some kind. But network leaders quickly realize that more help is required.

Human resources

Networks for social impact depend on human resources to coordinate their activity. After starting Graduate! Philadelphia, with the local United Way, Hadass Sheffer described adding organizational partners with varied expertise. These partners included separate agencies that knew about economic development, workforce investment, college education, and financial interests. In addition, she recruited nonprofits that served the target population of adult learners interested in returning to college. Sheffer's experience illustrates two human resources necessary for networks for social impact: knowledge and relationships. Graduate! Philadelphia's success was contingent on those with specialized knowledge, such as knowledge about local industries and financial aid—and relationships with the network's potential beneficiaries.

Networks organized around complicated problems may require fewer resources than complex problems (see Chapter 2 for the distinction). Because so much is unknown about complex problems, networks often recruit additional partners when they realize they need other knowledge. In Education for All, organizational leaders initially formed the network in response to literacy. But as the network continued its work, they realized that other community concerns impacted educational outcomes. It was not enough to have experts in education and literacy leading the charge; they also began to incorporate childhood health, trauma, and equity expertise. In trying to incorporate these perspectives, Education for All was bringing in diverse expertise.

Prior research distinguishes between two types of knowledge:[15] explicit knowledge[16] and tacit knowledge. Explicit knowledge is found within formal systems or conveyed via words or numbers. Many of the networks described in this book—WIN, MAAC, or LawHelp—rely on staff with specialized expertise in social work, mental health, or the law. These networks depend on individuals with substantial knowledge that includes licensing or credentials obtained through institutions and formal systems.

Senses, experiences, or intuition hold tacit knowledge. Explicit knowledge, in contrast, is located in systems or formal institutions.[17] For example, Education for All relied not just on best practices for improving literacy or career readiness, things we would recognize as explicit knowledge. They also relied on leaders who could identify community needs that went beyond statistics. They wanted leaders who could articulate the feelings and concerns that would dictate whether the community would accept the network's activities. Leaders often acknowledge that explicit knowledge is needed for the network to get started (e.g., the statistics that point to a problem, the abundance of best practices and data-proven interventions, the narratives about what has proven successful elsewhere). But tacit knowledge enables network leaders to understand whether these interventions will work in their community.

Relationships represent another form of human resources. Most communities offer white pages or websites that list organizations working in any specific area. However, networks are rarely successful just because they include all the relevant organizations. Instead, relationships enable organizations to succeed. For example, in an Education for All meeting in which leaders discussed recruiting new members, prospects were evaluated in part because of who they knew—and specifically, whether they had ties to underrepresented communities in the area.

---

[15] Elizabeth A. Smith, "The Role of Tacit and Explicit Knowledge in the Workplace," *Journal of Knowledge Management; Kempston* 5, no. 4 (2001): 311–21, http://doi.org10.1108/13673270110411733.

[16] Explicit knowledge may also be referred to as procedural knowledge or declarative knowledge.

[17] Robert Agranoff, "Inside Collaborative Networks: Ten Lessons for Public Managers," *Public Administration Review* 66 (2006): 56–65; Hubert Saint-Onge and Charles Armstrong, *The Conductive Organization* (Amsterdam: Elsevier, 2004); Michael Polanyi, *The Tacit Dimension* (London: Routledge, 1966); Jean Hartley and Maria Allison, "Good, Better, Best? Inter-Organizational Learning in a Network of Local Authorities," *Public Management Review* 4, no. 1 (January 2002): 101–18, https://doi.org/10.1080/14616670110117332.

Technological resources

Most reviews and frameworks underestimate or do not account for the effects of technical environments or technology on collaboration.[18] Technological needs are more challenging in a network, as organizations typically have their technological resources to complete their work in addition to whatever technologies a network creates for their shared work. Our research suggests that managing technical resources is an underrecognized challenge for networks. We have seen the negative consequences of a lack of technological resources. For example, in our research in Zambia, a network had no common repository to share notes or records. One of the partners lost the physical notes taken at previous meetings, requiring partners to reconstruct several months' worth of activities.[19]

Although setting up shared technological resources typically does not excite would-be collaborators, we have seen many network participants regret that they did not invest more in this collaboration stage. More recently, our research with communication scholar Jiawei (Sophia) Fu suggests that despite information communication technologies becoming more sophisticated and collaboration needs becoming more varied, many nonprofit organizations do not take advantage of these newer technologies. Rather than using shared repositories, case management software, teaching platforms, or various project management software, nonprofits tend to rely on email exchanges and phone calls to facilitate collaboration.[20]

Chapter 6 explicitly addresses the use of data systems and will go further into detail on the practice of collecting data and making data-informed decisions. In this section, we briefly touch on technology as a resource for coordinating work. Networks tend to start with simplistic repositories or databases before quickly realizing that they need more sophisticated technology as they scale up their efforts. WIN, AgeWell, and the Summit Education Initiative each invested in technology as their partnerships matured. Common concerns include partners realizing that they need more data, a system that can provide data in real-time, or systems that allow multiple partners shared access.

[18] John M. Bryson, Barbara C. Crosby, and Melissa Middleton Stone, "Designing and Implementing Cross-Sector Collaborations: Needed and Challenging," *Public Administration Review* 75, no. 5 (2015): 647–63, https://doi.org/10.1111/puar.12432.

[19] Katherine R. Cooper and Michelle Shumate, "Interorganizational Collaboration Explored through the Bona Fide Network Perspective," *Management Communication Quarterly* 26, no. 4 (2012): 623–54.

[20] Jiawei Sophia Fu, Katherine R. Cooper, and Michelle Shumate, "Use and Affordances of ICTs in Interorganizational Collaboration: An Exploratory Study of ICTs in Nonprofit Partnerships," *Management Communication Quarterly* 33, no. 2 (May 1, 2019): 219–37, https://doi.org/10.1177/0893318918824041.

Second, technology is a shared network resource; that is, it is a resource obtained by the network instead of contributed by a partner within the network. The Chicago Benchmarking Collaborative, featured in Chapter 6, came together to receive shared database funding. Other networks, such as WIN, collaborated with a technology provider to customize their system, which they launched one year after the program began. One organization may act as the gatekeeper for a shared technology or house a specific database. But networks typically come before the technological resources rather than the other way around.

Third, and finally, technology can be leveraged as a resource to benefit the network *only* when the network utilizes other resources—namely, the knowledge and skills required to use the technology effectively. A shared database is only useful to a network if network members maintain it and use it to inform their work. We will say more about this in Chapter 6.

Time

All member organizations in the network feel ongoing tension over how much time to give to the network versus organizational concerns. Organizations with more financial and human resources often have more time available for network meetings and activities. However, in this section, we focus on time as a resource to manage the network as a whole.

The processes involved in setting up a network, as described in Chapter 3, are time-consuming. The ongoing collaboration processes—creating agreements, selecting and building leadership, building legitimacy and trust, managing conflict, planning[21]—take time. Networks and their funders can frame these in terms of choices about how to manage their time. These choices include setting expectations for the network's longevity, setting deadlines for social impact, and funding cycle length.

First, networks can set expectations for the network's longevity. The social impact typology introduced in Chapter 2 implies that the type of social impact conditions expectations. Project-based impact often has an end date. Service-based impact may continue indefinitely or as long as services are needed. Introducing an innovation may take less time than scaling that innovation across a geographic area.

As described in Chapter 3, network leaders can frame social problems in different ways. This framing also has implications for the management of

---

[21] Bryson, Crosby, and Stone, "Designing and Implementing Cross-Sector Collaborations."

network time. Networks that use strategic ambiguity depict their work as long-term endeavors. When networks set goals to promote the well-being and life-long success of youth, for example, the framing predisposes the network to long-term action. In contrast, when networks focus on a specific problem, like having 60% of people in a geographic area have a post-secondary degree, the implication is that the network exists until they achieve the goal. Network participants anticipate that they may see slow, incremental progress among specific populations and will likely fall short of their goals for some time. Other networks might use a crisis frame in the hopes of mobilizing network efforts more quickly. For example, networks that emerge to address an increase in youth violence often have a sense of urgency. The crisis accelerates the action required by the network.

Second, networks manage their time by setting deadlines for social impact. In Chapter 3, we argued that setting a specific goal enabled networks to mobilize more effectively and evaluate whether they were achieving a social impact. Those specific goals often have a deadline. RE-AMP's social impact goals, for example, have always included a deadline. Gail Francis described their goal evolution this way: "When we started, we were about 20 organizations or so that [focused] specifically on the power sector and the 2030 goal." Then, they added an economic focus and new partners. They eventually landed on a 2050 goal. Many networks adjust their timelines as they go. In RE-AMP's case, this reflects the realization that the network needed more ambitious goals—and more time to meet its goals. For some networks that have achieved some wins, extending their goals or time frame can capitalize on network successes and extend network activities. For networks focused on complex problems, extending deadlines may be a disappointing but honest admission that more time is needed to achieve their goals. Admittedly, this might also be a tactic for as-yet-unsuccessful networks to buy some more time—and financial resources—to accomplish small wins. Like Education for All, other networks articulate both short- and long-term goals as a strategy for keeping network members engaged while also bracing them for a long commitment.[22]

Third, networks manage their time within the constraints of funding cycles. Many foundations work on a three-year grant cycle, thereby imposing a deadline or time frame around a network's activities. Although a network can and should seek multiple funding sources, funding cycles can alter network

---

[22] Katherine R. Cooper, "Paradox and Process: Navigating Tensions for Network Survival" (Presented at the National Communication Association, Baltimore, MD, November 2019).

activities as they consider what might be possible in the time allocated and how they will be required to report these activities.

Time is a resource that allows networks to achieve social impact; Jörg Raab, Remco Mannak, and Bart Cambre's study on crime prevention networks[23] demonstrates that network age is a necessary but not sufficient condition to achieving social impact. In their research, networks were at least three years old before their activities reduced recidivism. The reason is apparent in our interviews with network leaders. It takes much more time than expected to pull together the financial resources; identify all the sources of knowledge and human capital; develop trust; and put new programs, services, advocacy, or learning into action.

But for some networks, time simply runs out. In the case of the Ready, Set, Parent! collaborative program discussed at the beginning of this chapter, time constraints ultimately made the program unsustainable. Insurers were only willing to cover 48 hours of a family's hospital stay. Shelley Richards says, "There wasn't enough time in those 48 hours, and it started to become stressful for all the parties, for the mothers, the families, the nurses, and even us. Because it's like you can't put ten pounds of sugar in a five-pound bag."

However, time itself is not enough to achieve social impact, nor can a network have an impact by relying on an abundance of financial resources, knowledge, or goodwill among partners. Some research suggests that extensive resources are a necessary but insufficient condition for social impact.[24] Others indicated that network actors could make up for a lack of resources through their activities and structures.[25] Even when resources are abundant and accessible, networks may not achieve the outcomes or impact they seek. So, what prevents networks from achieving impact? In the next section, we explore some resource-related explanations for why networks might stop short of impact and consider how networks might address these challenges.

---

[23] Jörg Raab, Remco S. Mannak, and Bart Cambré, "Combining Structure, Governance, and Context: A Configurational Approach to Network Effectiveness," *Journal of Public Administration Research and Theory* 25, no. 2 (April 1, 2015): 479–511, https://doi.org/10.1093/jopart/mut039.

[24] Daniela Cristofoli and Laura Macciò, "To Wind a Skein into a Ball: Exploring the Concept and Measures of Public Network Performance," *Public Management Review* 20, no. 6 (June 2018): 896–922, https://doi.org/10.1080/14719037.2017.1363904; Provan and Milward, "A Preliminary Theory of Interorganizational Network Effectiveness."

[25] Raab, Mannak, and Cambré, "Combining Structure, Governance, and Context"; Weijie Wang, "Exploring the Determinants of Network Effectiveness: The Case of Neighborhood Governance Networks in Beijing," *Journal of Public Administration Research and Theory* 26, no. 2 (April 1, 2016): 375–88, https://doi.org/10.1093/jopart/muv017.

Dead ends to social impact

We begin our examination by focusing on how the management of resources, in all their forms, can impede a network from achieving social impact. The effective management of resources is one of the most challenging aspects of operating a network. There are several wrong turns that networks make along the way.

Networks compete with their partners for resources

Organizations are often encouraged to collaborate to scale up their efforts and resources.[26] Our previous research demonstrates that networks do not create more resources or capacity in and of themselves.[27] In many cases, partners find that their networked efforts provide them with more competitors instead of increased capacity.

The cases in this book suggest that organizations may continue to compete with their collaborators—or the network itself—even after forming a network. The directors of WIN, MAAC, and The Graduate! Network experienced this tension when they relayed their decisions to formalize their network as an entity with legal status—or not. MAAC and WIN opted to pursue legal status because it made their network eligible for more resources. However, The Graduate! Network—itself a 501(c)3—recommends that individual affiliates or programs, such as Graduate! Philadelphia, do not incorporate but find a fiscal agent. When Education for All leaders approached local businesses to secure funding for the network, several business leaders pointed out that they were already funding individual organizations located within the network. Asking for network contributions ran the risk of cannibalizing funds earmarked for social service organizations participating in the network.

---

[26] Beth Gazley and Jeffrey L. Brudney, "The Purpose (and Perils) of Government-Nonprofit Partnership," *Nonprofit and Voluntary Sector Quarterly* 36, no. 3 (September 1, 2007): 389–415, https://doi.org/10.1177/0899764006295997; M. May Seitanidi, *The Politics of Partnerships: A Critical Examination of Nonprofit-Business Partnerships* (London: Springer Science & Business Media, 2010); Morgane Le Pennec and Emmanuel Raufflet, "Value Creation in Inter-Organizational Collaboration: An Empirical Study," *Journal of Business Ethics* 148, no. 4 (April 1, 2018): 817–34, https://doi.org/10.1007/s10551-015-3012-7.

[27] Cooper and Shumate, "Interorganizational Collaboration Explored through the Bona Fide Network Perspective"; Fu, Cooper, and Shumate, "Use and Affordances of ICTs in Interorganizational Collaboration."

Network participants undervalue human resources

Financial resources are more straightforward to quantify than human resources. But human resources, including access to hard-to-reach populations and expertise, are more difficult to replace than financial resources. Networks reach a dead end when they undervalue human resources in comparison to financial ones. For example, in Education for All, Kate sat in on numerous meetings that dealt with this issue. The network required organizations to have "skin in the game" by making a financial contribution. Education for All expected participating organizations to pay tens of thousands of dollars. They chose this model to increase a sense of network ownership and reduce dependency on outside entities. However, problems began to surface when smaller organizations inquired about membership but could not make a substantial financial donation. Education for All leaders discussed the possibility of some in-kind contributions as opposed to monetary donations. But ultimately, they struggled to place a value on any of these human resources. Program expertise, access to underrepresented communities, or relationships with community leaders were undoubtedly valuable. But they could not determine how valuable they were—and whether they were equivalent to thousands of dollars in unrestricted funds.

Human resources, including expertise and personal relationships, are just as necessary for networks to achieve impact. Networks can create barriers to accessing these resources by undervaluing them. In networks organized for social impact, financial resources above other types can undermine the network's goals.

Resources run out before networks achieve impact

Resources ebb and flow throughout the network's life cycle. A network might form in response to a problem that the community perceives as urgent, only to see public interest wane over time. Funders can shift their priorities, offering extensive support for organizations working on a particular initiative or approach one year—and then move on to other interests the next year. These funding shifts represent environmental shocks that may place the network at a crossroads moment[28] (see Chapter 7 for more about crossroads moments). Shelley Richards, of EPIC, referred to their collaboration's federal grants as

---

[28] Bryson, Crosby, and Stone, "Designing and Implementing Cross-Sector Collaborations."

both a "blessing and curse" because they were substantial in size but always came to an end.

These environmental shocks include not just changes in financial resources but other resources as well. Individuals or organizations with critical expertise can leave the network. Relationships deteriorate. Or time simply runs out. Axiom two states that networks are sensitive to their environment. Network survival is no easy feat in settings with scarce or declining resources.

Network leaders mistake securing network resources for social impact

Securing resources and network survival is not the same as social impact. Social impact is more difficult to measure and requires more time than determining whether the network brought in more grant funding this year than in previous years. In many Education for All meetings, for example, partners struggled with interpreting shared data or how they could determine whether their programs were successful. However, partners always knew when new dues-paying organizations had joined or whether network leaders had secured a new grant. Securing resources—specifically, financial resources—demonstrate network success. However, that does not translate into social impact.

The risk of focusing on these resources is that network survival may become the primary goal. Because social impact networks form in response to wicked problems, the social issues they address are likely to persist. As long as network members value their participation and funders see some value in supporting it, the network will continue. The network's longevity might enable partner trust or demonstrate legitimacy to the community; it may also prove useful in securing additional financial resources. Just because the network continues to exist does not mean that it has generated any social impact. Networks that consume resources, year over year, without generating social impact detract from the social mission of the organizations that comprise them.

Funder guidelines and grant cycles prevent networks from achieving impact

Occasionally, when we teach an executive education session or run a workshop for nonprofit organizations, we will ask participants why they collaborate with others. They say the usual things. They wanted to have a more significant impact or wanted to do more in the community. And then, inevitably, someone will say: *We collaborate because funders made us collaborate.* Previous research,[29] ours included,[30] demonstrates that funders mandate partnerships and shape those partnerships in various ways. Sometimes a funder acts as a convener; in other circumstances, the pressure is more subtle. Funding applications may suggest or imply that applicants should work with others. In the Chicago Benchmarking Collaborative case, a funder told the lead organization that its proposal stood a better chance of being funded if they reapplied with collaborators. When funders mandate collaboration and networks as a panacea for all social problems, they do a disservice to the sector. Networks are more expensive and challenging to manage than single organizations. The drumbeat of collaboration at all costs reduces the effectiveness of many organizations doing great work.

Moreover, funders can set unrealistic expectations for networks. Networks require time before they produce a measurable social impact. As networks emerge and have some early successes, they may be able to scale up their activities—which means that the network will require more resources. And yet many funders seem to expect the network to do more with less.

We have suggested several resource-related dead ends that may keep a network from reaching social impact. Additionally, we offer one dilemma, or an area for ongoing network consideration, before introducing several pathways for networks to leverage the resources needed for social impact.

Dilemmas in managing network resources

As axiom three states, contradicting network demands present dilemmas for managers. These dilemmas are managed within the constraints of feedback and path dependence. In particular, the oversight of network resources presents a series of dilemmas.

---

[29] Kimberlie J. Stephens, Janet Fulk, and Peter R. Monge, "Constrained Choices in Alliance Formations: Cupids and Organizational Marriages," *Human Relations* 62, no. 4 (April 1, 2009): 501–36, https://doi.org/10.1177/0018726708101982; Richard A. Longoria, "Is Inter-Organizational Collaboration Always a Good Thing?" *Journal of Sociology and Social Welfare* 32 (2005): 123–38.
[30] Cooper and Shumate, "Interorganizational Collaboration Explored through the Bona Fide Network Perspective."

Assigning oversight of network resources

All networks face the "two hats problem."[31] Most participants have other jobs (i.e., their paid work) and work for the network (i.e., their non-paid work) on top of that. As a result, network members are often happy to cede the responsibility of obtaining and overseeing resources to other organizations. If the network has an administrative organization, they are often responsible for applying for grants, creating program budgets, or purchasing shared databases. After all, it is their job. In other networks, lead agencies may be responsible for network resources, especially if the network has designated funds, through a fiscal sponsorship agreement or their regular budget, for the organization.

The desire to delegate these responsibilities is understandable but not advisable. Kate recalls a network she visited where members met regularly. Leaders met in at least some iteration almost once a week, but they never reviewed the budget. There was seemingly never enough time to do a line-by-line review of the budget in any of these meetings. Organizational members affirmed the leader's responsibility for the finances without conducting an examination. When one partner's board requested in-depth reporting on the network's activities and funds, the network had to confront some troubling issues. Luckily, there was no criminal or negligent activity. But leaders realized that some organizational partners had failed to pay dues and that the cost of leasing office space for network meetings had increased.

One potential solution is for working groups or executive committees to oversee the network resources. This strategy may increase the sense of shared ownership if the composition is sufficiently diverse. If the network is big enough, we recommend rotating these responsibilities so that partners become comfortable with various network functions. Such arrangements enable the network to survive even in the event of the loss of a critical partner.

Network pathways to social impact

Resources are a necessary but not sufficient condition for social impact. However, not all networks have extensive resources. This section reflects on

---

[31] H. Brinton Milward, Katherine R. Cooper, and Michelle Shumate, "Who Says a Common Agenda Is Necessary for Collective Impact?," *Nonprofit Quarterly*, 2016, https://nonprofitquarterly.org/who-says-a-common-agenda-is-necessary-for-collective-impact/.

two paths that networks use to reach social impact when resources are not plentiful.

Begin a network to achieve outcomes, scale toward social impact as relationships and resources allow

For many networks, achieving impact is not the end goal (see Chapter 2); instead, they seek organization- or network-level outcomes. Social impact does not need to be an all-or-nothing approach; instead, partnerships can start small and scale up to more significant projects. The Chattanooga Museums Collaborative is an excellent example. This partnership began when the leaders of several Chattanooga-based museums—the Hunter Museum of American Art, the Tennessee Aquarium, and the Creative Discovery Museum—coordinated back-office functions. Ultimately, this arrangement proved successful. The museums had greater access to expertise, improved efficiency for each organization, and increased trust between organizations. Building on success, the partners ultimately launched a joint capital campaign. The 21st Century Waterfront Plan capital campaign was relevant to the museums because of their location on the waterfront. Leaders were considering their next stage of development independent of one another. One of the museum collaborators suggested that the museums instead think about the campaign's potential benefits for those who lived, worked, and played in the Chattanooga area. Together, the museums raised tens of millions of dollars from private donors, nearly half of a $120 million fund that revitalized the waterfront. Additionally, these three partners joined forces with the Hamilton County School District to receive funding for and create a museum magnet elementary school. They brought other financial resources to the table that were previously unavailable for the school, including a $500,000 Institute for Museums and Library Services National Leadership Grant. In this example, the Museums Collaborative moved from organizational and network outcomes to project-based social impact.

The social impact typology (Chapter 2) suggests several ways that networks might frame their activities. Networks can start with one approach before adding another as resources allow. For instance, a network might begin in pursuit of service-based impact, and, once they have been effective in that area, the network might add advocacy-based impact to reinforce their efforts further. In Zambia, for example, many of the organizations worked together on advocacy-based social impact through the donor-driven coalition. But they had previously worked together and continued to work together—by swapping client referrals. Similarly, Education for All leaders decided to focus on projects in the network's early stages but wanted to pursue advocacy initiatives once they had the resources.

Funders and communities may find a more incremental approach less appealing than a more audacious proposal. However, leaders suggest that less intensive interorganizational activity paves the way for later collaboration. For example, in the Berkshire United Way, leaders pointed to several collaborative endeavors initiated and sustained by various organizational sectors, including the business community. The "collaborative spirit"[32] of these endeavors paved the way for longer-term networks. Working together on smaller projects can build the trust that networks need to achieve impact.

Starting small also offers a network the chance to gather resources. Many networks report a flywheel effect for getting funding; once they have obtained a grant or two from a large "cornerstone" foundation, they have an easier time getting the next one. For example, Anna Henderson of WIN suggested that after their partnership won a Robert Wood Johnson Foundation LFP grant (an award given to 12 of the most innovative, new health-focused programs across the United States each year), she felt like they had been "vetted." Other foundations then wanted to fund WIN, which led the network to be more fiscally sustainable.

Allow resource constraints to encourage network specialization

The alternative to starting small is to accept that the network has limited resources and commit to stewarding those resources well. However, the critical part of this recommendation is the idea of communicating what it is that the network aims to accomplish—or has achieved. Pursuing resources solely for organizational outcomes is an appropriate form of collaboration (see Chapter 2). But the network should own their goal as well as their limits.

No single network does everything. Hadass Sheffer of The Graduate! Network described the network's decision to focus resources on serving individuals who want to return to college, as opposed to other areas relating to higher education, such as policy: "We pay attention to the individual. The entire model, whichever way you look at it, is focused on maximizing the benefits and attachments of the individual. . . . Because we're so focused on the people and making sure that things are happening on that level, we entrust most of our policy work to other

---

[32] Renee Guarriello Heath and Patricia M. Sias, "Communicating Spirit in a Collaborative Alliance," *Journal of Applied Communication Research* 27, no. 4 (November 1, 1999): 356–76, https://doi.org/10.1080/00909889909365545.

organizations." Networks can specialize in one part of the larger social issue. Rather than building a bigger network, they relinquish control of other aspects of the social problem to other networks or organizations.

Networks with more circumscribed goals can be tempted to exceed those goals when applying for grants. Networks can be blown off course by trying to fit a particular grant application or attract a specific partner. Although most networks find themselves having to make adjustments, these should be because they serve the network's broader purpose and the member and community needs. By knowing and articulating the network's focus, leaders can apply their energies accordingly. Rather than applying for every grant and trying to fit each box provided by a foundation, choose only those funders relevant to the network and build relationships with those funders.

Take an assets approach rather than a scarcity approach to network resources

When considering resources, a scarcity mindset can dominate the conversation.[33] Networks and communities can focus on the needed resources rather than the assets that already exist (see the "Tools for network instigators" in this chapter). A preoccupation with scarce resources may lead network leaders to fixate on obtaining those resources at the expense of other assets that the network does possess.

Network leaders may consider the and the members' resources located in their respective communities. The Graduate! Network's Sheffer described many assets in the original Philadelphia community that helped the local network succeed; these included physical locations where adult college students could complete their homework. Networks that take more of a grassroots approach to organizing may not attract many of the big grants. But these networks are typically able to access underserved communities in a way that some of the better-resourced networks are not.

Funders forge a path for social impact

Our final set of recommendations is not for network managers but funders. Our network participants frequently relayed funders' struggle to understand

---

[33] Alison Mathie and Gord Cunningham, "From Clients to Citizens: Asset-Based Community Development as a Strategy for Community-Driven Development," *Development in Practice* 13, no. 5 (2003): 474–86.

how their problem fits within a systems view. Leaders suggested that funders did not support adults' education initiatives to the same extent as they valued education for children or that funders did not see connections between education and economic development. Others suggested that funders wanted to pick and choose organizations to support as opposed to supporting the partnership. Robert Kret admitted that the Chattanooga Museums Collaborative turned down a donation from a funder who was primarily interested in only one museum. After walking away from the gift, the funder eventually came back and contributed to the joint capital fund because, as Robert suggested, the funder "saw the good that [the partnership] was doing for the whole community."

We make three recommendations for funders who want to support collaborative efforts. In combination, these pathways to social impact require time and tolerance to risk. With commitment, broad social impact across communities and social issues is possible.

First, funders should increase their support as the network scales up to impact. Funding must scale with the network's activities. Funders can accomplish this either by setting milestones for funding increases or by developing relationships with other funders. For example, in the Summit Education Initiative, leaders reported that funders understood that more resources would also be needed to support it as the work scaled up. In response to the increased demand and community expectations, they reported that their local United Way funder said, "Look, I know we are giving you more work because we are sending more people your way. Tell me how much more money you need, and I'll make sure you get it. You don't have to apply for it." Funders might invest in smaller, less-resourced networks that have the potential to reach impact. As the WIN example described earlier in this chapter makes clear, the first big grant's receipt makes the award of a second grant more likely. Yet some networks struggle to get that first grant.

Second, funders should invest in the infrastructure necessary to support a network. For example, funders might consider designating funds to create or maintain a shared database to track client outcomes. For instance, in the Chicago Benchmarking Collaborative, the Chicago Community Trust provided the money to purchase a shared database to enter student data and measure organizational results. They have also supplied incentives for individual organizations to use this database. Although not guaranteed from year to year, the Chicago Benchmarking Collaborative has provided financial incentives for each organization that entered their data and saw improvements in their client outcomes.

Funders may also invest in strategies to increase the human resources needed to achieve social impact. Although many networks described in this book focus on a single region, some networks—such as the NF Collective described in Chapter 5—include partners from around the country. Funders might consider allocating funds that enable partners to get together, build relationships, or invest in new training for network leaders.

Third, funders should extend their initial grant cycle for networks to at least five years. The majority of networks featured in this book reported that their efforts began with a grant for three years. But it takes longer for networks to achieve any real impact and to document that impact.

We have criticized funders in this chapter. But many funders are innovative and supportive partners of networks for social impact. The example of the Atlas Family Foundation and WIN demonstrates how funders can set the stage for effective networks. In this case, The Atlas Family Foundation had provided several area organizations with money and consulting hours to explore what an initial partnership might look like. Two years after launching WIN services—and with two independent evaluations as leverage—they found that partner agencies that were investing funds provided by WIN for their intended purpose of intensive case management were seeing stronger outcomes. Financial donations to the respective organizations continued, but with the mandate that funding had to underwrite case management to remain a part of the network. The foundation provided seed funding but did not dictate how the network would form. They stayed with the network for the long haul. The foundation provided funding for organizations to experiment with a network structure and various network activities before landing on the most impactful combination—and subsequently scaling up the resources to support the network's efforts.

Conclusion

Networks require extensive resources to achieve social impact, including financial resources, human resources, technology, and time. Axiom two states that networks are sensitive to their environment, including the ebb and flow of resources. The availability—or limitations—of resources provides opportunities for networks to sharpen their focus as they pursue social impact. But network leaders' efforts are not enough. This chapter argued that funders bear some responsibility for the networks they support and suggested funders' pathways alongside network leaders.

Resources can be a source of power. And resource differentials can be a source of tension between network partners. In the next chapter, we examine the role of power and conflict in networks for social impact.

Case study: Two networks combat gender-based violence

When Kate arrived in Zambia to study the response to gender-based violence, the timing appeared to be perfect. A major grant was recently awarded to a group of nonprofit organizations to support their efforts in fighting gender-based violence. There was a tremendous amount of energy and excitement around the partnership. Although the money was coming from overseas, agencies in Zambia coordinated the country's on-the-ground efforts.

The grant was expansive, providing funding for education, media campaigns, leadership training, and care centers. But some of the initial excitement over the grant quickly gave way to frustration. By selecting a lead organization, the funders had empowered this agency above the others. This particular agency oversaw the grant's financial administration, the partner agencies' training, and the evaluation of partner agencies' work. This arrangement created some tensions between the lead organization and partners.

The grant provided considerable resources for these programs, and the funder expected agencies to make regular reports about these activities' outcomes. But agencies did not always have the resources for determining the results. For example, agencies struggled to measure the impact of radio programs intended to raise awareness of gender-based violence. Additionally, because several agencies might work collaboratively on a particular program, reporting required multiple partners' efforts. Kate's meeting notes recounted a day when an urgent call from one grant partner to get some help in accounting at the funder's request upended the day's work for other partner agencies as they coordinated their response.

Another challenge was the amount of effort it took to publicize their efforts. The funding came with the expectation that the agencies would regularly publish stories in the local press; they were supposed to frequently air commercials and television and radio programs. The television and radio spots were expensive but seen as central to the campaign. Midway through the campaign, the agencies concluded that the grant funds allocated for media would not cover the costs. Newspaper coverage did not take up financial resources but took time. All partners and international funding agencies had to vet and approve each story before appearing in print. Partners verified the facts and added details to emphasize their own agency's contributions; other agencies would then want to revisit the changes made by those partners. Ultimately, it could take weeks or months for a story to appear in print. This delay was especially concerning because the funder had only allocated the grant money for three years; network participants were instructed by the international funder to consider whether their efforts would be sustainable beyond the grant's terms.

But this donor-driven network was not the only network working on gender-based violence. Many of the local agencies in Zambia had developed a grassroots referral network. In the referral network, agencies directed survivors of gender-based violence to seek complimentary services at other agencies. This network did not have regular meetings, and they did not publicize their efforts. Instead, only the participants' clients that they served knew about their activities. There was no leader and no central office space. Although a convener or lead agency did not exert control, some agencies wielded more influence. For example, many organizations could provide medical or legal help for survivors. But if a survivor needed to escape an abuser within her community or own home, only one organization could consistently provide housing or shelter. Time and time again, network participants said they turned to this particular agency when they had a client in need.

Questions to consider

1. What resources did the donor-driven coalition require? What resources did the grassroots coalition need?
2. What are some advantages or disadvantages of having a funder convene the network, as in the donor-driven coalition?
3. Some networks, upon having some success, might formalize or scale up their efforts. What would you recommend to the participants of the grassroots network?
4. In terms of a resources-to-outcomes ratio, which network approach do you think was more impactful in this environment?

Tools for network instigators

In this chapter's "Tools for network instigators," we focus on two resource management techniques about which we receive the most questions: fiscal sponsorship and community assets inventories. Fiscal sponsorship is the alternative to goal-directed networks forming a legal entity. Although we would not prescribe it for every network in the long term, most new networks go through a period of fiscal sponsorship before applying for and receiving legal status. Community asset inventories are an essential tool for network members to adopt an asset-based versus a need-based resource mindset. Also, they are often helpful in aiding leaders to appreciate resources beyond financial assets.

Fiscal sponsorship

Networks for social impact might choose different legal statuses—both as a strategy for attracting financial resources to the partnership and a means of managing those resources. In the United States, networks choose between gaining their own 501(c)3 status and fiscal sponsorship.

A fiscal sponsor ensures that social impact networks can receive donations without having the tax-exempt status that comes with registering as a 501(c)3. Instead, networks operate under the oversight of an existing nonprofit that can receive donations and provide financial oversight; in some cases, fiscal sponsorship may also provide infrastructure or additional administrative services that the network may need. Fiscal sponsors—typically nonprofit organizations themselves—receive an administrative fee for housing the network. In most cases, the networks maintain ownership of their brands and programs. Fiscal sponsorship is a voluntary arrangement that networks may terminate at any point. Although fiscal sponsorship has often been thought of as a strategy for networks in their early stages, some networks may use this as a long-term strategy. We recommend that potential partners specify these terms in the form of a fiscal sponsorship agreement. Templates and other guidelines are readily available online through the Council of Nonprofits and the National Network of Fiscal Sponsors.

Table 4.1[34] offers some guidelines for both the fiscal sponsor and the sponsored project:

---

[34] Adapted from National Council of Nonprofits, "Fiscal Sponsorship: Who Does What?," *Infographic*, accessed December 14, 2019, https://www.councilofnonprofits.org/sites/default/files/images/fiscal-sponsorship-infographic.png.

Table 4.1 Elements of Fiscal Sponsorship

Element	Role of Fiscal Sponsor	Implications for a Sponsored Project
Tax-exempt status	Lends credibility of 501(c)(3) status to project	Has an obligation to disclose to donors that it does not independently have tax-exempt status
Charitable contributions	Receives and acknowledges charitable contributions	Builds and maintains relationships with donors
Fees and funds	Retains control and discretion over funds	Pays administrative fee to and receives flow-through funds from sponsor
Oversight	Requests records and reports to fulfill oversight responsibilities	Complies with record keeping and other reports requested by fiscal sponsor
Communication	Communicates regularly with project leads	Communicates regularly with the fiscal sponsor

Table 4.2 Checklist for Potential Fiscal Sponsors

Will acting as a fiscal sponsor for a network enable us to ...	Yes	No
Test and accelerate public interests for effective social and civic action?		
Foster social innovation and entrepreneurship?		
Advance the emergence of able, creative community leadership?		
Promote well-managed solutions and fiscal efficiency in addressing social problems or challenges?		
Provide long-term, efficient, permanent project infrastructure?		
Transfer the knowledge, skills, and habits of excellent organizational operation from our own organization?		
Strengthen the presence, voice, and effectiveness of civil society?		

Although fiscal sponsorship offers numerous benefits to networks for social impact, the fiscal sponsor stands to benefit as well. The following considerations suggest a checklist[35] for potential network fiscal sponsors to determine whether the arrangement advances their mission:

[35] Adapted from National Network of Fiscal Sponsors, "Guidelines for Comprehensive Fiscal Sponsorship," website, accessed December 14, 2019, http://www.fiscalsponsors.org/pages/best-practices-fiscal-sponsorship.

Community asset inventory

There are considerable resources available to network leaders on how to secure grants and manage finances.[36] Community asset inventories,[37] in contrast, are designed to aid leaders in identifying many types of assets. A community asset inventory[38] requires groups to conduct interviews of association and institutional leaders. Examples of institutional leaders include officials from local schools, public hospitals or clinics, libraries, parks offices, chambers of commerce, and local businesses. Association leaders are individuals from the local neighborhood association, community centers, housing organizations, halfway houses, churches, advocacy groups, and senior groups. In these interviews, facilitators ask participants about the assets that the organization or association has, including:

- People
- Funding
- Physical resources
- Media materials
- Communication systems
- Relationships with the community
- Relationships with other organizations
- Aspirations
- Available time

The community asset inventory's goal is to help network leaders identify the asset in a community or network. They can also determine how the community might leverage existing assets to make a social impact and how organizations could work together.

---

[36] E.g., Richard F. Larkin and Marie DiTommaso, *Wiley Not-for-Profit GAAP 2018: Interpretation and Application of Generally Accepted Accounting Principles* (Hoboken, NJ: John Wiley & Sons, 2018); Robin Devereaux-Nelson, *How to Write a Nonprofit Grant Proposal: Writing Winning Proposals to Fund Your Programs and Projects*, 1st ed. (New York: CreateSpace Independent Publishing Platform, 2015).

[37] John L. McKnight and John Kretzmann, *Mapping Community Capacity* (Institute for Policy Research, Northwestern University Evanston, IL, 1996).

[38] Community Tool Box, "Chapter 3. Assessing Community Needs and Resources | Section 8. Identifying Community Assets and Resources," accessed December 10, 2019, https://ctb.ku.edu/en/table-of-contents/assessment/assessing-community-needs-and-resources/identify-community-assets/tools.

5
Power and Conflict

In 2014, President Obama launched My Brother's Keeper, a national initiative designed to close the opportunity gap for boys and men of color. When they heard about the initiative, Delia Farquharson and Francis Wynne thought that the model would be an excellent fit for their community of Mt. Vernon, New York. The two began to rally community members, reaching out to local elected officials, school board representatives, and leaders in children's mental health to set up a My Brother's Keeper coalition in their hometown. They received support from other community leaders once Farquharson and Wynne promised to lead it. Farquharson realized that this was because "nobody else wanted to commit" to overseeing the collaborative effort. But she and Wynne threw themselves into network building, recruiting partners, and organizing regular meetings to get the work underway. Their efforts culminated in a photo op on the steps of City Hall. Still, Farquharson suggests, there were signs that not all the organizational actors were committed to working together. Farquharson recalled an early meeting with a city council representative who warned her. "We were not ready as a community," Farquharson remembered him saying. "We were not ready to accept the big responsibility that is My Brother's Keeper to make it work."

Social problems, like closing the opportunity gap for boys and men of color, provide compelling reasons for various actors and organizations to come together. Who would *not* want to work together if it offered the chance to achieve greater social impact? Leaders are often frustrated by the lack of progress on the social issue. They are excited to realize that others are as motivated to act as they are. The thrill continues when members or funders dedicate new resources to the network. And then, eventually and certainly, there is conflict.

Research suggests that nonprofits idealize the potential benefits of collaboration and overlook some of the costs.[1] We suggest that most organizations,

---

[1] Eva Witesman and Andrew Heiss, "Nonprofit Collaboration and the Resurrection of Market Failure: How a Resource-Sharing Environment Can Suppress Social Objectives," *VOLUNTAS: International Journal of Voluntary and Nonprofit Organizations* 28, no. 4 (August 1, 2017): 1500–28, https://doi.org/10.1007/s11266-016-9684-5.

regardless of sector, tend to do the same at the beginning. Collaboration inevitably creates conflict. Management scholars Chris Huxham and Siv Vangen suggest that the potential for conflict is so great that organizations should avoid working together unless partnership is the only choice.[2] Networks represent a promising strategy, but conflict can disrupt activities before they lead to social impact.

In this chapter, we describe the challenges associated with network conflict. We first focus on power in networks and discuss the implications of power distribution and disparities. Next, we introduce the three types of conflict endemic to networks for social impact. Micro-level conflicts take place at the interface between individuals and organizations. Conflicts that occur between organizations and networks operate at the meso-level. When the broader community or system conflicts with networks, it is a macro-level conflict. Finally, we recommend how networks can recognize the types of conflicts that threaten their ability to achieve social impact and pursue several pathways to overcome them.

Power in networks

We begin our discussion of network conflict by examining power. Power disparities are not synonymous with conflict, but a failure to deal with power can result in network strife. Actors can utilize their power in different ways.[3] In goal-directed networks, they might display their power in setting the partnership's agenda or in their capacity to derail either the plan or progress on it. In serendipitous networks, they might demonstrate their power by arranging partnerships between unconnected organizations or encouraging other partners to exclude an organization. And, the distribution of power can ebb and flow across the networks' lifespans.[4]

[2] Chris Huxham and Siv Vangen, *Managing to Collaborate: The Theory and Practice of Collaborative Advantage* (London: Routledge, 2013).

[3] Cynthia Hardy and Nelson Phillips, "Strategies of Engagement: Lessons from the Critical Examination of Collaboration and Conflict in an Interorganizational Domain," *Organization Science* 9, no. 2 (April 1, 1998): 217–30, https://doi.org/10.1287/orsc.9.2.217; Jill M. Purdy, "A Framework for Assessing Power in Collaborative Governance Processes," *Public Administration Review* 72, no. 3 (2012): 409–17, https://doi.org/10.1111/j.1540-6210.2011.02525.x; John M. Bryson, Barbara C. Crosby, and Melissa Middleton Stone, "Designing and Implementing Cross-Sector Collaborations: Needed and Challenging," *Public Administration Review* 75, no. 5 (2015): 647–63, https://doi.org/10.1111/puar.12432.

[4] Chris Huxham and Siv Vangen, "Doing Things Collaboratively: Realising the Advantage or Succumbing to Inertia?," in *Collaborative Governance—A New Era of Public Policy in Australia?*, eds. Janine O'Flynn et al. (Australia: The Australian National University, 2009), 29–44, http://epress.anu.edu.au/anzsog/collab_gov/pdf/ch04.pdf.

Forms of power

Communication scholars Renee Heath and Matthew Isbell note that power is not possessed. Instead, it is relational and negotiated with others.[5] From this foundational claim, they invoke five bases of social power.[6] *Coercive power* refers to the ability of an actor to punish or threaten other actors. *Reward power* describes an actor's ability to compensate other members for participating. In networks, funders often exercise either coercive or reward power.[7] They may mandate collaboration or withhold funding for organizations that do not participate in a network. Funders can reward collaborative partners by continuing or increasing their budgets. Chris Huxham and Siv Vangen suggest that "common wisdom" dictates that "power is in the purse strings."[8]

Legitimate power, the third type, is associated with a specific position and the authority it denotes. The network administrative organization, for example, has legitimate power. Directors of network administrative organizations can compel other actors to comply with the network because of their official position leading the network. Sometimes actors have legitimate power related to the sector that they represent. For example, governments have legitimate power because they represent the public[9] or have the authority to decide on behalf of others.[10]

The fourth type of power, *expert power*, is based on the knowledge and credentials possessed by a specific network actor. For example, in education networks, individuals with a PhD in education have expert power. Expertise may be scientific, technical, social, or political.[11] Consequently, if organizations have come together in response to a complex problem, the network will have many actors with different forms of expert power.

Referent power is the fifth type. It refers to power earned due to charisma or likeability. For example, in the early days of Education for All, a local pastor shaped the conversation around equity. The pastor could not exert the other types of power but used his referent power to put equity on the agenda. Within a network, the most popular or charismatic actor wields influence. Referent

---

[5] Renee Guarriello Heath and Matthew G. Isbell, *Interorganizational Collaboration: Complexity, Ethics, and Communication* (Long Grove, IL: Waveland Press, 2017).

[6] John R. P. French and Bertram Raven, "The Bases of Social Power," in *Group Dynamics: Research and Theory*, eds. Dorwin Cartwright and Alvin Zander, 3rd ed. (New York: Harper & Row, 1968), 359–69.

[7] Katherine R. Cooper, "Nonprofit Participation in Collective Impact: A Comparative Case," *Community Development* 48, no. 4 (2017): 499–514, https://doi.org/10.1080/15575330.2017.1332654.

[8] Huxham and Vangen, "Doing Things Collaboratively."

[9] Michael McGuire and Robert Agranoff, "The Limitations of Public Management Networks," *Public Administration* 89, no. 2 (2011): 265–84.

[10] Barbara Gray and Jill Purdy, *Collaborating for Our Future: Multistakeholder Partnerships for Solving Complex Problems* (Oxford: Oxford University Press, 2018).

[11] Heath and Isbell, *Interorganizational Collaboration*.

power for organizations refers to their discursive legitimacy. Discursive legitimacy describes an organization's ability to be a public voice on a particular issue.[12] Organizations that the community respects and trusts have discursive legitimacy.[13]

However, power is not concentrated exclusively within organizations or institutions. Community power encompasses "the social and structural relationships among local residents and organizations that shape outcomes when disputes or competitions for resources might arise."[14] Members of the local community—including grassroots organizers, activists, leaders, and residents—also have a stake in the wicked problem. They exercise their power in various ways, including participation, protest, and even convening the networks in the first place. For example, Delia Farquharson and Francis Wynne, described at the beginning of this chapter, launched My Brother's Keeper as community members to support others *in* the community.

Power imbalances and the potential for conflict

Power is distributed unevenly across network partners; in fact, most researchers view power imbalance as part of network organizing.[15] Power disparities need not be harmful. The consequences are associated with the orientation that actors have toward power. They can exert *power to* move the network forward by participating in network action or decisions. Alternatively, they might exercise their *power for* other actors by representing or endorsing them. When actors use power to pressure other actors, impose actions upon them, or act independently of the network,[16] they display *power over* them. Power "incorporates both repressive and productive elements."[17] Network actors rely on power to accomplish network goals but may also use power to elevate some agendas over others.

Power disparities do not necessarily lead to conflict. Instead, network design (see Chapter 3) and network management (axiom three) exacerbate or ameliorate the potential for actors to use their power over others. When networks fail to establish decision-making processes for creating a shared

[12] Hardy and Phillips, "Strategies of Engagement"; Purdy, "A Framework for Assessing Power in Collaborative Governance Processes."

[13] Cooper, "Nonprofit Participation in Collective Impact."

[14] Brian D. Christens, *Community Power and Empowerment* (New York: Oxford University Press, 2019), 13.

[15] *See* Robert Agranoff, "Inside Collaborative Networks: Ten Lessons for Public Managers," *Public Administration Review* 66 (2006): 56–65; Huxham and Vangen, "Doing Things Collaboratively."

[16] Gray and Purdy, *Collaborating for Our Future.*

[17] Gray and Purdy, *Collaborating for Our Future,* 117.

agenda, power imbalances can also lead to conflicts that undermine agreeing on a shared purpose.[18] For example, when leaders use informal channels, rather than deliberation, to convince network leaders to pursue a strategy, they undermine others in their network. Such practices lead to distrust, weak commitment, or in some cases, overt conflict.[19]

Specific forms of network governance may minimize or exacerbate power disparities.[20] Distributed governance, at first blush, appears to be most equitable because it does not give one organization legitimate power. However, a lack of legitimate power can open the door for leaders to use other forms of power to advance their agendas. The designation of a lead organization or network administrative organization concentrates legitimate power but may reduce the exercise of other forms of power.

Researchers in community psychology and community development[21] further argue that network models vary in terms of their openness to community input. Networks that form with longer-term time horizons (see Chapter 4) and address complex problems have a more challenging time representing community members in their collaborative processes.[22] Most community members lack the necessary resources, including technical knowledge and time, to participate.

In the next section, we discuss network conflicts that are more or less attributable to power disparities. Power influences how conflicts evolve, regardless of their impetus. Perhaps more importantly, power affects the options available to network leaders to address all forms of conflict.

Interfaces for conflict

Conflict manifests itself at three interfaces. Micro-level conflict arises from tensions between individual and organizational demands. Strains between organizational and network interests are apparent in meso-level conflict. Macro-level conflict occurs when its surrounding community challenges the

---

[18] Bryson, Crosby, and Stone, "Designing and Implementing Cross-Sector Collaborations"; Huxham and Vangen, *Managing to Collaborate: The Theory and Practice of Collaborative Advantage*.

[19] Chris Ansell and Alison Gash, "Collaborative Governance in Theory and Practice," *Journal of Public Administration Research and Theory: J-PART* 18, no. 4 (2008): 543–71.

[20] Ansell and Gash, "Collaborative Governance in Theory and Practice."

[21] Brian D. Christens and Paula Tran Inzeo, "Widening the View: Situating Collective Impact among Frameworks for Community-Led Change," *Community Development* 46, no. 4 (August 8, 2015): 420–35, https://doi.org/10.1080/15575330.2015.1061680; Gray and Purdy, *Collaborating for Our Future*; Tom Wolff, "Ten Places Where Collective Impact Gets It Wrong," *Global Journal of Community Psychology and Practice* 7, no. 1 (2016), https://www.gjcpp.org/en/resource.php?issue=21&resource=200.

[22] Ansell and Gash, "Collaborative Governance in Theory and Practice."

network. Goal-directed networks experience conflict in all three interfaces. In contrast, serendipitous networks only experience micro-level conflict because they lack recognition. In other words, when there is no bounded and goal-directed entity, there is no basis for conflict. In the following section, we explore each of these interfaces for conflict, unpacking their implications for achieving social impact.

Individual-organization interface

Individuals plan and execute network activities.[23] Many of these individuals do so at the behest of their employers. The interface between these individuals and the organizations that expect them to act as representatives are ripe venues for conflict. As management scholars Chris Huxham and Siv Vangen[24] argue, membership and participation disagreements underlie this type of conflict.

Networks count organizations as members of their network, but individuals take part in network activity. Some individuals enthusiastically participate on behalf of an organization, but others do not share that same enthusiasm. For example, the Education for All network chose to form a steering committee. At a kickoff meeting, the participating organizations voted on nominations to the steering committee. However, instead of naming individual representatives, participants elected organizations. The organizations were then permitted to choose a person to represent them. Over the two years that Kate attended meetings, the committee's organizational composition stayed the same, but the individuals in the room changed. People retired, left their organizations, or remained at their organization but appointed a co-worker to take over their network responsibilities. Some representatives temporarily rotated out due to medical or family leave, during which some organizations opted to send a replacement while others did not. The replacements varied in their knowledge of and interest in participating in Education for All. Some found themselves appointed to join a network they had had no hand in building and in which they were mostly uninterested. Though their organization had been committed to these efforts, the individual was not.

For example, at one meeting Kate attended, Education for All leaders discussed that one of the network's founding organizations rarely attended

[23] Renee Guarriello Heath and Lawrence R. Frey, "Ideal Collaboration: A Conceptual Framework of Community Collaboration," *Communication Yearbook* 28 (2004): 192–233.

[24] Chris Huxham and Siv Vangen, "Ambiguity, Complexity and Dynamics in the Membership of Collaboration," *Human Relations* 53, no. 6 (2000): 771–806.

meetings. The organization in question, a nonprofit serving youth, had initially been represented by an individual who took several leadership roles within Education for All. Without that particular person, some of those committees stalled. Education for All leaders wondered whether they should compel the organization to send someone, even if their job was not an obvious fit for the position.

Of course, for every individual who was uninterested in participating in Education for All, the network gained a new member committed to the network—if not necessarily the vision set by the prior organizational leaders. Upon being appointed to represent their organization, some individuals questioned the decisions and actions of their predecessors.

Education for All illustrates the conflict between organizational membership and individual participation. In every network, representatives change over time. Individuals chosen because of their qualifications and interest in an organizational role are not necessarily qualified or interested in the network role.

In some networks, individuals unaffiliated with organizations can participate in the network (see Chapter 3). Social change often relies on the power and resources of those in the community, in addition to organizational resources.[25] However, networks struggle with how to include these people.[26] Even networks with a strong community presence faced this challenge; Delia Farquharson of My Brother's Keeper started her community coalition as a community member but then later launched a campaign to run for the city council. There were multiple reasons for running, but one reason was that she thought she could do more to serve the network in an official capacity.

Additionally, individuals have multiple stakes in social problems. These stakes impact their participation. For instance, Florence Young of Westbrook Children's Project noted that within their education-focused network, many of the leaders representing local organizations within the network also had children in the local schools. Although their official role was acting on an organization's behalf, their experiences as parents influenced their network roles—and beliefs about its goals. Another example of this conflict occurred within the Blue Ribbon Commission in North Carolina. Network leaders responded to community outcry after a local school was closed for low enrollment and low performance. It made reopening the school one of the commission's goals. The superintendent of the local school district had been part of the decision to close the school. But because of his position on the Blue

---

[25] *See* Christens, *Community Power and Empowerment.*
[26] Ansell and Gash, "Collaborative Governance in Theory and Practice."

Ribbon Commission board, he participated in the advocacy efforts to reopen the school.

Organization-network interface

Conflicts also arise at the interface between organizations and the network. Organizational autonomy and interdependence[27] define networks (see Chapter 1). Meso-level conflicts between organizations and networks are in the DNA of networks. Partners have different expectations for the network. Individuals are loyal to both their home organization and the broader partnership. Participants are more comfortable or familiar with particular stances on strategies and tactics. And some member organizations or community stakeholders attempt to exert control over the network.[28] We elaborate on each of these tensions.

Organizations have different expectations for the network

First, partners may have different expectations for the network.[29] These diverging expectations often have to do with framing the social problem (see Chapter 3). Different interpretations of the social issue are not, in and of themselves, a problem. Indeed, strategic ambiguity[30] relies on unity in purpose over uniformity in perception. Conflict arises when one partner tries to enforce its frame on others.[31] Conflict may also result when one partner tries to silence or minimize the influence of partners that do not share the same frame.

In Community Reach, partners portrayed a tension between education and economic development. Julian, a pseudonym for a leader of the economic development contingent, recounted efforts to minimize early childhood educators' influence: "One of the challenges and obstacles initially was making certain that we didn't have—this is going to sound horrible—we didn't have

---

[27] Ronald S. Burt, "The Network Structure of Social Capital," *Research in Organizational Behavior* 22 (2000): 345–423; W. W. Powell, "Neither Market nor Hierarchy: Network Forms of Organization," *Research in Organizational Behavior* 12 (1990): 105–24.

[28] Bryson, Crosby, and Stone, "Designing and Implementing Cross-Sector Collaborations."

[29] Differences in organizational frames and agendas may be reflective of organizational values, value or history. Differences in organizational values and identity represent real challenges for partners in collaboration (Gray and Purdy, *Collaborating for Our Future*; Bryson et al., "Designing and Implementing Cross-Sector Collaborations"), and are not necessarily well-explored in research. For example, in their 2015 review, Bryson et al. note that only one article that refers to cultural differences; see Siv Vangen and Nik Winchester, "Managing Cultural Diversity in Collaborations: A Focus on Management Tensions," *Public Management Review* 16, no. 5 (July 4, 2014): 686–707, https://doi.org/10.1080/14719037.2012.743579.

[30] Eric M. Eisenberg, "Ambiguity as Strategy in Organizational Communication," *Communication Monographs* 51, no. 3 (September 1, 1984): 227–42, https://doi.org/10.1080/03637758409390197.

[31] Art Dewulf and René Bouwen, "Issue Framing in Conversations for Change: Discursive Interaction Strategies for 'Doing Differences,'" *The Journal of Applied Behavioral Science* 48, no. 2 (2012): 168–93.

Community Reach being run by preschoolers. . . . we had to stomp our feet a little bit to get some things changed."[32] Mark (pseudonym), a superintendent of a school district, got the message. He suggested that many educators like himself had decided not to participate in Community Reach because the network had prioritized economic interests.[33]

Organizations may also have different expectations for resources. Resource disparities or constraints can contribute to meso-level conflict[34] (see Chapter 4 for a fuller discussion). Organizations are eager to initiate collaboration or network efforts because they think they will benefit financially from these partnerships. Jana Jones Halls of the Blue Ribbon Commission notes that "The reason there were so many people wanting to be involved is [that] we got a pretty significant grant just to get started. And a lot of the partners thought that there was going to be money at the table for them." When it becomes clear that the funding awarded to a network will support network infrastructure or joint initiatives instead of being distributed among participating organizations, organizational leaders may feel that they are doing a second job without compensation.

Organizations differ in their approach to network activity

Network partners have different approaches to network activity. They may have different practices for conducting meetings, for instance. Often public organizations are required to both keep detailed meeting minutes and make them available to the public. In contrast, many nonprofit organizations and businesses are not used to conducting meetings in public view. Organizations may also differ in how they seek funding, budget for programs, measure outcomes, make decisions, tolerate ambiguity, or liaise with the community. These differences are not in and of themselves a problem, but it can be difficult for partners to articulate and synthesize these orientations.

Different orientations are a function of the composition of networks designed to address complicated and complex problems. Differences in operating style are, in part, what drove Community Reach's economic development leaders to "stomp their feet a little." Businesses were accustomed to setting clear objectives and operating from a theory of action with few contingencies. In contrast, educators were willing to talk about the nature of the problem for longer and were hesitant to draw up any theory of action that

---

[32] Katherine R. Cooper, "Exploring Stakeholder Participation in Nonprofit Collaboration" (Dissertation, University of Illinois at Urbana-Champaign, 2014), 119, https://core.ac.uk/download/pdf/29152991.pdf.

[33] Cooper, "Nonprofit Participation in Collective Impact."

[34] Gray and Purdy, Collaborating for Our Future.

would apply to all children without accounting for what seemed to the business leaders to be an endless number of exceptions.

Organizations and networks have competing priorities

The network and each of its member organizations, in goal-directed networks, have a mission and need to generate sufficient resources to sustain their operations. Negotiating these dueling needs can prove challenging, as Florence Young of Westbrook Children's Project attests. She asks partner agencies to inform the steering committee if they apply for funding and plan to highlight their role in a network. The network will not apply for the same grant or contract so that they do not appear disorganized to funders.

By participating in a network, organizations become interdependent with one another. Organizational leaders, who are typically able to act as decision-makers within their organizations, are accountable to peers in new ways. Organizations' desire for independence comes up against new network constraints. The WIN and MAAC networks, for instance, wield considerable control over the standards by which each organization serves its clients. In WIN, organizations must employ a case manager, use a case-management software system, and allow WIN to act as a second supervisor for their case managers. MAAC evaluates how well its member organizations live up to a set of professional standards and may remove the organization from the network if its performance is not up to par. In both networks, organizations give up some of their independence to be part of something bigger.

Organizations try to sabotage the network

Some conflicts at the organization-network interface result from apparent differences in partner agendas or activities. But there may also be hidden agendas in which partners withhold information about their goals or interests.[35] Organizational plans may conflict with one another; each partner may also have multiple purposes. Negotiation of these agendas and interests is only possible if network partners are willing to talk about them in the first place.[36]

In some cases, organizations feel that their interests would be best served if the network dissolved.[37] Sometimes the partner joins the network because a

[35] Huxham and Vangen, "Ambiguity, Complexity and Dynamics in the Membership of Collaboration."

[36] H. Brinton Milward, Katherine R. Cooper, and Michelle Shumate, "Who Says a Common Agenda Is Necessary for Collective Impact?," *Nonprofit Quarterly*, 2016, https://nonprofitquarterly.org/who-says-a-common-agenda-is-necessary-for-collective-impact/.

[37] Katherine R. Cooper, H. Brinton Milward, and Michelle Shumate, "Teaching Simulation: The Toxic Node," 2019, https://www.maxwell.syr.edu/parcc/eparcc/simulations/The_Toxic_Node/.

funder mandated that they do so to continue receiving funding. Other times, large and influential organizations resent being tethered to smaller organizations in the network, but they fear the power that these organizations might claim if they banded together. Some organizations may become a toxic node in the network in these cases, actively working to sabotage the network's efforts.

Network-community interface

Axiom two states that networks for social impact are sensitive to changes in the environment. Conflict may also occur between the network and the broader community or social system. Research rarely addresses macro-level conflict in networks. The surrounding community poses a more significant asset—or threat—to network efforts than is typically acknowledged in the literature.[38] At least four types of conflicts, all related, occur at the interface between the community and the network.

The first type of macro-level conflict is a depletion of resources sector-wide. This type of conflict goes beyond "shocks" to the system, such as changes in a single funder's priorities.[39] Instead, it refers to more debilitating constraints, such as under-resourced schools. These system-wide constraints impede social impact just as much as a lack of finances or infrastructure. For instance, Florence Young of the Westbrook Children's Project pointed out that her state was cutting back on budgets for direct services organizations, Medicaid, and other projects designed to help people that the network serves. Funding cuts may result in fewer resources for the network in a broader community where those resources are badly needed, resulting in frustrations on both sides.

Second, networks rely on social capital (see Chapter 4), including capital contributed by the broader community in which the network resides. But communities do not always support local networks. Sometimes, cultural or regional differences prove challenging.[40] Hadass Sheffer of The Graduate! Network suggests that their network model has not been easy to replicate in every community. "We tried to replicate that process in the communities that we go to," Sheffer said. "Sometimes, it takes longer. Sometimes, they're very collaborative. We've found in the Midwest, people tend to be a lot more collaborative from the get-go. They understand that they all rise together

---

[38] For more on how the community context has been addressed in other fields, including community psychology, public health, and political science, see Wolff, "Ten Places Where Collective Impact Gets It Wrong."

[39] Bryson, Crosby, and Stone, "Designing and Implementing Cross-Sector Collaborations."

[40] Vangen and Winchester, "Managing Cultural Diversity in Collaborations."

or fall together. In Texas, we found the same thing. In the Northeast, that is not the culture." Others pointed out that their city or community was a more challenging environment to launch a network, as Delia Farquharson of My Brother's Keeper Alliance in Mt. Vernon acknowledged at the beginning of this chapter.

The third form of macro-level conflict arises when networks do not impact their community or take too long to achieve impact. Collaborative or network efforts may be ineffective or fail to produce value; partners can generate wrong solutions, create new problems for a community, or fail to address the most critical community problems.[41] For example, Education for All shifted its attention from literacy to equity in the face of community protests at the local school board. Those protests stemmed from community resistance to the network's literacy efforts for all children and frustration that educational outcomes were not improving for marginalized youth.[42]

Finally, networks for social impact can encounter local structural or systemic forces that prove insurmountable. Institutional racism or wealth inequality represents systemic forces entrenched within communities. There is very little research on how networks should address these systemic issues, but there is a growing awareness of the shortcoming. For instance, several years after writing their much-cited *Stanford Social Innovation Review* article on collective impact, consultants John Kania and Mark Kramer published another piece in which they acknowledged that their initial model did not account for equity issues.[43] Moreover, they conclude that their collective impact model's conditions could not create lasting change independently; instead, organizational partners needed to apply an "equity lens" to their individual and shared efforts.[44] Many network leaders are ill-equipped to address systemic bias and, consequently, the network's gains may not benefit all

---

[41] James E. Austin, *The Collaboration Challenge: How Nonprofits and Businesses Succeed through Strategic Alliances* (San Francisco: John Wiley & Sons, 2010); James E. Austin and Maria May Seitanidi, "Collaborative Value Creation: A Review of Partnering between Nonprofits and Businesses. Part 2: Partnership Processes and Outcomes," *Nonprofit and Voluntary Sector Quarterly* 41, no. 6 (2012): 929–68; Bryson, Crosby, and Stone, "Designing and Implementing Cross-Sector Collaborations."

[42] Katherine R. Cooper, "Disconnect, Collide, Diverge: Tracing Diversity Discourse in Community Collaboration" (National Communication Association (NCA) Conference, Convened Virtually, 2020).

[43] John Kania and Mark Kramer, "The Equity Imperative in Collective Impact," *Stanford Social Innovation Review*, 2015, https://ssir.org/articles/entry/the_equity_imperative_in_collective_impact.

[44] Both before and after Kania and Kramer's equity article, researchers and practitioners had criticized collective impact for a lack of attention to community or grassroots models. Critics suggested collective impact privileged certain leaders and tended to reinforce power dynamics described in community development and community psychology (Wolff, "Ten Places Where Collective Impact Gets It Wrong"); practitioners suggested that consultants had overlooked the fact that communities of color and those working with marginalized populations had been engaged in collective work for some time—and were now left out of formalized collective impact efforts (Vu Le, "Why Communities of Color Are Getting Frustrated with Collective Impact," *Nonprofit AF* (blog), November 29, 2015, https://nonprofitaf.com/2015/11/why-communities-of-color-are-getting-frustrated-with-collective-impact/).

populations. Network leaders often find that they must experiment with different approaches. In the Blue Ribbon Commission, Jana Jones Halls notes that working in a low-income community prompted additional challenges for their network because residents did not trust the local government or the school system. This distrust led the network to try a variety of different community engagement and involvement strategies over time.

In sum, power disparities are endemic to networks. These disparities, and the features of networks themselves, make conflict inevitable. This conflict occurs at three interfaces: individual-organization, organization-network, and network-community. Some of these conflicts are difficult for networks to overcome, and they result in dead ends on the road to social impact. Other conflicts never go away and require constant attention. And networks can productively manage some conflicts and power disparities, and, through that process, pave a pathway to social impact.

Dead ends for addressing conflict

When network leaders first encounter overt conflict, they often wonder if they have hit a dead end for their network. Conflict is not a dead end. The ways that networks address or fail to address conflicts have more to do with the outcomes.

Networks over-rely on partner goodwill instead of anticipating and addressing conflict

Conflict can catch network actors by surprise because they assume that partners are committed to the problem and want to support the network by giving their best efforts. Public administration researcher Robert Agranoff notes that "despite the cooperative spirit and aura of accommodation in collaborative efforts, networks are not without conflicts and power issues."[45] Because of the overwhelming positive bias toward collaborative efforts in research and practice, network actors may be unprepared to respond to individuals that intentionally disrupt the network.[46]

This bias leads network leaders to assume that partner goodwill is a substitute for anticipating and addressing conflict. For example, Education for All

---

[45] Agranoff, "Inside Collaborative Networks," 61.
[46] Cooper, Milward, and Shumate, "Teaching Simulation: The Toxic Node."

partners thought that a mutual concern for local children would encourage community organizations to join the partnership. But after local faith-based organizations and community organizations stopped showing up after the initial meeting, network leaders realized that there were deeper conflicts at play. In the NF Collective (see case study in this chapter), network leaders assumed that a shared commitment to fighting neurofibromatosis would bring foundations together; initial interest concealed more deep-rooted conflicts between partners. In both cases, when it erupted to the surface, the conflict fundamentally challenged the activities of the network, leading them to revisit its reason for existence. An assumption of partner goodwill means that network leaders may not only fail to anticipate conflict but fail to address conflict when it does arise.

Dilemmas in managing network conflict

Axiom three states that network dilemmas are born out of unresolvable tensions and managed within constraints. Some network conflicts, especially micro- and meso-level conflicts, are never entirely resolved. New individuals are hired by organizations or elected into office and join the network. Organizations and networks both require resources. No matter how good the management strategy, these conflicts will never go away. Instead, networks must continually manage them.

All networks experience turnover before reaching impact

Many of the networks we have studied experience significant turnover, which exacerbates conflict at the individual-organization and, at times, the organizational-network interface. Networks must continually manage turnover. Although organizations may remain within the network, leaders must build new individual connections.

Heather Rowles of MAAC noted that their network had an unusual approach to handling partner turnover. Their initial process to become a partner in the network was quite extensive. They required would-be partners to contract with MAAC for a year before they could apply for affiliate membership. As an affiliate member, the agency spends another year attending meetings and being vetted by MAAC members. After a year, the members take a vote on whether to promote the partner to full member status. This time-intensive process is necessary, Rowles suggests, because of the standards of care required of each agency and because of the vulnerable population the network serves. But interestingly, having gone through that process does not guarantee that every agency remains a member of the network. Said Rowles, "There is no way to prove that those [outgoing] leaders are going to be replaced by leaders who believe in collaboration and are willing to put forth all the effort it requires to be part of the collaboration." She pointed to two recent cases in which partner agencies lost their CEOs. In one case, the CEO was replaced by a deputy director who had worked with the outgoing CEO for years and was familiar with MAAC. Partners voted for this organization to stay on at full status. Another time, an agency hired a CEO from out of state that was not familiar with the MAAC model. In this case, the network voted to drop the agency to affiliate status for one year until being assured that the new CEO was willing to collaborate and understood the network's purpose. MAAC's long-standing partnership and the willingness of agencies to participate in this process suggests that they have found a way to manage turnover for their network. Although we stop short of recommending this approach for all networks, leaders need to develop a formal process for managing turnover. Without management, it can undermine the social impact of the network.

Organizational agendas compete with network agendas

The tension between organizational and network goals and needs is ongoing.[47] Meso-level conflict, expressed as dueling loyalties to organizational and network interests, represents a real threat to a network's ability to achieve impact. One common suggestion to bridging organizational-network goals is to create a common identity among partners.[48] In networks with diverse members, like cross-sector networks, a shared identity will not resolve real differences between organizations.[49] Instead, leaders must balance the needs of organizations with the network's aspirations. Networks that lean into

---

[47] Bryson, Crosby, and Stone, "Designing and Implementing Cross-Sector Collaborations"; Keith G. Provan, Kimberley R. Isett, and H. Brinton Milward, "Cooperation and Compromise: A Network Response to Conflicting Institutional Pressures in Community Mental Health," *Nonprofit and Voluntary Sector Quarterly* 33, no. 3 (September 2004): 489–514, https://doi.org/10.1177/0899764004265718; Huxham and Vangen, "Doing Things Collaboratively."

[48] Matthew A. Koschmann, Timothy R. Kuhn, and Michael D. Pfarrer, "A Communicative Framework of the Value of Cross-Sector Partnerships," *The Academy of Management Review* 37, no. 3 (2012): 332–54; Joop Koppenjan and Erik-Hans Klijn, *Managing Uncertainties in Networks. A Network Approach to Problem Solving and Decision Making* (London: Routledge, 2004).

[49] Milward, Cooper, and Shumate, "Who Says a Common Agenda Is Necessary for Collective Impact?"

organizational interests over network interests operate more like a serendipitous network and are unlikely to make a social impact. Networks that lean
more into their shared interests, at the expense of organizational interests,
have declining membership over time.

Network leaders are obligated to champion network interests to achieve an
impact. But they can also acknowledge distinct organizational identities. For
instance, in the Chicago Benchmarking Collaborative, individual organizations have received funding to support their organizational goals. After the
Blue Ribbon Commission became a nonprofit, network leaders demonstrated
that they were not trying to compete with partner organizations by incorporating their programs in the network's initiatives and directing network
funding back accordingly.

Organizational partners do not need to have uniformity to pursue a
common purpose. For example, in an article we co-authored with Brint
Milward,[50] we suggested that network leaders should anticipate that organizations have different interests. Consideration of organizational interests can
boost investment in the network. Rather than demanding that organizations
have the same agenda, network leaders should encourage their members to
be open about those agendas. We suggested that some networks have used
a *two tables solution* to encourage network members to articulate those
differences.

Although we depict organization-network loyalties as a tension and not
a dead end, organizational interests can threaten network effectiveness.
Florence Young of the Westbrook Children's Project noted that in her community, some stakeholders had an interest in addressing substance abuse in
a way that did not align with what the network was doing. After some initial
participation, Young said, "They stopped coming, and then they went into
the community and did their own thing, which I think they're still doing.
There's some communication there, but not a lot." In this case, failing to prioritize organizational interests led to competition in the community. Even as
some organizations opt out of the network, the network dilemma continues.
As Young notes, "I think the folks who are participating in the project at
whatever level they, for the most part, have a real understanding of what our
vision is and that we need not be looking at every shiny object that comes up
the street. It's hard to do because there's always something coming up that's
interesting or new."

---

[50] Milward, Cooper, and Shumate, "Who Says a Common Agenda Is Necessary for Collective Impact?"

Pathways to social impact amid conflict

Pathways to social impact in this chapter describe different strategies that networks can use to address conflict in their networks. None of these strategies will make conflict go away altogether. Conflict is native to the network approach. Conflict management is part of the job of network leaders.

Networks build and restore trust over time

In a collaborative setting, trust refers to the belief that partners (1) will make "good-faith efforts to behave in accordance with any commitments both explicit and implicit," (2) will "be honest in whatever negotiations preceded such commitments," and (3) will "not take excessive advantage of another even when the opportunity is available."[51] Trust is the most significant predictor of partnership effectiveness in serendipitous networks.[52] It reduces transaction costs, improves relationship stability, and stimulates learning, knowledge exchange, and innovation.[53]

Building trust is easier said than done. Trust takes time to build and maintain. Networks grow trust through repeated interactions where members demonstrate to one another that they will act consistently. Funders or network conveners who bring together first-time partners or partners that are relatively unfamiliar with one another on a three-year grant cycle should realize that a lack of time to build partner trust will likely limit the network's impact. Jana Jones Halls of the Blue Ribbon Commission noted that they had to rebuild trust after the network formalized as its own nonprofit. "There was a lot of mistrust after we became our own nonprofit," Jones Halls said. "When I came in, I had to spend the first year rebuilding relationships with all these partners that we needed, finding tangible reasons for us to partner, and making sure the partnerships benefited everybody."

Face-to-face dialogue is necessary to build and maintain trust.[54] Although networks can conduct task coordination at a distance, the real work of

---

[51] Larry L. Cummings and Phillip Bromiley, "The Organizational Trust Inventory," in *Trust in Organizations*, eds. Roderick Kramer and Tom Tyler (Thousand Oaks, CA: SAGE, 1996), 303.

[52] Yannick C. Atouba and Michelle D. Shumate, "Meeting the Challenge of Effectiveness in Nonprofit Partnerships: Examining the Roles of Partner Selection, Trust, and Communication," *VOLUNTAS: International Journal of Voluntary and Nonprofit Organizations*, August 8, 2019, https://doi.org/10.1007/s11266-019-00143-2.

[53] *See* Huxham and Vangen, "Doing Things Collaboratively"; J. K. Popp et al., "Inter-Organizational Networks," Collaboration across Boundaries Series (Washington, DC: IBM Center for the Business of Government, 2014); Keith G. Provan and Patrick Kenis, "Modes of Network Governance: Structure, Management, and Effectiveness," *Journal of Public Administration Research and Theory* 18, no. 2 (April 1, 2008): 229–52, https://doi.org/10.1093/jopart/mum015.

[54] Ansell and Gash, "Collaborative Governance in Theory and Practice."

establishing relationships is more straightforward when physically co-present, at least at first. In networks with a larger geographic footprint, like the NF collective (see case study in this chapter), leaders need to travel for trust.

Build network structures to address conflict

Networks may successfully navigate conflict by anticipating that it will occur and investing in conflict management strategies. Conflict is more likely at the beginning of collaboration than in any other phase of the partnership.[55] Many of the decisions we described in setting up the network (Chapter 3) have implications for conflict management.

Formalizing decision-making mechanisms, for example, can help the network manage organizational-network interface conflicts. When a conflict arises, networks can use the decision-making strategy on which everyone has already agreed. Consensus-based decision-making (see "Tools for network instigators" in Chapter 3), for example, is designed to help organizations work together to find solutions to legitimate disagreements.

Network governance strategies can exacerbate or mask conflict. Distributed governance, for example, requires greater coordination among network members. When organizations have not established trust or have a challenging history of working together, distributed governance structures make conflict more likely. When there are significant power disparities among network members, lead agency or network administrative organization governance structures can mask conflict. By acting as an intermediary between more and less powerful actors, the governing organization can blunt the tendency for groups to power over one another.

Recruitment strategies also have implications for conflict. Top-down recruitment makes toxic node types of conflict more likely than bottom-up recruitment strategies. From our experience with networks organized in response to gender-based violence, networks that choose their partners may be more productive.[56] Other studies also suggest that those actors that are working together voluntarily may be more cooperative than those who are mandated to work together.[57]

---

[55] Karin Ingold and Manuel Fischer, "Drivers of Collaboration to Mitigate Climate Change: An Illustration of Swiss Climate Policy over 15 Years," *Global Environmental Change* 24 (January 1, 2014): 88–98, https://doi.org/10.1016/j.gloenvcha.2013.11.021.4.

[56] See Katherine R. Cooper and Michelle Shumate, "Interorganizational Collaboration Explored through the Bona Fide Network Perspective," *Management Communication Quarterly* 26, no. 4 (2012): 623–54.

[57] John Charles Morris et al., *The Case for Grassroots Collaboration: Social Capital and Ecosystem Restoration at the Local Level* (Lanham, MD: Lexington Books, 2013).

Invest in network leaders with conflict management skills or technical assistance

Managing conflict is part of a network leader's job.[58] Network managers can help mitigate different interests[59] or build trust.[60] But the skills that a network manager uses to get people to the table may not be the same that they need to keep them there. Network managers can seek out training in conflict assessment, a process by which managers determine whether the conflict is productive and whether an intervention is possible.[61] They can learn about the conflict management styles they tend to use and which circumstances demand that the manager take a specific stance in response. They can brush up on strategies to address conflicts in a collaborative setting, such as perspective-taking or shuttle diplomacy.[62] Additionally, Renee Heath and Matthew Isbell[63] offer extensive communication practices for managing various substantive, procedural, or relational conflicts and specific resources to orient partners toward a common goal and move toward consensus.

In some circumstances, a third-party mediator is useful in alleviating conflict.[64] Some network leaders we interviewed reported that a mediator helped them. During a difficult time for AgeWell Pittsburgh, when partners were shutting down or repositioning programs, they noted that their "planning partner," the agency that convened the partnership, helped keep the network going. Alexis Mancuso said that this agency's role "was really big for us. Keep us at the table, keep us focused on the outcome, keep us focused on our mission and the strategy, and what we were attempting to do for the greater good of the community."

---

[58] Robert Agranoff and Michael McGuire, "Big Questions in Public Network Management Research," *Journal of Public Administration Research and Theory* 11, no. 3 (July 1, 2001): 295–326, https://doi.org/10.1093/oxfordjournals.jpart.a003504; Daniela Cristofoli and Josip Markovic, "How to Make Public Networks Really Work: A Qualitative Comparative Analysis," *Public Administration* 94, no. 1 (March 2016): 89–110, https://doi.org/10.1111/padm.12192.

[59] Agranoff and McGuire, "Big Questions in Public Network Management Research."

[60] Erik-Hans Klijn, Bram Steijn, and Jurian Edelenbos, "The Impact of Network Management on Outcomes in Governance Networks," *Public Administration* 88, no. 4 (December 2010): 1063–82, https://doi.org/10.1111/j.1467-9299.2010.01826.x.

[61] *See* Lawrence Susskind, Sarah McKearnan, and Jennifer Thomas-Larmer, "Conducting a Conflict Assessment," in *The Consensus Building Handbook*, eds. Lawerence E. Susskind, Sarah McKernen, and Jennifer Thomas-Larmar (Thousand Oaks, CA: SAGE, 1999), 99–136; Gray and Purdy, *Collaborating for Our Future*.

[62] Gray and Purdy, *Collaborating for Our Future*.

[63] Heath and Isbell, *Interorganizational Collaboration*.

[64] Barbara Gray, Peter T. Coleman, and Linda L. Putnam, "Introduction: Intractable Conflict: New Perspectives on the Causes and Conditions for Change," *American Behavioral Scientist* 50, no. 11 (July 1, 2007): 1415–29, https://doi.org/10.1177/0002764207302459; Barbara Gray, "Strong Opposition: Frame-Based Resistance to Collaboration," *Journal of Community & Applied Social Psychology* 14, no. 3 (2004): 166–76, https://doi.org/10.1002/casp.773.

Recognize that not all conflict has to be resolved

Some conflicts come to a clear resolution. We have seen micro-level conflicts come to a close when individual participants move on to other opportunities, for example. But, many network conflicts cannot and do not need to be resolved for the network to achieve impact.

Network researchers distinguish between mega-conflicts that pose a more significant threat to the network's existence and mini-conflicts that have the potential to be disruptive, but not crises. Examples of mini-conflicts include disagreements over agency turf, resources, staff time, and meeting locations.[65] Such conflicts can—and often do—distract network leaders from their shared goals. Networks achieve impact not because they manage to avoid conflict entirely but because they determine which conflict to resolve. Partners can learn to live with differences as part of their continued network involvement. Some conflict is useful for networks. Disagreement can prompt a deeper look at a problem and generate new insights among partners.[66]

Redistribute network power and invest in community power

Networks interested in long-lasting social impact in disenfranchised populations must address power disparities within their network and disempowerment of communities. Bringing community leaders to the table and holding community forums is insufficient to address systemic racism, income inequality, and generational poverty. Instead, networks will need to adopt empowerment practices[67] that redistribute power to these populations.

One way that networks can address these concerns is to reconsider how power is distributed throughout the network. Researchers Chris Ansell and Alison Gash[68] conclude that if significant power or resource imbalances between stakeholders prevent important stakeholders from participating in a meaningful way (see "Tools for network instigators" in this chapter), effective collaborative governance necessitates the empowerment and representation of disadvantaged stakeholders. Management researchers Barbara Gray and

---

[65] Agranoff, "Inside Collaborative Networks."

[66] Gray and Purdy, *Collaborating for Our Future*, 115.

[67] Marc A. Zimmerman, "Empowerment Theory," in *Handbook of Community Psychology*, eds. Julian Rappaport and Edward Seidman (Boston, MA: Springer, 2000), 43–63; Christens, *Community Power and Empowerment*; Christens and Inzeo, "Widening the View: Situating Collective Impact among Frameworks for Community-Led Change."

[68] Ansell and Gash, "Collaborative Governance in Theory and Practice."

Jill Purdy[69] further advocate for increasing the voice of what they refer to as low-power players.

How can networks encourage participation from low-power players? Research on gender diversity offers some suggestions. First, networks need to move beyond tokenism to a critical mass perspective in their representation. Tokenism refers to selecting a single person to represent an entire community. A critical mass perspective recognizes that real participation and empowerment in network decision-making require more representatives from the affected community. If the research on gender diversity applies, a critical mass is equal to 30% of decision-makers.[70] Networks that serve multiple groups may have difficulty embracing this recommendation because the communities are likely to be different from one another, have competing interests, and disagree on how to move forward.[71]

Second, networks can explicitly adopt norms of participation that center members of disenfranchised communities. These norms might include limiting the number of talking turns that influential individuals can use, promoting consensus-based decision-making processes, and inviting a trained facilitator to run meetings. They can encourage mindset shifts, like the VOICE heuristic (see "Tools for network instigators" in this chapter), to promote deliberation. Finally, they can conduct meetings at a time (e.g., outside of regular work hours), location (e.g., accessible for those with different abilities, can be easily reached by public transportation), and with the resources (e.g., child care, stipends) that enable community participation.

Practices that encourage the participation of low-power players in the network are tactics that networks can use to distribute power. Community empowerment, in contrast, describes the use of community development practices. Brian Christens, a community development scholar, argues that "there remain relatively few organizations that can effectively build community power while sustaining settings that facilitate participants' empowerment."[72] Some networks may engage in community organizing practices,

[69] Gray and Purdy, *Collaborating for Our Future.*

[70] Jasmin Joecks, Kerstin Pull, and Karin Vetter, "Gender Diversity in the Boardroom and Firm Performance: What Exactly Constitutes a 'Critical Mass?,'" *Journal of Business Ethics* 118, no. 1 (November 1, 2013): 61–72, https://doi.org/10.1007/s10551-012-1553-6; Mariateresa Torchia, Andrea Calabrò, and Morten Huse, "Women Directors on Corporate Boards: From Tokenism to Critical Mass," *Journal of Business Ethics* 102, no. 2 (August 1, 2011): 299–317, https://doi.org/10.1007/s10551-011-0815-z.

[71] J. Kevin Barge, "Dialogue, Conflict, and Community," in *The SAGE Handbook of Conflict Communication: Integrating Theory, Research, and Practice*, eds. John G. Oetzel and Stella Ting-Toomey (Thousand Oaks, CA: SAGE, 2006), 517–44;Sarah E. Dempsey, "Critiquing Community Engagement," *Management Communication Quarterly* 24, no. 3 (2010): 359–90; Miranda Joseph, *Against the Romance of Community* (Minneapolis: University of Minnesota Press, 2002); Heather M. Zoller, "'A Place You Haven't Visited before': Creating the Conditions for Community Dialogue," *Southern Communication Journal* 65, no. 2–3 (March 1, 2000): 191–207, https://doi.org/10.1080/10417940009373167.

[72] Christens, *Community Power and Empowerment*, 116.

supporting individuals in identifying their concerns, creating associations, and advocating for policy change. Some networks have fully embraced this strategy. The Blue Ribbon Commission established a Community Council made up of individuals. These individuals identified community needs, such as beautifying a local park and hosting community cookouts. The Blue Ribbon Commission provided resources for them to accomplish their goals. A network can also be in the business of building connections between community members, as depicted in the form of parent cafes organized by the Berkshire United Way. These cafes, hosted by the network's partner agencies, provide child care and dinner for parents to connect not only to local agencies but also to one another.

Redistributing power is the most controversial practice that networks can embrace; it can cause more conflict for network partners at the onset. My Brother's Keeper in Mt. Vernon sought to encourage participation from some of the community's younger stakeholders. They organized monthly gatherings for youth to voice their concerns and for adults in the community to listen. But when they shared some of those concerns, Farquharson noted, school district leaders took offense and accused the network of hosting gripe sessions to complain about schools. This type of reaction is typical. The centering of marginalized voices decenters the voices of those who have power.

Ultimately, we suggest that one of the reasons that networks struggle to achieve impact is because they are not taking enough risks. They coordinate organizational action along the lines they always have, without challenging or altering the system in which they operate. However, those same systems are at the root cause (see Chapter 2) of many social ills.

Conclusion

Conflict can be productive; it forces network actors to challenge their assumptions about one another and the problem at hand. However, managing conflict to achieve impact requires networks to invest in both structure and process. Decisions about network governance, network management, and resource allocation have implications for the concentration of power within networks. The process by which actors engage the network can distribute, disrupt, or engage that power.

Case study: NF Collective

Tracy Wirtanen, the CEO and founder of the Littlest Tumor Foundation, had long been engaged in the fight against neurofibromatosis (NF), a set of rare genetic disorders. Inspired by collective impact, Wirtanen thought that the time had come to rally together the NF community's varied members around the country. She hoped to "dissolve the silos" that existed between foundations, and others agreed that the time had come. Annette Bakker of the Children's Tumor Foundation noted that their grantees expected them to come together: "[They said], you asked us to come together, but you funders are not coming together.'" In December 2015, seven organizations participated in early conversations about a possible partnership. They had a second meeting in March 2016.

Despite their shared interests, the organizations struggled to find common ground in those early conversations. "When I first started the [Littlest Tumor] foundation. It was clear to me that there were divisions within the NF community," said Wirtanen. Others agreed and pointed to the history between organizations—in the 1980s, the Neurofibromatosis Foundation had had some of its people leave to start their own organizations. Others noted that some NF foundations were collaborating. For example, suggests Karen Peluso of Neurofibromatosis Northeast, "Those of us who were active lobbying Congress together communicated and communicated pretty well. But those that weren't involved with our advocacy group would sometimes take credit for the work that was being done by the advocacy group when they did not do it."

The organizations were unequally sized; there were two larger organizations, and the other foundations were much smaller. Bakker suggested that having "equally sized organizations" tended to result in "harmonious collaboration." These differences also translated to different representatives being "at the table"; smaller organizations were represented by executive directors or CEOs, whereas larger organizations sent the staff members whose activities were relevant to developing a potential partnership. Bakker suggested that it was difficult for larger organizations to work with smaller organizations. The disparity of resources limited organizational choices. In either situation, partners tend to be dissatisfied, Bakker acknowledged.

After their initial meeting, the partnership looked as though it might be over before it began. Some partners expressed a disinterest in working on joint advocacy projects because of existing efforts. Others who were not part of the initial meeting were not on board with the goals discussed previously. "I really thought, we're just not going to get anywhere with this," said Peluso. "But Tracy was very, very persistent. Tracy would not give up; she was going to get us together."

The partners came together from around the country to participate in a two-day retreat in Vermont in March of 2017. On the first day, an outside speaker facilitated exercises intended to get the potential partners talking to one another. On the second day, the partners' charge was to generate an idea that they could work on together. "Finally, one common thread that we kept getting was our concern for patients who live in remote areas, where they're not close to a clinician or NF specialist, and they don't get good care for their NF," Peluso said. "Their NF is very often misdiagnosed. And then, if they have an issue because of their NF, some of these doctors don't know how to treat them. We all agreed that this was an area that needed to be addressed." Simon Vukelj, based in New York as part of the Children's Tumor Foundation, recalled sitting next to Cindy Hahn of the Texas Neurofibromatosis Foundation and comparing websites. When they considered the perspective of someone newly diagnosed with NF who might be seeking information, Vukelj realized that "We're confusing our own patients. We're not all being clear about what the process should be in terms of who you should reach out to. I think it was a eureka moment for everyone in the room. It was so obvious and so easy that we could work on something like this together." In May of 2019, the partners launched the NF Collective website. It is a comprehensive website intended to serve people around the country as they begin their NF journeys, including a national directory of providers.

Members of the NF Collective suggested that several factors resulted in their ability to work together. Bakker championed the importance of having a common goal for partners to work toward. Both she and Wirtanen acknowledged that part of the network's success came from having the right individuals representing organizations. Ultimately, the partners agreed that having the right person at the network's helm makes a big difference. Individual characteristics matter, as Wirtanen was a vocal champion for the network.

It took over three years to get from the initial conversations to launching the website. The members of the NF Collective—as it is now called—noted ongoing discussions about who will update and manage the website. The partners are encouraged by the feedback they have received from users and see the potential for collaborating again. Wirtanen reports that the NF Collective is planning its next summit.

Questions to consider

1. What conflicts were present in this scenario? At what interface?
2. What specific strategies did they use to address these conflicts?
3. What forms of power were represented by network partners? What role did power play in this network?
4. Were the conflicts in the NF Collective resolved, or are they ongoing? How would you advise members of the collective as they continue to work together?

Tools for network instigators

In this chapter, we focused on the role of both process and structure to address conflict and manage power disparities. In Chapter 3, we described the designs in detail. In this "Tools for network instigators," we introduce two additional techniques to manage these processes. The Stakeholder Participation Tool allows networks to capture how involved stakeholders are in decision-making. The VOICE heuristic can reframe participants thinking about the goals of conflict and deliberation.

Stakeholder participation tool

Just because individuals are part of the network does not mean that they show up to meetings. Keeping track of meeting attendance is an excellent first step toward determining whether individual stakeholders are engaged in the network. The stakeholder participation tool (see Table 5.1 for an example), developed by a team led by public administration researcher Julia Carboni, is a helpful next step for determining which network stakeholders are more actively involved.[73]

Table 5.1 Stakeholder Participation Tool: Example Roster

Participant	January General Meeting	February Town Hall	February Operations Meeting	Centrality Calculation	Centrality Score
Housing Authority	X	X	X	$((2-1) + (2-1) + (3-1))/4$	1.0
ABC Nonprofit		X	X	$((2-1) + (3-1))/4$	.75
Community Organization	X			$(2-1)/4$	.25
University			X	$(3-1)/4$	.50
...					
Grand total minus number of events	2	2	3	$(2 + 2 + 3) - 3 = 4$	

[73] Tool adapted from Julia L. Carboni et al., "Using Network Analysis to Identify Key Actors in Collaborative Governance Processes," *Nonprofit Policy Forum*; Berlin 8, no. 2 (2017): 133–45, https://doi.org/10.1515/npf-2017-0012.

This tool relies on a concept from network analysis called centrality. Network centrality is a way of measuring a stakeholder's influence within the network. The step-by-step instructions suggest a method for quantifying both the influence of organizations and individual representatives in the network. Network leaders can then interpret these figures in terms of whether specific sectors or organizations are under- or overrepresented. Results may also indicate the extent to which individuals are directing the network's activity.

Evaluator instructions

1. Create a roster for each meeting or event that includes all possible organizational or citizen participants. Place an X next to each participating organization or citizen that substantially contributes to the discussion.
2. Use the roster to calculate the centrality of each organization. First, total the number of participants in each meeting. Second, for each meeting that a representative participated in, add the total number of participants minus 1. Third, divide that by the total of substantial participants minus the number of events.
3. Compare the centrality scores of each participant. Then group the participants into categories that are meaningful in your network. Evaluate if each participant type is contributing as you would hope to the network.

The VOICE heuristic

Conflict between network partners may not disappear, either because it's a conflict that is part of a network dilemma or a micro-level conflict that partners don't need to resolve. Many conflict management techniques assume that parties can and should arrive at a common understanding. We think it useful to suggest some resources for deliberation that permit conflict to remain unresolved. The VOICE heuristic[74] proposed by communication researchers Jessica MacDonald Milam and Renee Heath can reframe network participant thinking and offer a bridge between the network and the community it seeks to benefit.

---

[74] Jessica MacDonald Milam and Renee Guarriello Heath, "Participative Democracy and Voice: Rethinking Community Collaboration Beyond Neutral Structures," *Journal of Applied Communication Research* 42, no. 4 (October 2, 2014): 366–86, https://doi.org/10.1080/00909882.2014.911944.

Table 5.2 VOICE Heuristic[*]

Visible decision processes draw attention to:	How do we arrive at this decision? What process will we use? Who is involved and who needs to be involved? How will others be informed?
Ownership of political power asks that we:	acknowledge civic responsibility; consider the larger community affected by decisions; commit to participative processes.
Information balanced with deliberation considers:	Are our processes overemphasizing information exchange? Is this the best use of peoples' time? Is this taking up time we need to be deliberating? How should we best use meeting time?
Contestation requires that we consider:	collaborations a safe place for contestation; how we encourage quiet voices; how we draw out dissenters and diverse viewpoints; whether we overemphasize harmony.
Expression reminds us to limit expression and increase discussion by considering:	the structures and practices we use. Do they foster expression or voice? Are our forms expressing or integrating diverse views?

[*] Reprinted with permission from Jessica MacDonald Milam and Renee Guarriello Heath, "Participative Democracy and Voice: Rethinking Community Collaboration Beyond Neutral Structures," *Journal of Applied Communication Research* 42, no. 4 (October 2, 2014): 366–86, https://doi.org/10.1080/00909882.2014.911944.

Milam and Heath differentiate expression and voice. Expression enables participants to have a say, whereas voice incorporates a more comprehensive and participatory process. Voice refers not just to expression, but the elaboration and debating of ideas. The authors use the acronym VOICE to refer to a heuristic that allows for contestation and disagreement between partners. The acrostic in Table 5.2 provides some questions that may be useful for network leaders as they make decisions; it emphasizes how discussions can be structured to encourage voice instead of expression.

6

Using Data to Support Networks' Theory of Change

Funders, communities, and network leaders all recognize the value of data. Funders require data to demonstrate the effectiveness of their investments. Communities want data to ensure that clients and students are receiving quality services. But in our experience,[1] and according to the research on non-profit organizations,[2] many agencies and networks are collecting data that they barely use. In our study of collective impact networks across the United States, 46% of the networks we studied did some data-sharing. However, many of those networks were either selectively gathering network data, accessing secondary data sources, or using the data to produce benchmarking reports. We argue that evaluation is an underutilized catalyst for a more significant social impact. Data systems allow networks for social impact to assess community needs, benchmark member organizations' performance, evaluate the outcome of network activities, and work transparently and in partnership with the communities they serve.

In this chapter, we do not concern ourselves with serendipitous networks. There are many resources for organizations that want to use better evaluation practices for their own organization's operations, including with collaborators. Instead, we focus on orchestrated serendipitous networks and goal-directed networks.

Chapter 3 identified five theories of change, the way that network's actions lead to social impact: project, learning, policy, catalyst, and systems alignment mechanisms. In this chapter, we return to these theories of change to identify the best practices available for data use. Then we turn to two data uses methods that have the potential regardless of the theory of change: evaluating

---

[1] Katherine R. Cooper and Michelle Shumate, "Policy Brief: The Case for Using Robust Measures to Evaluate Nonprofit Organizations," *Nonprofit Policy Forum* 7, no. 1 (2016): 39–47, https://doi.org/10.1515/npf-2015-0029; Anne-Marie Boyer et al., "The Influence of Network Structure on Nonprofit Use of Outcome Data" (Association for Research on Nonprofit Organizations and Voluntary Action, Austin, TX: A. de Gruyter, 2018).

[2] Chongmyoung Lee and Richard M. Clerkin, "The Adoption of Outcome Measurement in Human Service Nonprofits," *Journal of Public and Nonprofit Affairs* 3, no. 2 (July 31, 2017): 111–34, https://doi.org/10.20899/jpna.3.2.111-134.

Networks for Social Impact. Michelle Shumate and Katherine R. Cooper, Oxford University Press. © Oxford University Press 2022. DOI: 10.1093/oso/9780190091996.003.0006

network processes and using evaluation practices for community empowerment. We end the chapter by returning to the dead ends, dilemmas, and pathways associated with data use for social impact.

Data use for project-based social impact

Networks make a project-based social impact when they create useful assets, programs, or services. Much like social impact projects initiated by independent organizations, standard program evaluation practices apply. Although a full review of these practices is beyond this book's scope, we distinguish between three common ways that social impact organizations utilize data.

According to research on human service nonprofits,[3] there are three primary purposes that social impact organizations have for collecting and analyzing data about their programs and services: compliance, negotiated uses, and directive purposes. *Compliance* describes how organizations are required to report on the efficiency, scope, and effectiveness of their programs, often resulting from government contracts or regulation. In these circumstances, social impact organizations and networks do not choose the metrics they will use or the most critical outcomes. Because there is often a common requirement for similar organizations to use the same metrics, those metrics may be comparable to other organizations as long as they have the same contract or the same regulations.

In contrast, data for *negotiated* uses describes when organizations use data to demonstrate their efficiency and effectiveness to stakeholders. These stakeholders include organizational funders such as corporate or private foundations, individual donors, and the community. Notably, because stakeholders differ, data for negotiated uses is rarely compatible across organizations. As such, organizations make claims of efficiency and effectiveness in isolation based on the organization's past performance, in the best cases. At its worst, organizations cherry-pick the best results from a more extensive data collection effort, only highlighting successes and hiding failures.

Finally, one of the most powerful levers for social impact is the varied uses that fall under *directive purposes*. Here, organizations collect data to make their programs or services more efficient, effective, or scale their efforts. Directive

---

[3] Chongmyoung Lee and Richard M. Clerkin, "Exploring the Use of Outcome Measures in Human Service Nonprofits: Combining Agency, Institutional, and Organizational Capacity Perspectives," *Public Performance & Management Review* 40, no. 3 (February 1, 2017): 601–24, https://doi.org/10.1080/15309576.2017.1295872.

purposes are the mechanism by which networks identify what aspects of the program, facilities, or services are working and what elements need improvement. Jody Fitzpatrick, James Sanders, and Blaine Worthen's excellent text on program evaluation[4] provides a thorough overview of directive data use for project-based social impact.

Most networks for social impact use data for a mixture of these purposes. For networks that hope to make a social impact through joint projects, we argue that the most significant catalyst for social impact is directive purposes. We include an instrument to evaluate these three types of data use in the "Tools for network instigators" section at the end of this chapter.

Data use for learning-based social impact

In many ways, data use for project-based social impact does not differ significantly from how independent organizations might conduct program evaluation. In contrast, data use for learning-based approaches demonstrates the unique advantages that networks have over independent efforts. Whereas independent organizations can learn from their performance and conduct audits of others' performance, networks enable cross-network learning in unique ways.

Continuous improvement describes a process where organizations identify their goals and then use performance feedback to obtain results.[5] Networks that promote organizational learning,[6] particularly learning about improving their programs and services, nurture social impact. They also have an advantage over isolated organizations; they can collect comparative data for organizational learning and continuous quality improvement. Different agencies often collect their program evaluation data in a vacuum. When presented with the data about their program's successes or failures, they often use their past performance to interpret it. For example, an organization that addresses veterans' housing needs might find that they place 75% of their clients in long-term housing within three months. The agency might compare that outcome to the last assessment outcomes to see if they are making gains or not. However, they do not know if they perform better than any other local

[4] Jody L. Fitzpatrick, James R. Sanders, and Blaine R. Worthen, *Program Evaluation: Alternative Approaches and Practical Guidelines* (Upper Saddle River, NJ: Pearson Education, 2017).
[5] Ingrid J. Guerra-López, *Performance Evaluation: Proven Approaches for Improving Program and Organizational Performance* (New York: John Wiley & Sons, 2017).
[6] Valerie B. Shapiro, J. David Hawkins, and Sabrina Oesterle, "Building Local Infrastructure for Community Adoption of Science-Based Prevention: The Role of Coalition Functioning," *Prevention Science* 16, no. 8 (November 1, 2015): 1136–46, https://doi.org/10.1007/s11121-015-0562-y.

agencies that provide housing. Network-level data can provide the missing insight. Organizations that offer similar services can compare their outcomes and outputs to each other. More importantly, they can ask questions about program delivery to determine how the implementation influences those outcomes.

Collecting data for organizational learning and continuous quality improvement provides a proven lever for network leaders to improve their social impact (see axiom 1). Researcher and family physician Christiane Horwood and colleagues conducted a randomized control trial to examine the benefits of continuous quality improvement among community health workers in South Africa.[7] They found that clients of providers assigned to the continuous quality improvement group had higher knowledge and were more likely to have adhered to health recommendations than clients of providers who were not in the intervention.

One of the critical challenges for communities of practice is identifying the individuals or organizations that perform best. Indeed, management scholars introduced continuous quality improvement with this insight in mind.[8] Without data, everyone believes that they are performing above average. However, with the right analysis tools, networks can identify top performers, and organizations can convene learning communities and professional huddles to continue to improve everyone's practice. In cases where no one is performing well, joint training can improve everyone's outcomes.

There are multiple ways to gather data to catalyze learning. However, there are five fundamental principles that we recommend:

1. Ensure that agencies are collecting the same metrics in the same way

Suppose organizations are going to compare their activities and outcomes. In that case, differences should not be attributable to the different metrics they use or how they collect those data. Networks who are embarking on developing a set of shared metrics for the first time are often surprised at how

[7] Christiane Horwood et al., "A Continuous Quality Improvement Intervention to Improve the Effectiveness of Community Health Workers Providing Care to Mothers and Children: A Cluster Randomised Controlled Trial in South Africa," *Human Resources for Health* 15, no. 1 (June 13, 2017): 39, https://doi.org/10.1186/s12960-017-0210-7.

[8] Stephen M. Shortell, Charles L. Bennett, and Gayle R. Byck, "Assessing the Impact of Continuous Quality Improvement on Clinical Practice: What It Will Take to Accelerate Progress," *The Milbank Quarterly* 76, no. 4 (1998): 593–624.

challenging it is to get everyone to agree and the level of detail required for that agreement.

Based on our interviews with network leaders, there are a few guidelines to keep in mind. First, all organizations do not have to collect only the metrics identified by the network. They can also collect additional information that they find helpful or that their funders require. For example, AgeWell Pittsburgh agencies have agreed upon 20 protective factors to ensure elder independence and well-being. However, each agency does not collect data on all twenty protective factors. Instead, they only collect data on the ones that their agency influences. Second, after identifying the overarching types of data that the network is interested in, it is often useful to get program level staff involved in designing how organizations will collect network data. They are often best equipped to have detailed conversations about how they will measure activities like attendance, engagement, and participation.

2.   Create systems for data entry that are easy to use and compatible with the systems that organizations are already using

Several technology platforms exist for agencies to share client or private data across organizations. Many networks we have encountered use cloud-based case management or customer relationship management systems for this purpose. When comparing these various software systems, ensuring that they allow data access at multiple levels is vital for complying with government privacy regulations. Cost is often a key factor, as well.

However, for the system to be useful, networks must consider the ease of use and compatibility with member organizations' existing data systems. Research on users' willingness to use new technology systems notes that perceived ease of use and usefulness predict whether individuals will use a new technology system.[9] Perceived ease of use results from the user's computer abilities and self-confidence in those abilities, system characteristics, training, user involvement in the design, and the nature of the

---

[9] Fred D. Davis, "Perceived Usefulness, Perceived Ease of Use, and User Acceptance of Information Technology," *MIS Quarterly* 13, no. 3 (September 1989): 319–40, https://doi.org/10.2307/249008; Fred D. Davis, Richard P. Bagozzi, and Paul R. Warshaw, "User Acceptance of Computer Technology: A Comparison of Two Theoretical Models," *Management Science* 35, no. 8 (1989): 982–1003; Viswanath Venkatesh and Fred D. Davis, "A Model of the Antecedents of Perceived Ease of Use: Development and Test," *Decision Sciences* 27, no. 3 (1996): 451–81; Nikola Marangunić and Andrina Granić, "Technology Acceptance Model: A Literature Review from 1986 to 2013," *Universal Access in the Information Society* 14, no. 1 (March 1, 2015): 81–95, https://doi.org/10.1007/s10209-014-0348-1.

implementation process.[10] Attention to each of these factors is critical. One of the most relevant system characteristics is whether it allows for importing data, either in real time or routinely, from other systems that network members use. In some cases, organizations will be able and willing to adopt a new data system exclusively. However, in other cases, funder or government guidelines will mandate that they enter data into another system. To reduce the burden of entering the same data twice, ideally, software should be able to import data from these mandated systems or sync with them automatically.

3. Incentivize data entry and goal setting

One of the reasons that the Chicago Benchmarking Collaborative, the case study included in this chapter, has been successful in their efforts is their incentive structure. Instead of incentivizing organizational improvement, when possible, they pay agencies for entering their data on time and participation in a goal-setting process. Goals should be specific and occur within a specified time.[11] There is a vast body of research on how goal setting influences performance. Edwin Locke and Gary Latham are the pioneers of goal-setting theory. Based on their summary of the research, goals affect performance for four reasons. First, they direct individuals' attention toward the specific activities needed to achieve the goal and away from unrelated activities. Second, goals energize those that make them, and more challenging goals are more motivating than less demanding goals, up until a point where the goal is not achievable. Third, individuals are more likely to persist in their efforts for longer when they set goals, as long as they have control over the time they spent on the task. Finally, goals lead to improved knowledge application and information seeking.

By rewarding member organizations for data entry and goal setting, instead of pay-for-performance, the Chicago Benchmarking Collaborative aligns with goal-setting research. When individuals set their own goals and receive regular feedback on how they are doing, they achieve higher performance.[12] In contrast, when goals are mandated, individuals have lower performance.

---

[10] Venkatesh and Davis, "A Model of the Antecedents of Perceived Ease of Use: Development and Test"; Viswanath Venkatesh and Hillol Bala, "Technology Acceptance Model 3 and a Research Agenda on Interventions," *Decision Sciences* 39, no. 2 (2008): 273–315, https://doi.org/10.1111/j.1540-5915.2008.00192.x.

[11] Edwin A. Locke and Gary P. Latham, "New Directions in Goal-Setting Theory," *Current Directions in Psychological Science* 15, no. 5 (October 1, 2006): 265–68, https://doi.org/10.1111/j.1467-8721.2006.00449.x.

[12] Locke and Latham, "New Directions in Goal-Setting Theory."

4. Establish a culture of formative assessment and learning instead of punitive evaluation

Focusing on rewards for the process instead of achievement highlights the fourth area of emphasis. One of the keys to sustaining continuous quality improvement is to structure the work to embrace a culture of growth. Samuel Silver, a professor of internal medicine, and colleagues'[13] review of the National Health Service (UK) Sustainability Model identifies three practices that help continuous quality improvement processes yield better performance and sustainability.

First, front-line staff and managers should receive regular feedback on their performance. In hospitals, this feedback might occur as frequently as every shift, but feedback occurs weekly, monthly, or quarterly in most networks we encounter. Silver and colleagues describe performance boards as another way to report feedback. Performance boards display the aim or priority at the top of the board, and the rows below depict the results. Where results diverge, they indicate current improvement activities.

Second, Silver and colleagues recommend that organizations document improvement activities. They should develop a written narrative that describes the action, steps, time required, and personnel responsibilities. These written documents then can be readily disseminated among network members as best practices, with clear guides describing what the organization did and how they implemented it.

Third, front-line workers should meet regularly in improvement huddles. These meetings allow front-line workers to assess what problems they might anticipate, process the feedback together, and identify what needs improvement. For example, the approximately 30 service coordinators who provide direct services on the ground for the AgeWell Pittsburgh network meet every other month. They talk about gaps in service, best practices, service delivery, and outcomes.

5. Use the appropriate statistics to make comparisons

Organizations should rarely compare their raw outcome scores to each other to determine best practices. Selection effects, meaning differences in the

---

[13] Samuel A. Silver et al., "How to Sustain Change and Support Continuous Quality Improvement," *Clinical Journal of the American Society of Nephrology* 11, no. 5 (May 6, 2016): 916–24, https://doi.org/10.2215/CJN.11501015.

qualities of whom different agencies serve, may be driving the results. Further, when networks conduct direct comparisons of outcomes, without statistical controls for selection effects, they unintentionally incentivize organizations in the network to engage in "skimming," or purposely taking on the least challenging cases. Using appropriate statistics and designs for program evaluation allows analysts to distinguish program outcomes from selection effects.[14]

Cross-sector networks for social impact may also have professionals that are familiar with these tools already. Sometimes, networks lack the funding to hire staff with appropriate design and statistical analysis knowledge. In these cases, networks may turn to members who have personnel with these competencies. For example, in many collective impact networks, Fortune 500 companies have made employees familiar with Lean Six Sigma,[15] a continuous quality management program, available to the network through an executive loan. Colleges and universities often have staff or students who have similar skills. Finally, many government agencies, especially professional agencies like Public Health Departments, have many professionals familiar with these techniques.

Using these guidelines, networks for social impact have a unique capability that individual organizations do not have. They can benchmark agencies and professionals to one another and, in doing so, promote organizational learning. Organizational learning is one of the critical factors that differentiate networks that achieve social impact from those that do not.[16] Organizations must perform their programs and services better if networks hope to move the needle on social issues in their community. Unsurprisingly, organizations are often better equipped to learn in networks with more effective processes.

Moreover, the intentional adoption of these practices helps guard against the limitations of the data. Self-report data is subject to bias; organizations often hold different perceptions of what constitutes "success," and the selection of performance criteria itself is subject to bias.[17] Thus, these practices prove useful in promoting organizational learning. They also appeal to networks convened for other types of social impact.

---

[14] Kathryn E. Newcomer, Harry P. Hatry, and Joseph S. Wholey, *Handbook of Practical Program Evaluation* (Hoboken, NJ: Wiley, 2010).

[15] M. P. J. Pepper and T. A. Spedding, "The Evolution of Lean Six Sigma," *The International Journal of Quality & Reliability Management; Bradford* 27, no. 2 (2010): 138–55, https://doi.org/10.1108/02656711011014276.

[16] Shapiro, Hawkins, and Oesterle, "Building Local Infrastructure for Community Adoption of Science-Based Prevention."

[17] K. Emerson and T. Nabatchi, "Evaluating the Productivity of Collaborative Governance Regimes: A Performance Matrix," *Public Performance & Management Review* 38, no. 4 (2015): 717–47.

Data use for policy-based social impact

In contrast, policy-based social impact requires different types of data. Some of this data is specific to the social issue that the network addresses. For example, environmental networks concerned about urban flooding may create detailed maps of which neighborhood houses have flooded basements in a metropolitan area. While these are powerful tools for policy change, especially when such research informs the creation of city, state, or national policy, they are too idiosyncratic to the social issue for a general discussion.

Regardless of the specific social issue, advocacy networks find two types of data useful in their work: public opinion research and power mapping. These data types correspond to the two mechanisms that advocacy networks often use to encourage policy change: grassroots and direct advocacy. Grassroots advocacy influences policy change by creating an indirect influence on policymakers through their constituents. In contrast, direct advocacy targets specific policymakers.

Public opinion research is a vital indicator of both progress and success in grassroots advocacy campaigns. While the methods of public opinion polling are beyond this chapter's scope,[18] in general, methods include media trend analysis, public opinion polling, focus groups, interviews, and instant-response sessions. Reliable public opinion research can provide critical insights into targeted groups' beliefs and attitudes, ongoing campaigns' effectiveness, and general shifts in opinions over time. We do not spend much time describing these techniques because they do not differ significantly for independent advocacy organizations and networks.

In contrast, power mapping, when done in a network, offers unique opportunities. Power mapping "identifies key actors within a particular field of action, defines the power that these actors have in relation to particular decisions or resources, and assesses the relationships of these actors with each other and with oneself."[19] Networks possess two critical advantages over independent advocacy organizations in power mapping. First, networks generally have a better-combined purview of the entire social terrain, including the relationships between powerful actors. Second, networks have more contact points between these powerful actors and themselves since they contain

---

[18] *See* Wolfgang Donsbach and Michael W. Traugott, eds., *The SAGE Handbook of Public Opinion Research*, 1st ed. (Thousand Oaks, CA: SAGE Publications Ltd, 2007) for chapters dedicated to the methods of public opinion research.

[19] Darren Noy, "Power Mapping: Enhancing Sociological Knowledge by Developing Generalizable Analytical Public Tools," *The American Sociologist* 39, no. 1 (2008): 4.

many organizations. Networks, like RE-AMP, often assemble organizations that are interested in the same policy objectives. In RE-AMP, subgroups called state tables build power for equitable deep decarbonization; and these groups sometimes become directly involved in state-level policy. Tools like power mapping can enhance these efforts.

Power mapping is not a single process but a collection of techniques. In general, networks will engage in five related processes, often iteratively as campaigns progress. First, they identify all of the institutions and individuals that influence their desired policy. Second, they will identify how much control each of these individuals and institutions has over the desired outcomes. Third, they will determine how much each of these individuals and institutions agree or disagree with their position. Fourth, they will map out the relationships these entities have with one another. Finally, they will identify all of the connections, both personal and institutional, with each of these targets. Based on this information, the network will identify priority targets for direct advocacy and which organizations or individuals should contact them. Then after a while, the network revisits the map, noting changes in relationships and positions.

Data use for catalyst-based social impact

Where policy-based social impact requires tracking attitudes and shifting opinions, catalyst-based social impact networks must track fidelity to the model that they are promoting. These networks' key idea is to scale up an existing model or best practice to other communities, organizations, or networks. Implementation science, the study of the implementation of various types of programs and services, has found significant differences in how closely professionals adhere to evidence-based practices.[20] These differences in adherence, or fidelity, explain a significant amount of variations in impact. Some scholars suggest if programs were implemented with fidelity, they would be 12 times more effective.[21]

---

[20] Shannon Stirman et al., "Relationships between Clinician-Level Attributes and Fidelity-Consistent and Fidelity-Inconsistent Modifications to an Evidence-Based Psychotherapy," *Implementation Science* 10, no. 1 (August 13, 2015): 115, https://doi.org/10.1186/s13012-015-0308-z; e.g., Bonnie Klimes-Dougan et al., "Practitioner and Site Characteristics That Relate to Fidelity of Implementation: The Early Risers Prevention Program in a Going-to-Scale Intervention Trial," *Professional Psychology: Research and Practice, Children's Mental Health* 40, no. 5 (October 2009): 467–75, https://doi.org/10.1037/a0014623.

[21] Joseph A. Durlak and Emily P. DuPre, "Implementation Matters: A Review of Research on the Influence of Implementation on Program Outcomes and the Factors Affecting Implementation," *American Journal of Community Psychology* 41, no. 3 (March 6, 2008): 327, https://doi.org/10.1007/s10464-008-9165-0.

Consider Take Stock in Children,[22] a Florida-based program that pairs adult mentors with elementary or middle school at-risk youth. In 1995, the program reported robust results: 94% percent of the students completed the program, and 80% went to college. Based on these results, the organization scaled its effort from one site serving Pinellas County to 31 local affiliates serving 50 counties. The program did not have any fidelity measures in place, and its results varied widely across affiliates. Without appropriate performance measures and training, the program struggled to scale up its promising results. After it instituted these measures, they ensured program adherence and saw similar outcomes for students.

Networks that aim to scale up their efforts or replicate a single network's success in different communities face a similar challenge. Evidence-based programs and previous successes are no predictor of future success without proper attention to implementation. Collecting data across agencies running similar programs can bring implementation differences into relief and help professionals identify the best practices, including appropriate adaptations that enhance the program's efficacy.

AmericaServes networks provide a robust example of how to scale networks across geographies. Their networks utilize the same platform, UniteUs, to manage referrals across their networks. Their networks share a management model that includes a coordination center to handle both intake and manage referrals. However, the quality of their scale-up, now to 17 U.S. communities, uses standard metrics across networks to assess how well the network is adhering to core principles. They established a set of central performance measures related to social impact, focusing on speed and accuracy.[23] They use metrics like the number of clients served, percentage of cases resolved, and average days required for a provider referral to compare networks to each other and to identify networks in need of technical assistance or different types of intervention. These metrics are publicly available on a real-time dashboard.

Power Scholar Academy, a joint program of BellXcel and the YMCA, provides a more human capital-intensive example. Partheev Shah of BellXcel described how data and technical assistance were two of the tools that allowed them to scale the program from a pilot program that served 300 students to a program that served 7,000 students a summer. Shah commented, "I think it

---

[22] McKinsey & Company, "7 Elements of Nonprofit Capacity Building" (Reston, VA: Venture Philanthropy Partners, 2001), http://bonner.pbworks.com/w/file/fetch/106093761/Effective%20Capacity%20Building%20in%20Nonprofit%20Organizations.pdf.

[23] Nick Armstrong et al., "Adapting the Collective Impact Model to Veterans Services: The Case of AmericaServes," in *Bulletproofing the Psyche: Preventing Mental Health Problems in Our Military and Veterans*, eds. Kate Hendricks Thomas and David L. Albright (Santa Barbara, CA: Praeger, 2018), 209–27.

starts with a commitment nationally that the fidelity and quality of the implementation are critically important." But beyond commitment, BellXcel and YMCA committed resources not only to observing the outcomes of the project but sending experts to coach local program implementers on what was working and what was not. In short, catalyst-based social impact is not just about getting more communities to adopt an evidence-based program, like Power Scholars Academy. It's also about making sure that those communities adopt it with fidelity and providing the technical assistance needed for implementation.

Data use for systems alignment-based social impact

While networks that have a catalyst theory of change are often interested in assessing network performance on a standard set of measures, those using a systems alignment approach have a more difficult task. They collect data to diagnose how and why existing organizations are not serving their communities well. Their two jobs are to identify system-level gaps in coverage and leaky pipelines across organizational activities. *Gaps in coverage* describe groups of people or areas that are receiving fewer or no services. *Leaky pipelines* describe critical moments in a person's or areas' life cycle that require intervention. Identifying these vital moments highlights one of the opportunities that networks have over individual institutions. The networks can identify when individuals transition from services offered by one organization to another well or poorly.

To identify gaps in coverage, network leaders map out which clients or areas are receiving services (see the "Tools for network instigators" in this chapter for an example). These maps allow the network to redirect organizations' efforts so that they better serve the entire community. Consider, for example, the Chicago Literacy Alliance. The alliance is currently a network of over 140 organizations; all focused on some aspect of literacy in Chicago. In the early 2000s, the alliance mapped out all of the network's literacy programs against which Chicago Public Schools they were serving. They discovered that some schools had over a dozen organizations serving them, and just down the street, another school would only have just a few or none. By using this information, literacy programs could reduce duplication of services by better covering the underserved schools.

Identifying gaps in services can also be an essential tool to address a program evaluation challenge, *confusing selection effects with program effects*. Some people or groups are more likely to sign up for services, come to classes, or attend meetings. When an agency compares the outcomes for this group against outcomes for the entire population, it is tempting to conclude that their program or services made the difference. However, the results might be attributable to the differences between individuals who elected to participate in those programs or services and individuals who did not. Participants differ from the population, and those differences explain their improved results. Program evaluators describe the resulting difference as selection effects.[24] For example, those individuals might have had more considerable resources or more discretionary time. They might have higher self-efficacy or a feeling that they could impact the outcomes of their own lives. Or they might have greater trust in organizations. All of these factors could influence their results, with or without the programs or services. To distinguish selection effects from program effects, program evaluators have to conduct comparative research[25] on participants and non-participants to account for these factors. Alternatively, if the goal is to move the needle on social issues, they could address gaps in participation.

The process of assessing which groups and areas that are not receiving services is a challenging endeavor. The analysis usually requires participation from a government agency with access to population-level records. Public Health Departments, school districts, city government, and agencies that distribute basic human services or income often have comprehensive records of who lives in a particular region. Networks can match the cities' records with agencies' records of their clients to identify which individuals are underserved. Existing programs can be aligned to attract these underserved individuals, or network partners may need to create brand-new programs to reach the groups. Without such analysis, agencies can become self-satisfied in addressing the needs of clients who are the easiest to reach.

Leaky pipelines, similarly, find gaps in services or interventions but do so considering the life cycle of the client or the area. Cradle-to-career education networks, like the Summit Education Initiative discussed in Chapter 1, trace how the effects of interventions early in a student's career can be amplified or diminished at different points in their journey through school. In doing so, they identify areas where to strengthen the pipeline. For example, Summit assesses every preschooler who will be entering kindergarten the next year. Through this assessment, they identified preschools that were more effective than others. However, beyond this comparative evaluation, they also

---

[24] Gary T. Henry, "Comparison Group Designs," in *Handbook of Practical Program Evaluation*, eds. Kathryn E. Newcomer, Harry P. Hatry, and Joseph S. Wholey (Hoboken, NJ: Wiley, 2010), 125–43.
[25] Henry, "Comparison Group Designs."

identified when students would benefit most from a summer bridge program between preschool and kindergarten. Environmental advocacy networks, similarly, can determine where pollution impacting waterways occurs upstream. In doing so, they can direct their efforts to the source of the problems.

Identifying leaky pipelines requires data about clients or areas that extend beyond an end-of-program assessment. Social impact networks are uniquely equipped to collect this type of data as coordinators of services across organizations. Privacy concerns mandate both permissions to retain the data and use databases that manage access levels across agencies. However, such systems can give the network a unique purview of the entire ecosystem of activities and outcomes.

The Campaign for Grade-Level Reading in Delray Beach, Florida, USA, provides a useful example. The City of Delray Beach leads the network, which includes 15 other organizations serving youth. Consistent with the Campaign for Grade-Level Reading's foci, the network targets kindergarten readiness, summer learning, and absenteeism. One of the first relationships they developed was with the Palm Beach Public Schools, which is the district that covers the Delray Beach area. Through a data-sharing agreement, the network can analyze outcomes for all public school students in Palm Beach. They can determine which students do not receive city and nonprofit services. Further, they can observe student outcomes over time as they progress through the public school system. The network won the All-American City award for their efforts.

Data use for network management

Network processes play an essential role in ensuring that networks achieve social impact. Networks that function well facilitate social impact (see axiom 1). Here we draw attention to two crucial network processes that deserve attention: evaluating network functioning and mapping new relationships as they form in the network.

Evaluating network functioning describes the four key processes that improve networks' social impact:[26] goal-directedness, efficiency, cohesion, and opportunities for participation. *Goal-directedness* refers to how the network makes decisions, governs itself, and carries out meetings. *Efficiency* refers

---

[26] Valerie B. Shapiro et al., "Measuring Dimensions of Coalition Functioning for Effective and Participatory Community Practice," *Social Work Research* 37, no. 4 (December 2013): 349–59, https://doi.org/10.1093/swr/svt028; Shapiro, Hawkins, and Oesterle, "Building Local Infrastructure for Community Adoption of Science-Based Prevention."

to how task-oriented the network's governing body is and how quickly they move from talk to action. *Cohesion* is the sense of unity and "group spirit" in a network. When network participants are directly asked for their contributions individually, and there is relatively equal involvement, networks are said to have higher *opportunities for participation*. Valerie Shapiro, a professor of social work, and colleagues have an easily accessible instrument that measures coalition functioning.[27]

Our study of 13 matched education reform networks used this instrument to measure the 26 networks' functioning. In our experience, network members rank coalition functioning high, a mean score of 4 on a 5-point scale. Moreover, we found no significant difference in average coalition functioning scores, across dimensions, for more centrally governed, goal-directed networks versus less formal or developed networks. We suggest that this is because the measure evaluates network management, not network governance. It also means that network management processes are orthogonal to the adoption of any network governance model.

According to Shapiro and colleagues' research,[28] one of the critical mediators between coalition functioning and improved social impact, along with organizational learning, is forming new connections among organizations. Network leaders, as we have seen, have two ways to influence the formation of new ties.[29] They can create circumstances for organizational leaders to encounter one another and allow them to find opportunities for collaboration or "blind dates." Or they can broker new relationships among organizations, identifying viable partnerships, or as "arranged marriages." Whichever tactic a network employs, the only way to determine if those activities are effective is to measure the addition of new collaborations among member organizations. Small networks can use the organization/project pivot table, described in the "Tools for network instigators" section, to map these collaborative networks themselves and then examine changes in the connections among organizations. Suppose the teams want to use social network analysis techniques. In that case, they can transform this pivot table into a network by converting a two-mode network into a one-mode network with their choice of social network analysis software. However, if the network is large or if the team does not

[27] Shapiro et al., "Measuring Dimensions of Coalition Functioning for Effective and Participatory Community Practice."

[28] Shapiro, Hawkins, and Oesterle, "Building Local Infrastructure for Community Adoption of Science-Based Prevention."

[29] Raymond L. Paquin and Jennifer Howard-Grenville, "Blind Dates and Arranged Marriages: Longitudinal Processes of Network Orchestration," *Organization Studies* 34, no. 11 (November 1, 2013): 1623–53, https://doi.org/10.1177/0170840612470230.

have social network analysis expertise, researcher Danielle Varda has developed an inexpensive tool designed to measure changes in networks for social impact over time.[30] Because of its ease of use and low cost, we recommend it as a starting point to identify collaborations and as a process metric, examining network change for larger networks.

Data use for community empowerment

The last of the data-use opportunities that networks have is community accountability. Networks for social impact often have no mandate to respond to the community. Networks that do not include government institutions determine services and set goals for communities but are not elected by its citizens. Even networks that include democratically elected government officials have less accountability to citizens since those officials rarely have complete decision-making authority over the network's actions. Thus, community accountability is a discretionary choice for networks.

However, community accountability has several benefits that social impact networks may want to harness (see Chapter 5). First, it helps to build trust and goodwill among community members. Trust is often essential for networks to achieve cooperation and reduces the likelihood of resistance or outrage. Second, community accountability creates opportunities for individuals to participate in network activities. At a minimum, accountability allows community members to provide feedback on network activities and, at best, will enable them to set goals and monitor the network's progress at achieving those goals. Finally, community accountability is often a powerful tool to motivate partners to stay engaged with the network and to change their organization's activities. We are not advocating the use of data to "shame" organizational partners into compliance. However, we observe that the public sharing of progress creates an urgency for change in ways that internal communication among partners sometimes cannot.

We introduce a continuum of data use that opens up the network to the community. At the minimum, social impact networks give accounts to communities about their activities, goals, outputs, and outcomes. They often do so in reports, published once a year or once a quarter. Providing information to

[30] Danielle M. Varda, "Data-Driven Management Strategies in Public Health Collaboratives," *Journal of Public Health Management and Practice* 17, no. 2 (April 2011): 122, https://doi.org/10.1097/PHH.0b013e3181ede995.

the community is not transparency; it is disclosure.[31] Networks that give accounts are mainly using data for negotiated purposes.

At the next level, networks for social impact can strive for greater transparency. Transparency is "the deliberate attempt to make all legally releasable information available—whether positive or negative in nature—in a manner that is accurate, timely, balanced, and unequivocal, for the purpose of enhancing the ability of publics to hold organizations accountable for their actions, policies, and practices."[32] When networks for social impact use data for transparency, they allow stakeholders to participate in the evaluation, hold network members accountable for their action or inaction, and report factual information about performance, whether good or bad.

Community data dashboards allow networks for social impact to achieve greater transparency. Data dashboards[33] are visually appealing ways to display data against targets. They are one step beyond merely reporting results in an annual report because they are typically comprehensive, encouraging networks to release positive and negative data without comment. When networks aim for greater transparency, they begin to move from negotiated uses to directive uses because they invite community members into network activities and outcomes. Higher Expectations for Racine County, a network dedicated to creating a fully capable and employed workforce for Racine County, Wisconsin, USA, utilizes this approach. Although they release annual reports of their results, they increase their transparency with a publicly accessible dashboard. There the community can visualize subsets of data based on their interests rather than relying on the public reports.

Community members can become even more involved in the network at the end of the continuum[34] when they become part of the process of evaluating the network's work. Jennifer Greene[35] describes one such approach. In it, the program evaluator begins with the goals of the organization or network. They collect preliminary data and write nontechnical evaluation summaries of the

[31] Brad Rawlins, "Give the Emperor a Mirror: Toward Developing a Stakeholder Measurement of Organizational Transparency," *Journal of Public Relations Research* 21, no. 1 (January 2009): 71–99, https://doi.org/10.1080/10627260802153421.

[32] Rawlins, "Give the Emperor a Mirror," 75.

[33] Robert Rothman, *Data Dashboards: Accounting for What Matters* (Georgia: Alliance for Excellent Education, 2015); "How Dashboards Can Help Your Nonprofit Achieve Its Goals," *Webinar, Nonprofit Quarterly*, December 6, 2018, https://nonprofitquarterly.org/how-dashboards-can-help-your-nonprofit-achieve-its-goals/.

[34] see David M. Fetterman and Abraham Wandersman, *Empowerment Evaluation Principles in Practice* (New York: Guilford Press, 2005).

[35] Jennifer G. Greene, "Stakeholder Participation and Utilization in Program Evaluation," *Evaluation Review* 12, no. 2 (April 1, 1988): 91–116, https://doi.org/10.1177/0193841X8801200201; Jennifer C. Greene, "Communication of Results and Utilization in Participatory Program Evaluation," *Evaluation and Program Planning* 11, no. 4 (January 1, 1988): 341–51, https://doi.org/10.1016/0149-7189(88)90047-X.

results. In these summaries, they provide no recommendations. Then, they gather community members to discuss the results, focusing on two research questions: (1) What can be learned from the results so far? And (2) For each of the policy areas or programs identified (including additional ones generated by the participants), what recommendations are "appropriate, meaningful, and feasible"? After each meeting, the evaluator adds the meeting summaries to the next community group's results to consider. This process may lead the evaluator to collect additional data if the group identifies this as a recommendation before moving forward. Once the evaluator has received all the relevant feedback and collected any other data, they provide the community's recommendations to the network.

Communities benefit from social impact networks when they consolidate network members' evaluation into a single data platform. This consolidation makes reviewing the activities of network members less time-consuming for citizens than evaluating each organization individually. In short, member organizations can become more accountable to the community, and the community may have a higher capacity for involvement through their participation in network-based evaluation and reporting.

Data use represents an opportunity for networks to enhance the social impact that they make. Whether that social impact is through a project, learning, policy, catalyst, or systems alignment mechanisms, there are ways to make the network activity more effective. And all networks might benefit from a more significant examination of how evaluation can enhance their functioning and community engagement. However, there are some network dilemmas to navigate and practices to avoid on the road to social impact.

Dead ends for data use to support theories of change

When it comes to data use, networks often engage in practices that we consider dead ends. Dead ends, in this case, do not necessarily mean that the network will end. Instead, it means that the network will either fail to achieve social impact or do more harm than good.

Failing to measure social impact

The first dead end is failing to evaluate social impact. Many networks capture measures of individual, organizational, or network outcomes (see Chapter 2). They can report on individuals' satisfaction with network events. They might report an increase in organizational efficiency, especially if the network offers services that the organization would have independently bought on the market. Or networks can say how many member organizations they have or how much money they raised over the past year. These measures are reasonable and perhaps even necessary, but they do not measure social impact.

Although networks that eschew evaluation may be making a social impact, there is no evidence of it without evaluation. Moreover, while we would not recommend networks abandoning their data compliance requirements, these requirements rarely give network managers the ability to determine what influence network activities had on the measures. Measuring social impact allows networks to evaluate if their efforts produced the change they sought to make.

Many networks we interviewed, especially in our interviews with educational network leaders across the United States, made evaluation their last priority. There was never enough funding or time to invest. They often lacked the staff and did not budget the funds to hire the technical assistance necessary to conduct an evaluation. Instead, they were left to wonder if they were making any difference at all.

Poor data design and analysis practices

Poor data design and analysis practices are another dead end. When networks design data systems that incentivize skimming or set low goals, they provide potent inducements for organizations to displace their social impact goals to demonstrate gains in the data. Further, networks will make inaccurate assessments about the effectiveness of network or organizational programs and activities without appropriate statistical controls. Such faulty conclusions about efficacy can undermine effective programs' impact at reaching the most challenging populations or areas.

Measuring outcomes without tracking activities

In 2016, we hosted a Collective Impact Summit at Northwestern University.[36] One of the panels that we insisted on including was on evaluation. We brought

---

[36] For a report of the findings from the Collective Impact Summit, *see* Michelle Shumate and Katherine R. Cooper, "Collective Impact: What We REALLY Know" (Evanston, IL: Network for Nonprofit and Social Impact at Northwestern University, May 23, 2016), http://nnsi.northwestern.edu/cireport.

in educational evaluation experts from across the country to give us their input, including Shaun Dougherty, Tim Sass, and Elizabeth Farley Ripple. Many collective impact networks claim that because they see gains in educational outcomes after their network started, they had evidence of their impact. The experts said no. Educational outcomes change for various reasons, including shifts in the community's demographics, changes in state-level education policy, and improvements in schools. The network could not claim responsibility. The reason, they argued, is because the network could not demonstrate the effect of its activities on particular students.

The Collective Impact Summit discussion illustrates a broader point about data use. When networks claim geography-level, not just client-level, social impact (see Chapter 2), they need to have data that link their activities to the outcomes. Otherwise, their claims about their influence are spurious.

Indeed, networks that make a social impact through project, learning, catalyst, and systems alignment mechanisms need data not just on their social impact but on their activities. Without such data, they cannot determine which of their activities produced any effect, created a greater impact, or detracted from the impact. These insights are important because they enable networks to scale up what is working and disinvest from what is not.

Network dilemmas for data use to support theories of change

The ongoing, contradicting demands of networks present dilemmas for network managers. Although data use should enable networks to identify pain points and opportunities for growth, its use cannot be divorced from the values.

Understanding the limits of data and using it anyway

The first dilemma requires network managers to hold two truths about data in tension: *you cannot manage what you cannot measure*, and *everything does not boil down to numbers*. Management consultant Peter Drucker is often credited with the first truth. And indeed, much of this chapter is dedicated to helping networks measure their outcomes. We are certainly not advocating for data use malpractice (see "Dead ends" in this chapter).

However, one of the lessons learned from decades of Lean Six Sigma management is that there is a dark side to all of this measurement. The selection of some measures and not others is fraught with political agendas (see Chapter 5 for more on network conflict). And real issues that are not part of logic models or measurement models can and do affect the social impact that networks make. We suggest that effective network leaders hold these two truths in tension. While the limitations of measurement should not inhibit its use, data is not the whole story.

Balancing the negotiated and directive use of data

At the beginning of the chapter, we described both negotiated and directive uses of data. Although we primarily applied this distinction to project-based mechanisms for social impact, the two uses illustrate a more generic tension. Networks must balance using evaluation to demonstrate their progress and successes with its application to make tangible improvements in their activities. Networks that only use data to report their success to communities or funders neglect data systems that are powerful network improvement engines. However, networks that only engage in continuous quality improvement or public opinion polling, among other directive uses, fail to capitalize on data to increase motivation, enhance legitimacy, and recruit new members to join a network. Effective network leaders will balance these two purposes of data use.

Pathways for data use to support theories of change

Using data to support social impact mechanisms is an underutilized management tool. Networks that use data effectively can be more strategic about where to dedicate their resources and time. They can generate greater external legitimacy for their efforts because they have the data to demonstrate their impacts. Useful data keeps organizational leaders at the table because they can see the fruits of their actions. There are several pathways to data use that pave the way to social impact.

Create a culture that values data use

When consultants or opinion leaders first introduce the idea of utilizing data for learning, decision-making, and systems alignment, some organizational leaders are intimidated. They fear that they or their organization will be judged based on the data. They operate using a fixed mindset[37] about the data, the same way that some students have a fixed mindset about their grades. They think the data will show how good or bad they are. This fixed mindset is especially prevalent when funders play an outsized role in setting the evaluation criteria (see Chapter 4 for more about funders and networks). When networks operate with a fixed mindset, the choice of metrics is fraught with politics and issues about data ownership.

One of the pathways for data use for social impact is to encourage a growth mindset. In a growth mindset, data is an indicator of how things are going. It's not a final evaluation of a person's, organization's, or program's worth. A growth mindset looks at unfavorable data and says, "that shows we are not where we want to be, yet."

Network leaders can model a growth mindset by sharing their organization's data and identifying areas where they can grow. They can also promote a culture that values data by celebrating the improvements that organizations make in the face of challenging information. They can create routines and rituals around sharing data and setting new goals. Finally, they can publicize successes, repeating stories about when their data-use process helped them achieve a more significant social impact.

Use data to support the network's mechanism of social impact

One of this chapter's contributions is that it demonstrates the wide variety of ways that data use can support social impact. In keeping with the systems approach of this book, the most critical aspect of data use is that it supports the entire set of activities that the network is doing. Alignment is what allows networks to make a social impact.

Axioms 3 and 5 combined emphasize that there are many ways to make a social impact, but not all methods are available to networks. Nowhere else in this book is this principle more evident. Networks can choose to use data to enhance their social impact in various ways, including program evaluation, continuous quality improvement, public opinion research, power mapping, gap analysis, identifying leaky pipelines, process evaluation, and community-led evaluation. However, no network can or should use all of these techniques.

---

[37] Carol Dweck, "What Having a 'Growth Mindset' Actually Means," *Harvard Business Review Digital Articles*, January 13, 2016, 2–4; Harvard Business Review Staff, "How Companies Can Profit from a 'Growth Mindset,'" *Harvard Business Review*, November 1, 2014, https://hbr.org/2014/11/how-companies-can-profit-from-a-growth-mindset.

Using too many of them would be both costly and would detract from the network's work.

The mechanism or mechanisms for social impact that the network chooses to employ should drive the data techniques employed. Both social issue analysis and the theory of change inform the appropriate types of data to collect, its analysis, and how network leaders interpret it to support social impact. In short, the applicable data method is contingent upon the earlier choices and actions of network leaders. And although networks may try to revisit these initial decisions, it is more difficult to change the network's purpose and theory of change. We describe such challenges in Chapter 7.

Case study: Chicago Benchmarking Collaborative

The Chicago Benchmarking Collaborative (CBC) is a data-focused partnership made up of six area education and human service agencies serving thousands of low-income individuals.[38] Christopher House served as project manager for the CBC. Traci Stanley, director of quality assurance at Christopher House, coordinates the network. Her role includes the management of data submission for all seven agencies—on a variety of measures including demographics and outcomes related to education, employment, and socioemotional functioning—plus the creation of data reports, scheduling, and facilitation of regular meetings, and review of improvement plans based on observed data patterns.

Data-sharing is central to the CBC's mission of collective program improvement. After studying multiple data-sharing platforms, the CBC chose a case management software package that offered secure data-sharing—critical to protecting clients' identities. It was also customizable, meaning it could accommodate the different programming offered by each agency in the CBC. "Once case management software is purchased, organizations can reconfigure data elements instead of paying the software makers for changes," Stanley said.

The case management software also enabled tracking children's progress over time, even if they changed programs within a given CBC agency. "Ideally, I get children in as infants or two-year-olds," said Julie Dakers, Christopher House director of early childhood and youth development services, "and I can track their progress, even if they transition into our school-age and youth leadership programs. I can paint a picture of them over time, and that's exciting." The software also facilitated the retention of data regarding why children left specific programs. As Edgar Ramirez, Chicago Commons, then-associate executive director summed up, "The data is the glue that keeps this group together."

CBC member organizations met regularly to develop programming goals, strategies, and components. Member agencies set goals for each organization since the CBC did not encourage program-level collaboration. Christopher House acted as project manager for these activities. "We have an annual timeline that's broken down by month of the activities that happen and the deadlines," Stanley said. "I ensure everyone is collecting data and knows how to enter

---

[38] This case is adapted from Michelle Shumate and Liz Livingston Howard, "Making the Most of the Chicago Benchmarking Collaborative," *Kellogg School of Management Cases*, n.d., https://store.hbr.org/product/making-the-most-of-the-chicago-benchmarking-collaborative/KE1066.

information into the database correctly." In general, CBC members met several times during the year to share and study data and develop goals and practices. These meetings focused on a comprehensive report that compared the outcomes of member agencies. After the school year, CBC partners would meet to look at the past year's educational data and identify data points to target for improvement during the summer. "By September/October," Stanley said, "teams at each organization are meeting and talking about selecting data points that they want to focus on and developing SMART goals for improving results."

SMART is an acronym for specific, measurable, agreed upon, realistic, and time-bound. For example, if 2014 data showed that 42% of students in a particular age group showed a 1-point increase in literacy scores, a SMART goal might be to achieve a 10-point gain. If accomplished, the data would show that 52% of students indicated that level of improvement. Improvement plan activities designed to reach that goal might include intentional lesson planning, provision of books and educational toys to support lesson planning, specific opportunities for professional development, and partnerships with local universities to offer family literacy nights or similar events.

Beyond standard academic outcome measures such as grade point averages and test scores, CBC partners could target improvement in socioemotional measures such as students' feelings of competence as learners, measured by a research-based survey provided to youth in the programs. Agencies set targets based mostly on the performance demonstrated by other CBC member organizations on a given measure. CBC expected teams to turn in their plans to Stanley by October's end. In collaboration meetings held around mid-February, teams would examine fall data and adjust improvement plans before spring data collection. Spring data gathering included a group of post-assessments, such as where graduating high school seniors in the program had been accepted to attend college. After complete data were available, CBC agencies met to compare progress against improvement plans, set new goals and tactics, and subsequently reported their progress, completing that year's cycle.

Questions to consider

1. For the member agencies, what are the advantages and disadvantages of doing joint program evaluation?
2. What would be the most challenging about setting up a system like CBC?
3. Should agencies directly compare their results to each other? Why or why not?

Tools for network instigators

The data use in networks tool

In this section, we draw attention to two tools that are less familiar to network leaders. This first is a tool for networks that utilize project-based mechanisms for social impact. The Data Use in Networks tool[39] assesses how networks use evaluation processes for their joint programming (see Table 6.1). Scholars have empirically validated the measure for organizations, and we have amended it to focus on networks. The second set of tools is for networks that

Table 6.1 Data Use in Networks Instrument

Instructions: Read the following items and consider whether your coalition collects data for this purpose. Circle your answer.

Our coalition collects data to . . .

	NEVER	RARELY	SOMETIMES	OFTEN OR ALWAYS
1. Improve management decisions	0	1	2	3
2. Improve strategic planning	0	1	2	3
3. Improve services for clients	0	1	2	3
4. Appraise employee performance	0	1	2	3
5. Support budget decisions	0	1	2	3
6. Do outreach and public relations	0	1	2	3
7. Report to the board	0	1	2	3
8. Improve communication between administrators and elected officials	0	1	2	3
9. Respond to public demands for accountability	0	1	2	3
10. Respond to pressure from community groups	0	1	2	3
11. Comply with government requirements	0	1	2	3
12. Report to funders	0	1	2	3
13. Get new funding	0	1	2	3

Scoring sheet

Use the below guide to calculate your quiz scores. You should have three separate scores for groups A–C.

Group A: Directive Uses—Total score for Questions 1–6: _____/18.

Group B: Negotiated Uses—Total score for Questions 7–9: _____/9.

Group C: Compliance Uses—Total score for Questions 10–13 _____/12.

[39] Survey adapted from Lee and Clerkin, "The Adoption of Outcome Measurement in Human Service Nonprofits."

use systems alignment to make a social impact. These tools are designed to help networks track which organizations address particular targets, focus on specific network goals, and enact appropriate programs, either alone or in collaboration with other organizations in the network. Although these pivot tables alone do not make a robust data system that will allow for a predictive model, they help track effort.

Pivot Tables

For systems-alignment mechanisms, an essential tool is pivot tables based on a project database. The project database should include the following information:

1. Project Name
2. Project Leader Information
3. Project Description
4. What network goal(s) or leading indicators does the project address?
5. Which organizations are involved in the project?
6. Which target area or groups does the project serve? (e.g., City Y School, Great River Basin, preschool children).

The reason to place this information in a database is that it only needs to be entered once to create a variety of helpful reports. Each of these elements is essential to building pivot tables to address gaps in system-level service and engagement. We would suggest that networks create these pivot tables as reports that they can run on at least a quarterly basis. They provide a snapshot of the activity of the network. Each has its purpose.

(A) Goal/Project Pivot Table
The goal/project pivot table allows you to identify which goals receive the most attention and receive less care (see example in Table 6.2). One way to think about the pivot table is that a row with many blank spaces suggests little network activity toward accomplishing that goal.

(B) Target/ Project Pivot Table
The target area or group/project pivot table identifies areas of the community or geographic region receiving services (see example in Table 6.3). This pivot table helps determine the gaps in service described earlier in this chapter.

Table 6.2 Example Goal/Project Pivot Table

	Backpack Buddies	Church Food Pantry	WIC Accepting Farmers Market	Community Garden	Cooking Class
Educate on healthy cooking techniques					
Provide low- or no-cost health food options					
Build community social capital					

Table 6.3 Example Target/Project Pivot Table

	Backpack Buddies	Church Food Pantry	WIC Accepting Farmers Market	Community Garden	Cooking Class
Neighborhood North					
Neighborhood West					
Neighborhood South					
Neighborhood East					

(C) Goal/Target Area Pivot Table

Similar to the target area or group/project pivot table, this pivot table aims to identify gaps in service or leaky pipelines (see example in Table 6.4). This table allows network leaders to see if the enacted approach to the social problem matches the logic model (e.g., the goal targets the right age group). Alternatively, they can determine how the network addresses specific goals for particular targets (e.g., green infrastructure has not been implemented in these communities but not by design).

(D) Organization/Project Pivot Table

This table helps to manage organizational involvement in a network (see example in Table 6.5). If not carefully managed, many networks can operate using the 80–20 rule, where 20% of the organizations are responsible for

Table 6.4 Example Goal/Target Pivot Table

	Neighborhood North	Neighborhood West	Neighborhood South	Neighborhood East
Educate on healthy cooking techniques	■		■	
Provide low- or no-cost health food options	■	■	■	
Build community social capital			■	■

Table 6.5 Example Organization/Project Pivot Table

	Backpack Buddies	Church Food Pantry	WIC Accepting Farmers Market	Community Garden	Cooking Class
District School A	■				
District School B					
District School C				■	
Junior League	■				
United Church		■			
SW Community Org.				■	■
City Government			■		
Public Health Agency			■		

almost all of the network's work. This table should identify all of the organizations in the network and identify the projects in which they are involved. By examining this table, network leaders can determine which organizations should be encouraged to participate in new ways and which organizations are already overextended.

7
Remaining Agile and Adaptable

In interviews with networks older than five years, a theme re-emerged over and over—change. None of these networks continued to operate the same way they had at emergence (see Chapter 3). Summit Education Initiative (see the case in Chapter 1) disbanded the network entirely and restarted from scratch. AgeWell Pittsburgh began with a home-visiting program that they abandoned after funding ended. For other networks, the change was not as dramatic. The Wisconsin Association of Independent Colleges and Universities began as a coalition for government relations. Over time, they added services to help their members control costs.

This chapter is about how networks, like these examples, reinvent themselves, mature, learn, grow, and dissolve. This chapter highlights two axioms of this book. In combination, both axioms help us understand the mechanisms by which change occurs and the degree of change required.

Axiom three states that network dilemmas brought on by ongoing contradictions are never solved, just managed within constraints. In this chapter, we focus on how network instigators' choices influence the mechanisms of network change. Allowing relationships to form among a set of organizations more organically (i.e., a serendipitous network) or creating a commonly understood network entity with some degree of shared goals (i.e., a goal-directed network) creates critical differences in the origins and patterns of network change.[1] The choices of the organizations in the network and environmental changes that affect the entire field drive serendipitous network evolution. In contrast, goal-directed networks move forward as an entity, driven not just by member organization changes but due to network leadership, maturation, and the degree to which the network fits the overall environment.

Axioms two states that networks are sensitive to their environment. Both the networks and their environment drive the degree of change. Following

---

[1] Michelle Shumate and Zachary Gibson, "Interorganizational Network Change," in *Oxford Handbook of Organization Change and Innovation*, eds. Marshall Scott Poole and Andrew Van de Ven, 2nd ed. (Oxford: Oxford University Press, 2021); Martin Kilduff and Wenpin Tsai, *Social Networks and Organizations* (Thousand Oaks, CA: SAGE, 2003).

Networks for Social Impact. Michelle Shumate and Katherine R. Cooper, Oxford University Press. © Oxford University Press 2022.
DOI: 10.1093/oso/9780190091996.003.0007

strategic management scholars' work,[2] we characterize the degree of change for serendipitous and goal-directed networks as either incremental or radical.[3] Incremental changes may originate from either the network or the environment. It is expected and routine. Radical change is far more disruptive. At the network level, radical change appears as dramatic alterations to membership, changes in the network's goals, shifts in resource allocation, the adoption of new modes of program and service alignment, and network governance changes. At the environmental level, radical changes can include the approval of significant policy changes in a social issue area, dramatic swings in public opinion regarding a social issue, population movement, and industry-disrupting innovation.

We organize this chapter around these two distinctions. Table 7.1 summarizes the four types of network change. Recognizing the nature of network change is essential to its effective management.

Table 7.1 Types of Network Change

Degree of Change	Serendipitous Network	Goal-directed Network
Incremental	*Causes of change*: organizational learning, organizations changing their relationships with others in the network, organizations leaving or joining the field, the maturation of the industry or field *Management techniques*: enhance organizational adaptative capacity, conduct regular environmental scans, recognize the field's stage of development	*Causes of change*: planned change from network leadership, field-level shifts, network maturation *Management techniques*: utilize network change management techniques appropriate to the level of agreement and stakes organizations have in the issue
Radical	*Causes of change*: usually from the environment, including social issue change, shifting resources for entire field, and disruptive innovation *Management techniques*: use relationships with other organizations to buffer the impacts of change, consider if change has led to crossroads for organization and make decisions appropriately	*Causes of change*: resources are discontinued, significant leadership transitions, rapid change in how the social issue is viewed by external stakeholders, network leadership induced *Management techniques*: make decisions based on the type of crossroads faced by network

[2] Alan D. Meyer, Geoffrey R. Brooks, and James B. Goes, "Environmental Jolts and Industry Revolutions: Organizational Responses to Discontinuous Change," *Strategic Management Journal* 11 (1990): 93–110.
[3] Meyer and colleagues' model of network change includes four terms to describe the origin and degree of variation: adaptation, evolution, radical, and revolutionary. Although we draw on this model, we've reduced the number of terms to enhance readability.

Incremental change and serendipitous networks

The dual motors that drive change in serendipitous networks are the choices organizations make and change in the environment. Organizational change as an engine occurs through learning, changing partnership portfolios, and entering or exiting a field. In part, serendipitous network change is an outcome of accumulating these organization-level actions (see axiom one). Additionally, it results from the maturation of the field.

Network instigators, especially hosts, can encourage serendipitous network change by creating organizational learning opportunities and forming new relationships. For example, professors Jean Hartley and Maria Allison[4] describe the learning that occurred in the Better Value Development Programme, a hosted serendipitous network of academics and 23 local authorities in the United Kingdom. One hundred and eighty-one individuals met for monthly workshops. They reported two types of knowledge gains. First, they noted that they gained new information about best practices and programs. Hartley and Allison describe this as explicit knowledge, or knowledge that is easily codified and written down. Second, participants suggested that they learned how they were progressing compared to other local authorities, including the processes that these authorities were using. Hartley and Allison describe this information as tacit knowledge or know-how. When organizations capitalize on this new learning, it creates change in the organizational field.

A changing partnership portfolio is the second source of incremental network change. Few relationships between organizations endure over time. For example, in Kimberly Isett and Keith Provan's research on mental health providers in Tucson, Arizona, USA, 41% of ties remained stable across three years. Typically, organizations in serendipitous networks form relationships with one another based on trust and risk aversion.[5] First, organizations develop trusting relationships with partners. They manifest this trust through

---

[4] Jean Hartley and Maria Allison, "Good, Better, Best? Inter-Organizational Learning in a Network of Local Authorities," *Public Management Review* 4, no. 1 (January 2002): 101–18, https://doi.org/10.1080/14616670110117332.

[5] Mark Lazerson, "A New Phoenix?: Modern Putting-Out in the Modena Knitwear Industry," *Administrative Science Quarterly* 40, no. 1 (1995): 34–59, https://doi.org/10.2307/2393699; Ranjay Gulati, "Social Structure and Alliance Formation Patterns: A Longitudinal Analysis," *Administrative Science Quarterly* 40, no. 4 (1995): 619–52; Ranjay Gulati and Martin Gargiulo, "Where Do Interorganizational Networks Come From?," *American Journal of Sociology* 104, no. 5 (March 1, 1999): 1439–93, https://doi.org/10.1086/210179; Brian Uzzi, "Social Structure and Competition in Interfirm Networks: The Paradox of Embeddedness," *Administrative Science Quarterly*, 1997, 35–67; Andrea Larson, "Network Dyads in Entrepreneurial Settings: A Study of the Governance of Exchange Relationships," *Administrative Science Quarterly* 37, no. 1 (March 1992): 76–104, https://doi.org/10.2307/2393534.

the formation of repeated partnerships and adding informal ties to con-tractual ones.[6] For example, in Michelle's research on HIV/AIDS interna-tional NGOs (INGOs) serendipitous network from 1985 to 2001,[7] the most consistent predictor of a partnership between organizations was a previous partnership.

However, the accumulation of changes in networks is substantial. Besides changing the portfolio of ties, organizations enter and leave fields. New entrants and exiting organizations create variations in the distribution of resources, po-tential partners, and the competitive landscape. For example, in the study of HIV/AIDS INGOs, an organization's average lifespan was approximately four and a half years.[8] Network leaders and scholars often underestimate the dyna-mism of organizational fields.[9]

In addition to the network change originating from organizations, seren-dipitous network change occurs due to maturation in the field. When organ-izations seek out new partners, they tend to form relationships in the early stages of the network with partners of partners, forming triads or small clusters of relationships among a set of organizations.[10] In later stages of net-work formation, they rely on reputation to select partners. For example, in research on four INGO communities from 1990 to 2004,[11] INGOs tended to form partnerships with partners of partners from 1990–1998. However, from 1998–2004, the tendency disappeared. Drawing upon strategic management research,[12] we note that identity and legitimacy drive partner selection in the early stages of an industry or social issue. However, as industries or social is-sues mature, organizations focus on the resources that potential partners have to share.

Organizations hoping to survive, manage, and thrive amid incremental change have two tools from which to draw. First, they can enhance their

---

[6] Kimberley Roussin Isett and Keith G. Provan, "The Evolution of Dyadic Interorganizational Relationships in a Network of Publicly Funded Nonprofit Agencies," *Journal of Public Administration Research and Theory: J-PART* 15, no. 1 (2005): 149–65.

[7] Michelle Shumate, Janet Fulk, and Peter R. Monge, "Predictors of the International HIV/AIDS INGO Network over Time," *Human Communication Research* 31 (2005): 482–510, https://doi.org/10.1111/j.1468-2958.2005.tb00880.x.

[8] Shumate, Fulk, and Monge, "Predictors of the International HIV/AIDS INGO Network over Time."

[9] Howard E. Aldrich, *Organizations Evolving* (London: SAGE Publications, 1999).

[10] Lazerson, "A New Phoenix?"; Gulati, "Social Structure and Alliance Formation Patterns: A Longitudinal Analysis"; Gulati and Gargiulo, "Where Do Interorganizational Networks Come From?"; Uzzi, "Social Structure and Competition in Interfirm Networks"; Larson, "Network Dyads in Entrepreneurial Settings."

[11] Nina F. O'Brien et al., "How Does NGO Partnering Change Over Time? A Longitudinal Examination of Factors That Influence NGO Partner Selection," *Nonprofit and Voluntary Sector Quarterly* 48, no. 6 (December 2019): 1229–49.

[12] Julie M. Hite and William S. Hesterly, "The Evolution of Firm Networks: From Emergence to Early Growth of the Firm," *Strategic Management Journal* 22, no. 3 (March 2001): 275–86, https://doi.org/10.1002/smj.156.

organization's ability to adapt through learning. Second, they can manage their portfolio of relationships so that they have access to the best information.

First, learning is contingent on participation and organizations' ability to assimilate what individuals learn as part of their networking activities. Researchers refer to some organizations' capability to learn from and adapt to changes in their environment as absorptive capacity.[13] Absorptive capacity is about the design of three sequential learning processes: exploratory learning, contextualizing the knowledge in the organization (i.e., transformative learning), and then implementing changes as a result. The "Tools for network instigators" section of this chapter describes how managers can increase their organization's absorptive capacity.

Second in serendipitous networks, organizations can enhance their ability to manage an evolving landscape by managing their network ties. Scholars suggest that organizations connected to other organizations that are not connected to one another have a distinct advantage;[14] they have access to better information than other organizations. This recommendation runs counter to the strategy that most organizations use to form relationships— choosing partners of partners. However, organizations that are already connected share information. In contrast, having connections to organizations that do not have a partnership with partners allows organizations access to non-redundant information.

In sum, incremental serendipitous network change originates from the accumulation of organizational actions and the field's maturation. Organizations can manage this changing landscape by enhancing their absorptive capacity and managing their network portfolio to capture new information. However, these strategies alone are insufficient to address radical network change.

Radical change and serendipitous networks

A radical change in serendipitous networks almost always results from revolutionary changes in the network's environment (see axiom two). Examples

[13] Peter J. Lane, Balaji R. Koka, and Seemantini Pathak, "The Reification of Absorptive Capacity: A Critical Review and Rejuvenation of the Construct," *The Academy of Management Review* 31, no. 4 (2006): 856, https://doi.org/10.2307/20159255.

[14] Gautam Ahuja, "Collaboration Networks, Structural Holes, and Innovation: A Longitudinal Study," *Administrative Science Quarterly* 45 (2000): 425–55, https://doi.org/10.2307/2667105; Giovanni Battista Dagnino, Gabriella Levanti, and Arabella Mocciaro Li Destri, "Structural Dynamics and Intentional Governance in Strategic Interorganizational Network Evolution: A Multilevel Approach," *Organization Studies* 37, no. 3 (March 1, 2016): 349–73, https://doi.org/10.1177/0170840615625706.

of revolutionary change include, but are not limited to, changes in the social issue, resources in the field, and disruptive innovation. Evolutionary scholars describe these moments of transition as a punctuated equilibrium. A change occurs in the environment, leading to a radical shifting of network members and ties. After the situation stabilizes, models of incremental network change are re-established.

Communication scholars have conducted some of the best work on radical serendipitous network change among social impact organizations. For example, researchers examined Croatian civil society before and after the 2000 presidential elections.[15] A presidential election does not always equate to a radical network change. In democratic societies, the peaceful transfer of power is taken for granted. However, the 2000 presidential election in Croatia was no regular election. In 1990, a newly elected President Franjo Tudjman had led Croatia to end all formal ties with Yugoslavia. The way that this break with Yugoslavia occurred led to the Bosnian and Croatian civil wars. In 1999, Tudjman became ill and died. These events left a political opening with the potential for dramatic consequences. In the lead up to the 2000 elections, USAID stepped in to fund democratic, free-media coverage, and civil society efforts. A government-oriented NGO (GONGO), an election monitoring agency, stepped in to ensure a fair and peaceful election. The network included 18 core players who were tightly connected. USAID sat at the center of the networks, with the highest centrality, while the GONGO acted as a broker, connecting unconnected parts of the network. After the 2000 election, USAID and the GONGO had achieved their goal, a fair and peaceful election. They pulled back their financial support, offering primarily informational support to civil society organizations. Two new funders entered the space, but with less funding than previously available. After the election, the density of network ties decreased by half. While the network before the election was wholly connected, with brokers holding together clusters in the networks, the network had several unconnected components after the election. In short, the network was beginning to fall apart.

The Croatian example demonstrates how changes to funding environments can radically shift serendipitous networks. A study of Children's Human

---

[15] Maureen Taylor and Marya L. Doerfel, "Building Interorganizational Relationships That Build Nations," *Human Communication Research* 29, no. 2 (2003): 153–81; Maureen Taylor and Marya L. Doerfel, "Evolving Network Roles in International Aid Efforts: Evidence from Croatia's Post War Transition," *Voluntas: International Journal of Voluntary and Nonprofit Organizations* 22, no. 2 (2011): 311–34.

Rights NGOs[16] illustrates how shifts in the legitimation of a social issue can transform serendipitous networks for social impact. The research focuses on the network that advocated on behalf of the U.N. Convention on the Rights of the Child. The advocacy and drafting of the convention began in earnest in 1978 and continued until its ratification in 1989. Their study of the 113 NGOs involved over 24 years found that the convention's approval dramatically reshaped the network. The rate of change, or the amount of change that occurred during a period, jumped for five years.

Not only did the rate of change increase, but the rules for forming partnerships shifted. Before the ratification, organizations tended to partner with older organizations, who had more existing partners, and which a current partner had a relationship. After confirmation, NGOs began a period of searching for younger partners. The new partners often did not have many existing partners and were relatively unknown in the network. Instead, something about the convention's ratification changed the rule of partner selection—perhaps suggesting a later stage of development or greater legitimacy for the network.

In times of radical serendipitous network change, organizations often have to undergo radical change themselves. It may be tempting to pull back from partners, waiting for the dust to settle. But network research suggests that organizations with ties to a variety of partners, including partners with resources, tend to weather radical network changes better than organizations that do not.[17] Put more bluntly, organizations that adopt a network strategy are more likely to survive.[18]

During moments of radical change, serendipitous networks transform their membership and relationships. One type of network change that we have not addressed thus far is when serendipitous networks become goal-directed networks.[19] While we discuss the process of network formation in Chapter 3, here we note that one form of network change that can occur is that serendipitous networks can become a more goal-directed network. And when networks become more goal-directed, different mechanisms for change operate, and other management methods are then available.

[16] Drew B. Margolin et al., "Normative Influences on Network Structure in the Evolution of the Children's Rights NGO Network, 1977–2004," *Communication Research* 42, no. 1 (February 1, 2015): 30–59, https://doi.org/10.1177/0093650212463731.

[17] M. S. Kraatz, "Learning by Association: Interorganizational Networks and Adaptation to Environmental Change," *Academy of Management Journal* 41, no. 6 (1998): 621–43.

[18] Mark A. Hager, Joseph Galaskiewicz, and Jeff A. Larson, "Structural Embeddedness and the Liability of Newness among Nonprofit Organizations," *Public Management Review* 6, no. 2 (2004): 159–88.

[19] M. P. Koza and A. Y. Lewin, "The Coevolution of Network Alliances: A Longitudinal Analysis of an International Professional Service Network," *Organization Science* 10, no. 5 (September 1999): 638–53.

Incremental change and goal-directed networks

Most process models of networks for social impact assume that networks, after emergence, will continue to change. This change has four reasons: feedback loops, network orchestrators' actions, network maturation, and environmental shifts. The first two focus on network instigators and leaders' intentional acts to improve their networks. The latter two focus on changes in networks, regardless of network leaders' desires or actions. These represent forces that network leaders must navigate.

Purposeful change

Although the number of stages varies, scholars generally agree that networks move from an early stage of assembly to later stages where they capture more significant value and encourage more remarkable growth.[20] Leaders continue to shape their networks, though their roles change as they move from network instigator to network manager.[21] While the emergence of a network results from an incremental set of enacted decisions, network management never ends (see axiom three). Rosabeth Kanter describes this phase of collaboration as housekeeping.[22] The analogy is apt. Much like housekeeping, networks have to consistently respond to changes and work just to stay in the same place. Brint Milward and Keith Provan[23] refer to these tasks as network management. Leaders must manage accountability, legitimacy, conflict, design, and commitment. Network management is "a continual balancing act" (p. 7), and initial designs do not always work in the long term. Sometimes networks get the results that they desire immediately. However, most of the time, they learn by trying a strategy and discovering its problems.

Consider, for example, the lessons that The Graduate! Network learned as they tried to scale the successful Graduate! Philadelphia network to Chicago and Connecticut. The Graduate! Network aims to build pathways for adults

---

[20] Shumate and Gibson, "Interorganizational Network Change."

[21] Raymond L. Paquin and Jennifer Howard-Grenville, "Blind Dates and Arranged Marriages: Longitudinal Processes of Network Orchestration," *Organization Studies* 34, no. 11 (November 1, 2013): 1623–53, https://doi.org/10.1177/0170840612470230; Katherine R. Cooper et al., "*The Role of Conveners in Cross-Sector Collaborative Governance*" (Association for Research on Nonprofit Organizations and Voluntary Associations, San Diego, CA, 2019).

[22] Rosabeth Moss Kanter, "Collaborative Advantage: Successful Partnerships Manage the Relationship Not Just the Deal," *Harvard Business Review* July–August (1994): 96–108.

[23] H. Brinton Milward and Keith G. Provan, *A Manager's Guide to Choosing and Using Collaborative Networks*, vol. 8 (IBM Center for the Business of Government Washington, DC, 2006).

to return and complete their college degrees. The Graduate! Philadelphia network was so successful that they were approached by leaders in Chicago and Connecticut to duplicate their results. Graduate! Philadelphia acted as consultants, but the communities each wove their networks. In Chicago, one of the local partnership's lead agencies competed with the local collaborative for funds. Both of those programs failed early. Through that process, The Graduate! Network fine-tuned their model. Forty-one communities now have strong networks running, using the principles laid out, including independent fundraising. Networks have an opportunity to evolve if they learn from their own mistakes.

Other times, network changes originate from managers trying to solve a problem or becoming aware of a better practice that another entity uses. For example, public managers may become aware of innovations that they want the network to implement and catalyze them through their actions.[24] Or, network leaders may wish to encourage the formation of new ties between organizations in their network.[25] They might assume that network change is implemented in ways described by traditional change management models.[26] However, research suggests that these network leaders face challenges and dilemmas that organizational leaders do not.

Laurence O'Toole[27] argues that these unique challenges arise from networks having more uncertainty and less institutionalization than organizations. First, networks have more unknowns than organizations do. That uncertainty stems first from leaders' imperfect knowledge of the interdependencies among actors. Without knowing the interdependencies, it is unclear how any action might ripple across the network. Second, if network actors are happy with the current network dynamics, they may be unwilling to accept changes that undermine the equilibrium that they have developed. Finally, network leaders have uncertainty because all parties have conflicting interests, making collective action problems potentially more challenging. Member organizations will balance priorities that improve their organization's position while considering priorities that will enhance the network as a whole. How each member will weigh their contributions to the whole is based, in part, on their assessment that other organizations will make similar contributions.

[24] Laurence J. O'Toole, "Networks and Networking: The Public Administrative Agendas," *Public Administration Review* 75, no. 3 (May 2015): 361–71, https://doi.org/10.1111/puar.12281.
[25] Dagnino, Levanti, and Mocciaro Li Destri, "Structural Dynamics and Intentional Governance in Strategic Interorganizational Network Evolution."
[26] John Hayes, *The Theory and Practice of Change Management* (London: Palgrave, 2018).
[27] O'Toole, "Networks and Networking."

Box 7.1 Incremental Change Management Techniques for Network Leaders

---

- Directly advocate for the change
- Arrange new relationships between organizations in the network
- Creating sub-agreements
- Reducing the number of players involved in the change
- Making the change try-able and communicating results
- Offering training and new information to organizations
- Incentivizing the formation of serendipitous ties

Scholars[28] astutely argue that network leaders' options are more constrained than leaders of organizations. In some cases, where clear agreements and organizational interests happily coincide, they can directly encourage network change. In other cases, they may have to adopt a different repertoire of activities. Drawing on their work and our work examining network change in federated nonprofits,[29] we introduce a set of network management techniques that network leaders can use to encourage planned change (see Box 7.1). We have arranged them from the most directive tactics to the least. Directive tactics typically work best when there is broad agreement about the move, the stakes of the network change are smaller, and fewer actors need to be involved. In these cases, change can be quick and meet little resistance. Less-directive tactics face less resistance but are more likely to result in many unpredicted types of change occurring in the network since network members can adopt partially, modify the proposal, or reject the change altogether.

First and at the top of the box is the most straightforward of the incremental change management techniques, directly advocating for the change. In organizational change management, scholars call this technique "mandating the change," but leaders rarely can mandate organizations' actions in their network. Instead, they can consistently introduce the change using the network's decision-making process, whether that be a whole network vote, the consensus of an operations team, or advocating the independent adoption of the change by each organization in the network. As established in the early phases

---

[28] Dagnino, Levanti, and Mocciaro Li Destri, "Structural Dynamics and Intentional Governance in Strategic Interorganizational Network Evolution"; O'Toole, "Networks and Networking."
[29] Michelle Shumate, Liz Livingston Howard, and Waikar Sachin, "Driving Strategic Change at The Junior League (A)," *Kellogg School of Management Cases*, 2017, https://doi.org/10.1108/case.kellogg.2016.000101.

of network emergence, the network's decision-making structure constrains the leader's available activities.

Second, network leaders can change the "network game" by establishing new relationships among network leaders.[30] Leaders can accomplish this in two ways. They might seek to arrange the relationship by directly encouraging the relationships and facilitating its creation. Brokering relationships is one of the most direct moves that a network leader can make, and it is often a move with high costs in terms of time and effort. In contrast, they might set the stage for new ties to form, usually by engaging in hosting activities for particular groups of actors. Hosting, as described in Chapter 3, is much less costly but also more unpredictable.

Third, network leaders can manage conflicts of interest and resistance to change by influencing the agreement's terms. O'Toole describes two such strategies, reducing the number of participants needed for a deal and forming sub-agreements. Both tactics involve some risk since both can upset the equilibrium of relationships in the network. Reducing the number of participants needed for agreement can be accomplished in two ways. First, a small group of network organizations can be encouraged to adopt a change, independent of others. Second, while the general idea of the proposal might be agreed upon by the whole network, a subset of actors can determine how to implement it. Also, network leaders can attempt to form "side" agreements with other actors in the network. These agreements may protect some actors' interests in the face of a change or buffer the actors from negative consequences.

Fourth, leaders can make the change triable for organizations. Often this means creating pilot programs where one or a small set of organizations adopts an innovation at a small scale. Managers can share the pilot results with the entire network and, depending on the results, might be more widely adopted. For example, the Chicago Benchmarking Collaborative (see Chapter 6) considered a wide variety of mechanisms to raise early childhood reading scores. One possibility was to engage in a campaign to encourage parents to read to their young children for 20 minutes a day. Rather than have the entire network adopt the program at once, Christopher House piloted the program. Based upon the result of the pilot, the rest of the agencies agreed to perform the campaign.

Fifth, and among the least directive methods, network leaders can introduce information or training about the change. Like the empirical-rational

---

[30] O'Toole, "Networks and Networking."

strategy,[31] this method assumes that the change will have obvious benefits when member organizations learn about alternatives. However, research suggests this strategy is only likely to be successful when members are unhappy with the status quo.

Unplanned change

Often, network leaders do not plan for the changes that their networks make. Both environmental shifts and network maturation prompt network changes. These shifts require a reassessment of the network's tasks. For example, in a study of hospital federations,[32] the researchers noted how the federation shifted functions across the life cycle. In the transition to a federation stage, leaders focused on establishing roles and coordination mechanisms. In the subsequent stage, which they entitle maturity, leaders shifted to attaining the network's goals and maintaining members' commitment. These shifts are part of the natural maturation process of networks.

Network maturation has to do with two factors: changes in the field in which the network is embedded and the codification of agreements. Over time, organizational fields change both how they see the organizational problem and the network.[33] Changing frames used to describe the social problem influence networks, and networks affect how external actors understand that social frame. In contrast, the degree to which external actors are receptive to the new network shapes its activities.[34] In the early stages, when the network is not yet known, it struggles for legitimacy among external audiences. However, once the network has become accepted as a legitimate entity in later stages, it can operate differently from in its earlier stage. For example, the Multi-Agency Alliance for Children began in 1996 as the Metro Atlanta Agency for All Children. They recognized that they served children from a broader

[31] Robert Chin and Kenneth Dean Benne, *General Strategies for Effecting Changes in Human Systems* (Human Relations Center, Boston University, 1969); Myungweon Choi and Wendy E. A. Ruona, "Individual Readiness for Organizational Change and Its Implications for Human Resource and Organization Development," *Human Resource Development Review* 10, no. 1 (March 1, 2011): 46–73, https://doi.org/ 10.1177/1534484310384957.

[32] Thomas A. D'Aunno and Howard S. Zuckerman, "A Life-Cycle Model of Organizational Federations: The Case of Hospitals," *The Academy of Management Review* 12, no. 3 (1987): 534–45, https:// doi.org/10.2307/258519.

[33] Barbara Gray and Jill Purdy, *Collaborating for Our Future: Multistakeholder Partnerships for Solving Complex Problems* (Oxford: Oxford University Press, 2018).

[34] Benjamin Huybrechts and Helen Haugh, "The Role of Networks in Institutionalizing New Hybrid Organizational Forms: Insights from the European Renewable Energy Cooperative Network," *Organization Studies* 39, no. 8 (August 2018): 1085–108, https://doi.org/10.1177/0170840617717097.

geographic area as they gained recognition for the network and their work. The attention allowed them to change their name to reflect their new service area, all of Georgia. In other words, recognition of the network allowed them to continue to grow and operate differently.

Both of these perspectives suggest that network change occurs because of external recognition. However, network maturation also has to do with the codification of particular network routines. When partners work in productive ways in a series of interactions, the result can be greater trust and willingness to deepen those relationships.[35] In other words, network history can make certain activities possible that would have been too risky or too hard in previous years. Consider the case of the Chattanooga Museums Collaboration. When they first began their collaboration, it was limited to technical services, like sharing accounting, human resources, and information technology support. Because of that endeavor's success, they bundled their health insurance, liability insurance, and retirement plans. Each of these new endeavors created opportunities for personnel from the museums to work together. When then-mayor Bob Corker proposed that they collaborate on the waterfront redevelopment plan, they had already developed the relationships that made a joint capital campaign possible.

In goal-directed networks, incremental change often depends on factors like the network's maturation, trust development, feedback cycles from the network's activities and the environment, and network learning. A repertoire of change management techniques is essential for the housekeeping of the network and network growth. However, they are insufficient to grapple with radical change.

Radical change and goal-directed networks

Incremental change for goal-directed networks often involves questions like growth, changing practice, or increasing the interdependency among actors. In contrast, radical network change demands that networks consider their very existence and identity; these are "critical crossroads."[36] Deborah

---

[35] Gulati, "Social Structure and Alliance Formation Patterns: A Longitudinal Analysis"; Paul H. Schurr, Laurids Hedaa, and Jens Geersbro, "Interaction Episodes as Engines of Relationship Change," *Journal of Business Research* 61, no. 8 (August 2008): 877–84, https://doi.org/10.1016/j.jbusres.2007.09.006; Bart Nooteboom, "Trust, Opportunism and Governance: A Process and Control Model," *Organization Studies* 17, no. 6 (November 1, 1996): 985–1010, https://doi.org/10.1177/017084069601700605.

[36] D'Aunno and Zuckerman, "A Life-Cycle Model of Organizational Federations."

Agostino, Michela Arnaboldi, and Martina Dal Molin[37] put it this way: "if the challenge of a crossroads is overcome, then a new phase in the collaboration is activated; otherwise, the collaboration itself will dissolve."

Agostino and colleagues identify the two most prominent reasons for crossroads-level changes, resource shift, and leadership transitions. Resource shifts describe when a significant funding source for a network withdraws its support. Shelley Richards of Every Person Influences Children (EPIC) described this circumstance well. The Ready, Set, Parent! was designed to help new parents gain the skills they needed to take care of their newborn child in the best way they could. The education program took place following the birth of a new baby during the hospital stay. During their tenure, insurance shortened allowable hospital stays, reducing the amount of time their program could operate. Then the funding pieces ran out (see Chapter 4). In all, the network lasted six years from inception to dissolution.

The emergence of the COVID-19 pandemic illustrates another type of shift, increasing demand. During the pandemic, human service and education networks had to radically re-envision their services and meet more significant needs than they had encountered previously. The pandemic is ongoing as of this book's writing, and we have yet to see how networks will adapt.

Leadership transitions can also bring about radical network change. Deborah Agostino and colleagues give an example of this type of radical change in their study of an Italian university network. The leader of the network, a former scientist, resigned. The network realized that one person was doing all the coordinating, to date, and that one person was gone. It left the network adrift as they tried to recalibrate. In our study of community-education networks, network leader transitions were common. In many of the networks we studied for four years, the senior leader of the network left. However, not all of these transitions led to radical network change. In circumstances where leadership is centralized in one person, the network had to regroup, consider its priorities, and then decide how to move forward. In networks with a strong team of leaders, the change was incremental.

We find two additional sources of change in our research: social issue-driven change and management-led crossroads. Social issue-driven change describes the rapid transformation of the public or stakeholders' views about a social issue. Those radical changes can leave once progressive networks behind or make conservative networks socially unacceptable. For example, the

---

[37] Deborah Agostino, Michela Arnaboldi, and Martina Dal Molin, "Critical Crossroads to Explain Network Change: Evidence from a Goal-Directed Network," *The International Journal of Public Sector Management; Bradford* 30, no. 3 (2017): 258, http://dx.doi.org.turing.library.northwestern.edu/10.1108/IJPSM-04-2016-0078.

Netherlands Climate Action Accord is the second national effort to set climate change policy. The first accord was considered successful, but after the Paris Agreement in 2016, the network set an even higher goal.

Similarly, management can manufacture a radical network change if they feel that the network's performance has made incremental change management impossible. Summit Education Initiative took this path (Chapter 1). The board of the network shut down its operations based on performance. The network had a substantial endowment, and the need for better education remained high. The board itself was the impetus for the network's crossroads.

The successful management of radical network change for planned networks depends on the nature of the change (see Box 7.2). Based on our interviews and review of the research, we offer several strategies that networks have used to navigate these crossroads successfully and create a new normal for the collaboration. All except management-led crossroads are a renegotiation of the decisions made during network emergence (Chapter 3). Network leaders have to navigate those decisions once again.

In contrast, management-led crossroads require significantly more effort to manage. Drawing on crisis management theory,[38] when a crisis results from attributable leadership behavior, the outrage is higher than when it's the result of circumstances out of the organization's control (i.e., a shift in funding). When management takes dramatic action to reshape the organization, trust and legitimacy are both at risk. Not only will any network formed out of the response have to make the many choices necessary in network emergence, they will also have to repair the goodwill lost as a result of the board's actions.

Network death and reincarnation

Not all networks survive a crossroads moment. Sometimes networks in whole, or part, end. Networks disband for a variety of reasons. They may dissolve because the project is complete, or the partners explicitly decide that the time has come to part ways. In other circumstances, networks die through neglect, as fewer and fewer organizations attend meetings. Regardless of the reason, we describe these cases as network death. Network death is not always a bad thing. The choices that network leaders make in setting up the network are path-dependent (see Chapter 3), and network death allows them to clear

---

[38] Jonathan Bundy et al., "Crises and Crisis Management: Integration, Interpretation, and Research Development," *Journal of Management* 43, no. 6 (2017): 1661–92, https://doi.org/10.1177/0149206316680030.

Box 7.2 Managing Change at a Crossroads

Resource-Driven Change
1. Identify other sources of revenue, with a preference for diverse revenue streams
2. Consider whether a formal organization is needed to replace the network structure

Leadership Transition-Driven Change
1. Identify stakeholders of the network
2. Identify internal champions
3. Develop new consensus on goals moving forward, considering changing environment
4. Identify new leadership team

Social Issue-Driven Change
1. Consider whether the network has fulfilled its purpose
2. Identify whether there are new needs the network should address that are tangential to the original mission

Management-Led Crossroads
1. Establish the reasons for the urgency
2. Conduct interviews with stakeholders and an environmental scan to re-establish the network
3. Act transparently and consistently to rebuild trust

---

the slate. Many of these same leaders will try again with another initiative and make different decisions along the way.

In many communities, the process of network formation and dissolution is cyclical. Jana Jones Hall, former executive director of the Blue Ribbon Commission in Wilmington, North Carolina, USA, described it this way in an interview: "In our community, it happens a lot. About every three years, if we have an uptick in crime, people come together and try to form coalitions or specific groups to address it. Sometimes not as successfully." Returning to axiom four, not all networks organized for social impact achieve that impact. Many, if not most, will disband before they reach their goals.

But in the face of network death, there is hope. Goal-directed networks can become serendipitous networks.[39] Network dilemmas may continue beyond death (axiom three). Network reincarnations are both the beneficiaries of the previous network's actions and can be locked in by these actions. When goal-directed networks end, the remnants are often a serendipitous network of latent ties. It is easier to form a new network if organizations are already familiar with each other. The work is faster when organizations have done this kind of thing before.[40] But previous networks can lock in participants. They can reconstitute the network, failing to consider other relevant stakeholders. They may include organizations that were part of an earlier network action, failing to recognize their limited stake in the new one. They may structure their interactions in ways that resemble the old network, rather than the best way to get things done in the new network. Despite its limitations, network reincarnations mean that what was once dead can be reborn into a new network, with the potential to make a social impact.

In this chapter, we have argued that network change can be incremental and radical. Leaders manage this change depending on whether networks are goal-directed or serendipitous. In serendipitous networks, member organizations seek to learn from their partners and adapt to the changing pattern of ties among organizations. They must pay attention to those patterns because the rules for success shift in moments of radical transformation. In contrast, in goal-directed networks, incremental and radical change occurs for the whole network. Here, we describe both loci of action when describing dead ends, dilemmas, and pathways for managing network change.

Dead ends for managing network change

Critical crossroads are life or death moments for networks by definition. If the network does not change, then it will cease to exist. If network leaders fail to attend to incremental network change or manage planned change poorly, they can find themselves at a crossroads of their own making.

---

[39] Francesca Mariotti and Rick Delbridge, "Overcoming Network Overload and Redundancy in Interorganizational Networks: The Roles of Potential and Latent Ties," *Organization Science* 23, no. 2 (April 2012): 511–28, https://doi.org/10.1287/orsc.1100.0634; DaJung Woo, "Exit Strategies in Interorganizational Collaboration: Setting the Stage for Re-Entry," *Communication Research*, June 4, 2019, 0093650219851418, https://doi.org/10.1177/0093650219851418.

[40] Mariotti and Delbridge, "Overcoming Network Overload and Redundancy in Interorganizational Networks."

Failure to adapt to a changing environment

Whether as a result of resistance or other factors, the failure to adapt to a changing environment is a dead end. Organizations that fail to adapt can find themselves in a weak position in the field of organizations addressing a social issue, outpaced by others. Networks that fail to adapt often see their programs become less effective over time and are less attractive to funders than they once were or have declining network memberships. Ultimately, when networks reach a critical crossroads moment, failure to adapt means network death.

Organizations can find themselves at a critical crossroads as well. When organizations are at a crossroads, and networks are not, there is temporal asynchronicity (see Chapter 1). Temporal misalignment means that the rate of change for an organization in the network and the network is not in synch. In such cases, networks will either need to slow their pace or find ways for organizations to disengage from their work, at least for a time.

Remaining in a network when the organization is at a crossroads moment

Remaining in a network when the organization is at a critical crossroads is a dead end. Collaboration has become such a standard prescription that leaders cannot imagine leaving a network. However, remaining in a partnership is costly and, in circumstances where an organization must reinvent or disband, unwise. Organizations at a crossroads need their time and slack resources for reinvention and adaptation. Leaders may take leaves of absence from networks or leave altogether. But, unless they are mandated to stay in collaborations, they should walk away.

Dilemmas in managing network change

Both organizational and network leaders face similar managerial dilemmas when addressing network change. They meet them in the context of either their organization or in the context of a network. However, while the challenge is the same, network leaders typically have less control and certainty than their organizational counterparts.[41]

Adaptation and scaling what works

First, managing change requires navigating the contradicting demands between adaptation and scaling what works. Both organizations and networks face unrelenting pressures for change. To reap benefits from learning, both organizational[42] and network scholars[43] argue networks must scale what they have discovered. It is simply too costly to continue to identify new practices, make new connections, or gather information without reaping the rewards of applying that new knowledge or those new relationships at scale. Effective leaders pivot back and forth, navigating the need to adapt and take new ground.

Addressing resistance and making needed changes

Second, both organizational and network leaders engaging in planned change manage the dilemma of addressing resistance and making needed changes.[44] Although this tension is present for organizational leaders, network leaders feel it more acutely. Albeit challenging for leaders to replace individuals in their organizations who disagree, they do not lose the role as a result of their exit; they can hire someone else to fill that position. In contrast when organizations that disagree with a change may leave the network, key competencies or access to populations may leave with them. Some organizations are simply irreplaceable. However, networks or organizational leaders who cave to resistance too much will fail to make the changes needed. For network leaders, this often means the network will fail to achieve the desired social impact.

[41] O'Toole, "Networks and Networking."

[42] James G. March, "Exploration and Exploitation in Organizational Learning," *Organization Science* 2, no. 1 (1991): 71–87.

[43] Christian Stadler, Tazeeb Rajwani, and Florence Karaba, "Solutions to the Exploration/Exploitation Dilemma: Networks as a New Level of Analysis," *International Journal of Management Reviews* 16, no. 2 (April 2014): 172–93, https://doi.org/10.1111/ijmr.12015.

[44] Laurence J. O'Toole, "Implementing Public Innovations in Network Settings," *Administration & Society* 29, no. 2 (May 1, 1997): 115–38, https://doi.org/10.1177/009539979702900201.

Pathways for managing network change

When managing network change, networks and organizations find them-selves facing constraints based on their past decisions. Previous decisions seem to lock them out of some ways of dealing with a changing environment and into ways of managing planned network change. No matter the pathway that led the network forward, there are two pathways for networks to achieve social impact.

Managing the tempo of planned change

For network leaders who are enacting planned change or proactively addressing other types of change, the primary pathway to success is man-aging the tempo of change. Network instigators must pay attention to the magnitude of the planned change. Changes that have greater visibility, influ-ence more people, and that are faster are more likely to spur resistance than changes without any one of those attributes.[45] Network leaders should choose among the different techniques for managing network change, recognizing that more directive techniques are unlikely to be successful in the face of re-sistance. They can often break larger-scale change into smaller bites, slowing the tempo of change and decreasing resistance.

Recognize the type of change

This chapter introduces four types of change: incremental and radical change for serendipitous and goal-directed networks. One of the pathways forward for network leaders is to diagnose which kind of change is occurring correctly. Incremental change requires different change management strategies than radical change for both organizations in networks and network leaders.

This chapter illustrates axioms two and three, the choices that network instigators make in shaping the network, including whether it's serendipitous or goal-directed, and the environment shapes its trajectory. Following axiom five, different paths can achieve social impact. There are a variety of tools to manage change. The critical issue is choosing the appropriate management techniques for the situation (also see "Tools for network instigators").

---

[45] Choi and Ruona, "Individual Readiness for Organizational Change and Its Implications for Human Resource and Organization Development."

Conclusion

Networks dream that their trajectory will be linear—gaining ground through each iteration. But network management and organizational management in networks is more like playing chess. Depending on the moment in the game, the best strategy might be a strategic retreat. In these moments, network members may feel like the network is going backward; they revisit conversations that they settled at the network's beginning stages. However, a strategic retreat is sometimes necessary and can ultimately lead to better outcomes than continuing a predetermined but maladaptive way of operating.

Case study: Westside Infant-Family Network

Back in 2006, Anna Henderson had recently moved to Los Angeles. While networking in the nonprofit community, she ran into an agency executive director, who identified her as an ideal candidate to serve as the executive director for the newly formed Westside Infant-Family Network (WIN). The network, consisting of six agencies, was established to provide infant and early childhood mental health resources to families dealing with multiple generational challenges. Often, infants and children who have experienced trauma miss their developmental markers and exhibit early behavioral issues, such as chronic aggression. These issues can start a chain of adverse outcomes beginning with preschool expulsions and frequently ending with life-long problems with school, work, and relationships. WIN would provide in-home case management, which gave families access to essential resources, like diapers, housing assistance, and food. Once the family stabilized, WIN would offer in-home therapy to the parents and child together, from bilingual, masters-level therapists.

The idea was innovative, and within the first year of their operation, the Robert Wood Johnson Foundation recognized their work. However, WIN's results were uneven. Some network partners were achieving remarkable results for infants and parents, while others were not. Henderson looked into the numbers and discovered the difference. WIN raised about $300,000 per year to distribute to network partners. The successful partners used their $50,000 for in-home case management, while the other partners did not. After a contentious debate, WIN restricted the funds to in-home case management. The vote nearly ended the network, and some of the original partners left.

When the network started, WIN was operating under one of the network partners' fiscal agency (see Chapter 4 for more on fiscal agency), the Westside Children's Center. Under fiscal agency, WIN was largely ineligible for many government grants. Because it was applying for foundation funding under its host's banner, there were significant opportunities for confusion and perceived funding competition with its host. WIN's fiscal sponsorship agreement constrained what it was able to achieve. In 2011, Henderson finally convinced the network that WIN had to become a 501(c)(3), a legal designation for nonprofits in the United States. This independence allowed it to raise more funds and shifted the entire governance structure of the network. Because it would be a conflict of interest for agencies that receive money from WIN *and* comprise its board, they recruited an independent board of directors. New board members brought their clinical expertise to the table, while others brought backgrounds in law and entertainment. All brought personal and professional networks that supported WIN's fundraising efforts.

WIN's holistic approach to working with families through care coordination of food, health, housing, preschool, advocacy, and mental health across multiple agencies created additional challenges. Partner agencies provided various kinds of services, and each had different referral processes, cultures, and expectations. Henderson identified a technology provider from San Francisco, AJWI, who created a HIPAA-compliant data system that allowed the agencies to serve families in real time. The technology allowed the agencies to develop a shared service plan for each client tagging each task to individual staff members across agencies.

The system helps staff understand their roles and alert them early when tasks remain unmet, thereby giving staff a feeling of agency and setting them up for success. Moreover, because the system reports on benchmarks to each staff member and supervisor monthly, network leaders could address coordination problems early, and the supervisor and supervisee could troubleshoot issues together. Many case managers feel this system allows them to do their most vital work—but in some cases, the performance-based system created a new challenge for the network. For agencies that were well-resourced and had stable staff, the system worked great. However, for agencies that struggled more and had a higher case-manager turnover, the new performance culture was not a great fit. For those agencies, WIN negotiated to bring case management under their roof. In some cases, that ended the partnership, but for agencies where there was alignment in expectation, like Venice Family Clinic, the partnership has only strengthened over the years. As of 2019, WIN has eight agency partners, including Venice Family Clinic, a cornerstone partner since 2003.

WIN's outcomes are impressive. They continue to surpass their benchmarks to increase healthy childhood attachment and appropriate development and reduce parental stress and depression. The model works, but Henderson is still not satisfied. As she noted, "last year, we were serving 400 children and parents a year in our intensive, in-home clinical program, up from about 100 families. It's a drop in the bucket. We have never had an opening on our therapeutic side." She continues to look for solutions to scale their work, including inviting sister agencies to accept cross-referrals from WIN's waiting list. Other providers are often suspicious at first, looking for the "catch." But, as Henderson puts it, "We have to work together if we are ever going to reach impact at scale here." And so far, that "collaboration-with-high-expectations" thinking is working. In 2018, WIN received $16 million from the Los Angeles Department of Mental Health *Innovations 2* initiative to create a more trauma-resilient community across west-central and south Los Angeles. Now, the question is this: Can they build the infrastructures to scale while holding on to innovation and quality?

Questions to consider

1. What changes did the WIN network make during Henderson's tenure? What prompted each of those changes?
2. WIN lost member agencies as a result of some of the changes that they made. How should networks balance member wishes with the desire to change?
3. In 2016, WIN invited four other early childhood mental health providers to join their network to scale up the impact they were making; many people might consider these organizations "competitors." What are the intended and potential unintended consequences of this change?

Tools for network instigators

Selecting the right tools for managing change depends on identifying who is doing the changing and the change's nature. Strategies that are appropriate to address organizational change within a network are different from tools that help networks manage their transition as a whole. Additionally, organizations' and networks' tools to manage incremental change are different from the tools they should use when confronting radical change. We recommend using the decision tree and supplemental resources to help network instigators get to the right tool for the right situation (see Figure 7.1).

Strategic planning for networks

Goal-directed networks, like all organizations, require planning. Radical change that threatens the identity, core activities, or the whole network requires revisiting all of the questions that they answered during the emergence of the network (see Chapter 3). Networks can address these crossroads moments through a strategic planning process. At its best, strategic planning should not take years to accomplish or result in a lengthy strategic planning document. Instead, it is a process that allows networks for social impact to take stock of where they are, where they want to be, and to take

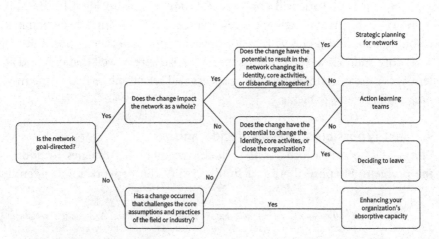

Figure 7.1. Choosing the right tools.

measured steps to accomplish their goals.[46] A typical process follows the following steps.

1. Prepare to plan

Preparing to plan involves identifying the stakeholders that are affected by this process. One of the mantras of successful strategic planning, coined by management consultant Jim Collins,[47] is that you have to determine who needs to be on the bus before driving it anywhere. The step may also mean identifying if your network needs technical assistance to navigate this strategic planning process. A great facilitator can often help keep conversations on track and help manage timelines.

2. Gather the necessary information and evaluate your assumptions

This step typically involves conducting a situational assessment, usually known as a SWOT analysis. Our experience is that networks are often keenly aware of their strengths and weaknesses but need a little prompting to identify the environment's opportunities and threats. Both are necessary foundations for reflection. Networks in this step should consider their mission, values, vision, and mandates. In this step, networks should answer this question: Have we already outlived our reason for being? If the answer is yes, the network may decide at this point to disband, knowing that it accomplished its purpose. If the answer is no, this may be an opportunity to reaffirm why the network came into being.

3. Prioritize the strategic issues that the network faces

Assuming the network will continue, the next task is to identify the most pressing problems the network faces. Typical problems include a change in resources, a longtime network leader moving onto another opportunity, or a network split. However, other issues may arise here as well that demand attention. A great strategic planning process will select one or two of the most pressing problems to tackle.

4. Identify possible strategies, decide, and act

The next step in the process is to identify potential strategies to address the problem. Suppose there is a funding shift; the network might identify

---

[46] J. M. Bryson, *Strategic Planning for Public and Nonprofit Organizations: A Guide to Strengthening and Sustaining Organizational Achievement (4th Edition)* (San Francisco: Jossey-Bass, 2011); John M. Bryson, Barbara C. Crosby, and Melissa Middleton Stone, "Designing and Implementing Cross-Sector Collaborations: Needed and Challenging," *Public Administration Review* 75, no. 5 (2015): 647–63, https://doi.org/10.1111/puar.12432.

[47] Jim Collins, *Good to Great: Why Some Companies Make the Leap . . . And Others Don't* (New York: Harper Collins, 2001).

strategies such as applying for a foundation grant, become a nonprofit that is eligible for a state contract, or asking network members like the United Way, community foundation, or corporations to support the network. Network leaders should evaluate each of the strategies based on an established set of criteria. Then the network should use its decision-making apparatus to decide and implement the plan.

5. Evaluate results, and perhaps try again

After the network has taken action, they should evaluate the results. At best, strategies are informed guesses about how to address a problem. Sometimes they do not work. The strategic planning leadership is responsible not only for adopting an approach the first time but re-evaluating after an agreed-upon period and, if necessary, selecting a different strategy to address the issue. When the group agrees the actions resolve the strategic issue, the process ends.

Action learning teams

Action learning teams are great tools for networks or organizations to manage incremental change. They are, first and foremost, about learning. Many action learning implementations assume that coming up with solutions is most important. However, such an outlook undermines the foundations of the action learning process.[48] Action learning teams consist of four to eight members, and in networks, those members are typically part of different organizations to maximize diversity. In large networks, they should also represent different types of organizations. Networks give the team an urgent or essential problem, task, or project, which ideally is owned by one or more network leaders. The leader, or a consultant, acts as a coach, helping to direct inquiry. One of the most challenging ground rules is that all participants must lead with questions, not answers or knowledge in the discussion. This ground rule exists because if the team is sharing what it already knows, it's not learning.

Beyond identifying adaptations that the organizations or network need to make, action learning teams have some additional benefits. First, they promote the development of collaborative leadership within the organization and network. Action learning teams are a great way to grow leadership talent who can identify a problem, evaluate possible options, implement a solution, and

---

[48] Michael J. Marquardt et al., "Fundamentals of Action Learning and How It Works," in *Action Learning for Developing Leaders and Organizations: Principles, Strategies, and Cases* (Washington, DC: American Psychological Association, 2009), 21–49, https://doi.org/10.1037/11874-002.

learn from the results. Second, action learning teams promote a learning culture, where innovations and experiments are commonplace.

Depending on whether the change affects organizations in the network or the whole network, the activities' sequence may differ. Paul Coughlan and David Coghlan[49] describe a sequence for *organization-focused change*: self-assessment, action planning, action learning, evaluation, and distillation.

1. The action team leader would encourage organizations to complete a self-assessment on the focal topic.
2. Depending on the results of that self-assessment, each organization would develop a preliminary plan of action. That plan of action would receive feedback from both peers in the action learning team and the coach. The coach would also provide additional resources to refine the proposal further.
3. The organization would then implement the plan and regularly provide the team with updates on the results.
4. After a set period, the organizational leaders would be encouraged to reflect on the results of their plans, any modifications they made from the original strategy, and evaluate the outcomes.

In contrast, action learning teams seeking to create changes for the *network* might operate differently. For example, in 2004, the Association of Junior Leagues International (AJLI) faced a crossroads-level change for its association.[50] AJLI was the headquarters of 294 local Junior Leagues, each with its independent legal status. In short, it was a network. Since its founding in 1901, this voluntary women's association has seen several changes. However, it had not kept up with changes in women's responsibilities, including the number of women working outside of the home full time. Its membership was in decline. The association used action learning teams, composed of members' organizations from different regions and of various sizes, to develop its strategic plan as an association.

1. AJLI gave each team a specific association-level objective to refine.
2. The association gave each member organization a small grant to research and tried a different approach to the problem.

[49] Paul Coughlan and David Coghlan, "Action Learning: Towards a Framework in Inter-Organisational Settings," *Action Learning: Research and Practice* 1, no. 1 (April 2004): 43–61, https://doi.org/10.1080/1476733042000187619.
[50] More about this case is available in Michelle Shumate, Liz Livingston Howard, and Waikar Sachin, "Driving Strategic Change at The Junior League (A)," *Kellogg School of Management Cases*, 2017, https://doi.org/10.1108/case.kellogg.2016.000101.

3. The organizations then reported back, and the association communicated the lessons learned to the broader network of organizations, suggesting several successful pathways to change.

Enhancing absorptive capacity

Organizations that are experiencing rapidly changing environments need to be more agile. One way to ensure that an organization is learning as much as possible is to improve its absorptive capacity.[51] Four processes are essential for using knowledge to align an organization with the demands of a changing field: acquisition, assimilation, transformation, and exploitation. For each process, we identify best practices for enhancing an organization's ability to learn.

Acquisition refers to the use of external resources, such as networks, consultants, journals, and conferences, to obtain information. Organizations can promote information acquisition by incentivizing employees to learn more about the social issue they address and the core business environment. In an extensive review, George Huber[52] describes two types of learning from external environments, grafting and scanning. Traditionally, management scholars define grafting as acquiring knowledge by hiring individuals that possess that knowledge. However, networking can also be a form of grafting.[53] To encourage learning through networks, organizations should encourage individuals who have sufficient background to participate in network meetings and activities that allow them to form relationships with others who are knowledgeable in desirable areas. These relationships facilitate the exchange of information. Scanning requires individuals to purposefully seek out information through consuming existing research and by conducting their research. Giving individuals the resources, time, and incentives to engage in scanning is essential. Organizations that invest in scanning and grafting through networking acquire more knowledge than organizations that do not.

Assimilation refers to how information is communicated, particularly across organizational units and up the chain of command. Employees learning new things improve the organization if it only enhances their performance or knowledge. The primary driver of enhanced assimilation is communication

[51] Lane, Koka, and Pathak, "The Reification of Absorptive Capacity."
[52] George P. Huber, "Organizational Learning: The Contributing Processes and the Literatures," *Organization Science* 2, no. 1 (1991): 88–115.
[53] Andrew C. Inkpen, "Learning Through Joint Ventures: A Framework of Knowledge Acquisition," *Journal of Management Studies* 37, no. 7 (2000): 1019–44, https://doi.org/10.1111/1467-6486.00215.

across vertical and horizontal barriers.[54] Vertical barriers describe how organizational hierarchy can limit the flow of information from front-line employees to senior leaders. Organizations can overcome vertical boundaries by creating opportunities for front-line workers to give feedback to senior leaders. There are a host of different ways to accomplish this goal.[55] Organizations can hold regular executive roundtables where front-line employees meet with senior leaders (sometimes over lunch). They can encourage senior leaders to do daily rounding where they interact with front-line staff once a day. They might set up an employee council made up of front-line workers as an advisory group. Horizontal barriers describe the silos that sometimes form between functional units in an organization. The most common way to address horizontal boundaries is to develop cross-functional teams or task forces.[56] By encouraging individuals from different units to work together, they gain access to knowledge commonly held in other groups.

Transformation occurs when information is collected, organized, and made meaningful. Data without context is useless. Many of the communication structures that enhance the assimilation of knowledge also contribute to its transformation. However, organizations that hope to apply knowledge to current and future organizational problems must intentionally give individuals the chance to engage in sensemaking. Information overload and overwork deter individuals from engaging in sensemaking and applying new knowledge. In contrast, when organizations invest in learning-centered opportunities, such as grand rounds, learning communities, or action learning, they open up space to transform knowledge.

Exploitation describes the application of new knowledge in everyday work. In this stage, leaders know more, and that knowledge affects decisions about work routines. Much of the research on knowledge exploitation suggests that organizational size, inertia, and bureaucracy each inhibit the application of knowledge in everyday work.[57] In contrast, when an organization encourages a learning culture by rewarding risks and learning from failures, individuals are more likely to apply new knowledge to their everyday work.

---

[54] Abdelkader Daghfous, "Absorptive Capacity and the Implementation of Knowledge-Intensive Best Practices," *SAM Advanced Management Journal (07497075)* 69, no. 2 (Spring 2004): 21–27.

[55] Marcel Schwantes, "6 Things Good CEOs Always Do to Connect with Employees," *Inc.com*, April 14, 2017, https://www.inc.com/marcel-schwantes/7-things-good-ceos-always-do-to-connect-with-employees.html.

[56] Daghfous, "Absorptive Capacity and the Implementation of Knowledge-Intensive Best Practices."

[57] Daghfous, "Absorptive Capacity and the Implementation of Knowledge-Intensive Best Practices."

8
Frontiers for Networks for Social Impact

In the wake of COVID-19, networks have emerged as central features of national response strategies. For example, in the United States, United Ways mobilized to provide additional funding to a network of providers, seeking to address community needs. In other places, networks pivoted their work—moving meetings online and focusing on emerging needs. The global pandemic reaffirms our commitment to networks' potential for social impact and the importance of network change in the face of environmental uncertainty.

In this chapter, we revisit the central themes of this book. Our goal is to reflect on the configurations and processes associated with more significant social impact. We provide both a summary of our key arguments that connect the configuration and process approaches to network effectiveness and practical guidance to leaders navigating network design and management challenges. We begin this chapter by revisiting the axioms that we introduced in Chapter 1 and illustrating how these axioms are apparent in networks that have made an impact. Many pathways to social impact exist. By summarizing our model, we offer several cases to demonstrate those characteristics that impactful networks tend to have in common. Finally, we conclude this chapter by providing implications for researchers, practitioners, and funders.

The axioms of social impact networks

In Chapter 1, we introduced the five axioms that represent the core argument of this book. These axioms integrate the configurational and process approaches to networks and are foundational to a systems approach to social impact. Configurational models[1] take a snapshot of the dynamic work of

---

[1] E.g., Daniela Cristofoli, Benedetta Trivellato, and Stefano Verzillo, "Network Management as a Contingent Activity: A Configurational Analysis of Managerial Behaviors in Different Network Settings," *Public Management Review* 21, no. 12 (March 20, 2019): 1775–800, https://doi.org/10.1080/ 14719037.2019.1577905; Steffie Lucidarme, Greet Cardon, and Annick Willem, "A Comparative Study of Health Promotion Networks: Configurations of Determinants for Network Effectiveness," *Public Management Review* 18, no. 8 (September 2016): 1163–217, https://doi.org/10.1080/ 14719037.2015.1088567; Jörg Raab, Remco S. Mannak, and Bart Cambré, "Combining Structure, Governance, and Context: A Configurational Approach to Network Effectiveness," *Journal of Public*

Networks for Social Impact. Michelle Shumate and Katherine R. Cooper, Oxford University Press. © Oxford University Press 2022.
DOI: 10.1093/oso/9780190091996.003.0008

networks. Although process models[2] inherently address networks' dynamism, they do not offer a prescription about the best way to configure networks to achieve social impact. We offer a systems approach[3] that integrates these two lines of research, addressing the possible configurations of the parts needed for success and how the system must adapt to a changing environment.

The axioms describe the fundamental assumptions of our systems approach. They describe the conditions under which networks can and do make a social impact. In this section, we bring together the chapters' themes illustrating the axioms that inform theory and practice.

1. Outcomes are interdependent

Chapter 2 describes four levels of outcomes that result from network activity: individual, organizational, network, and social impact. Individuals accrue personal outcomes, such as new skills and feelings of satisfaction, because of their network activity. Organizational members experience outcomes, like greater prestige, access to resources, and organizational learning, from their network participation. Network outcomes describe the joint gains from the partnership, including continued funding, growth, and new relationships among member organizations. Finally, social impact describes the outcomes experienced by the community as a result of their actions. Axiom one states that the different levels of these outcomes are interdependent.

Chapter 1 introduces three types of interdependence that occur between levels: competition, aggregation, and temporal. Competition describes the ways that outcomes at one level reduce those that accrue at another level. In essence, outcomes at one level can constrain the possible impact at another. Aggregation describes how outcomes at one level can add up to results that occur at a higher level. Finally, temporal interdependence describes how change that occurs at one level may impact the rate of change that occurs at another level.

Administration Research and Theory 25, no. 2 (April 1, 2015): 479–511, https://doi.org/10.1093/jopart/mut039.

  [2] E.g., Barbara Gray and Jill Purdy, *Collaborating for Our Future: Multistakeholder Partnerships for Solving Complex Problems* (Oxford: Oxford University Press, 2018); Amelia Clarke and Mark Fuller, "Collaborative Strategic Management: Strategy Formulation and Implementation by Multi-Organizational Cross-Sector Social Partnerships," *Journal of Business Ethics* 94, no. 1 (July 1, 2010): 85–101, https://doi.org/10.1007/s10551-011-0781-5.
  [3] Marshall Scott Poole, "Systems Theory," in *The SAGE Handbook of Organizational Communication: Advances in Theory, Research, and Methods*, eds. Linda L. Putnam and Dennis K. Mumby (Thousand Oaks, CA: SAGE, 2014), 49–74.

Competition occurs across all four levels but appears especially common between organization and network outcomes. Chapter 4 described circumstances in which networks may compete for a finite pool of resources with their member organizations. We saw this conflict play out in networks as they weighed whether to pursue their legal status as a nonprofit. When networks become a legal entity, as the Blue Ribbon Commission did, organizational- and network-level resources compete. Such competitions can reduce the available resources for social impact.

Outcomes can reinforce one another through *aggregation*. Consider the ways that networks can use data about organizations to improve their practices (Chapter 6). Here, drawing from the research on Communities That Care,[4] we know that organizational learning and new network connections predict social impact. They do so through aggregation, where every organization improves the quality of the services they offer. Their improvement, in aggregate, enhances the quality of programs and services in a community.

Finally, network outcomes influence one another through *temporality*. In Chapter 7, we note that organizations and networks sometimes find themselves at different stages. Organizations may experience a critical crossroads, threatening their very survival, while networks may be experiencing incremental change. Similarly, personnel changes, such as a new job or a retirement, can dramatically affect the stability of the network and its ability to make a social impact. Finally, networks can mature in ways that leave some of the organizations unable to continue participation. For example, as Westside Infant-Family Network improved its logic model and evaluation standards, agencies that shared the same expectations for outcomes adapted, and others chose not to continue (see case study in Chapter 7).

Network leaders aiming to make a social impact should carefully consider their theory of change. They ought to consider how the network action—not just the programs or organizational actors in the network—contributes to social impact. Pragmatically, axiom one calls for network leaders to move beyond network management tropes, such as "we can achieve more together." Instead, leaders ought to have a concrete articulation of what type of social impact they aim to achieve and how the network will get there.

---

[4] M. Lee Van Horn et al., "Effects of the Communities That Care System on Cross-Sectional Profiles of Adolescent Substance Use and Delinquency," *American Journal of Preventive Medicine* 47, no. 2 (August 1, 2014): 188–97, https://doi.org/10.1016/j.amepre.2014.04.004; Valerie B. Shapiro, Sabrina Oesterle, and J. David Hawkins, "Relating Coalition Capacity to the Adoption of Science-Based Prevention in Communities: Evidence from a Randomized Trial of Communities That Care," *American Journal of Community Psychology* 55, no. 1 (March 1, 2015): 1–12, https://doi.org/10.1007/s10464-014-9684-9.

2. Networks are sensitive to their environment

Environments vary in terms of a wide range of resources. In Chapter 4, we defined resources as the properties that might be possessed, acquired, or manipulated by network members or actors in a network's environment. They include financial resources, human resources, technological resources, and time. Networks with more of these resources in their environment have an easier time achieving social impact at scale or through centralized network governance. Networks with fewer resources may find that decentralized network governance and a focus on smaller-scale social impact are their only options.

Conflict within an environment also influences networks. In Chapter 5, we described how networks could come into conflict with their communities. Communities' expectations can change network activities; the extension or withdrawal of community support may contribute to whether networks can achieve impact. In Education for All, the network's initial goal of improving youth outcomes met a lukewarm response. Network leaders pivoted to an equity goal after sensing growing support for addressing racial disparities in the community.

Environmental changes can also lead networks to a critical crossroads[5] that challenge their very existence and identity (Chapter 7). These changes include resource shifts and social issue changes. Dramatic environmental shifts, like COVID-19, have the potential to lead both organizational members and networks to these crossroads moments. When the resources that a network has access to decreases, it cannot maintain business as usual. Instead, leaders must make dramatic changes to their network's governance, staffing, social issue framing, and structure.

This axiom should serve as a warning to leaders fascinated by network management trends. When technical associations and consulting firms draw successful case studies as evidence for their prescriptions to other communities, leaders should treat these claims with skepticism. A network design's effectiveness depends on its environment—and especially the resources available to do the work. And models built in previous years may not fit in the future.

---

[5] Deborah Agostino, Michela Arnaboldi, and Martina Dal Molin, "Critical Crossroads to Explain Network Change: Evidence from a Goal-Directed Network," *The International Journal of Public Sector Management; Bradford* 30, no. 3 (2017): 255–69, http://dx.doi.org.turing.library.northwestern.edu/10.1108/IJPSM-04-2016-0078.

3. Networks' dilemmas are never solved, just managed within constraints

Axiom three describes the ways that network dilemmas require managers to pivot between two contradicting values. In many ways, this axiom draws from network management[6] and orchestration literature.[7] However, we push the argument further by drawing on a systems view. Through that lens, recursive feedback loops and path dependence shape these demands. Together, they explain why network leaders experience a pull toward one or the other in a given moment.

Feedback loops describe how different network actions create information that influences the processes, structures, and resources of the network. Networks and organizations can increase their sensitivity to feedback by effectively using data (Chapter 6). Networks that collect routine data on organizations' activities and the connections among them can detect changes in the network and respond accordingly. In contrast, networks that fail to collect such data may only become aware of such changes in the face of network-organization conflict (Chapter 5) or reaching a critical crossroads (Chapter 7).

Whether serendipitous or goal-directed, organizations in networks can increase their sensitivity to feedback from the environment by improving their absorptive capacity[8] (Chapter 7). They do so by building structures and incentives that promote the acquisition, assimilation, transformation, and exploitation of information from the environment. Organizations with higher absorptive capacity can gather more information from their network ties and use that information better.

Path dependency suggests that choices that networks make, often in the very early stages of setting up the network (see Chapter 3), influence the options that those networks have in later stages. Each choice that a network makes in this initial assembly (Chapter 3) walls off options in later stages. For example, the choice of network instigator role and recruiting strategy makes some types of governance structures more likely. Network conveners often become the lead organization in networks. Using a hybrid recruiting strategy often results in complicated governance strategies, including participatory governance and centralized governance elements. Similarly, the process of

[6] E.g., H. Brinton Milward and Keith G. Provan, *A Manager's Guide to Choosing and Using Collaborative Networks*, vol. 8 (IBM Center for the Business of Government Washington, DC, 2006).
[7] E.g., Raymond L. Paquin and Jennifer Howard-Grenville, "Blind Dates and Arranged Marriages: Longitudinal Processes of Network Orchestration," *Organization Studies* 34, no. 11 (November 1, 2013): 1623–53, https://doi.org/10.1177/0170840612470230.
[8] Abdelkader Daghfous, "Absorptive Capacity and the Implementation of Knowledge-Intensive Best Practices," *SAM Advanced Management Journal (07497075)* 69, no. 2 (Spring 2004): 21–27.

recruiting and setting membership criteria can have dramatic consequences for networks later. If community members do not play a role in networks' decision-making structures, community-organizational conflict is more likely to occur (Chapter 5).

Together, feedback loops and path dependence explain the pull that network leaders feel toward one or the other side of network dilemmas. When leaders repeatedly invest in one side of that contradiction, the opposing side's pull grows stronger. For example, encouraged by an enthusiastic response to its efforts to include community input on their network's goals, a network may invite further community participation. The more people that they add, the slower their progress toward meeting their goals. This choice creates new constraints for future action, illustrating path dependence. In this example, a network that spends a lot of time gathering community input may soon face pressures to move things along more efficiently in the interest of achieving some outcomes. We suggest that the more a network pulls to one side of that dilemma, the more the other side pushes back, constraining the future network choices.

Throughout the book, we identify dilemmas that the network leaders must manage. Every choice that a network makes results in both feedback and results in a different set of options at the next stage of the network evolution. In this book, we identify eleven managerial dilemmas. These dilemmas invoke contradictions between:

- Efficiency and inclusivity (Chapter 3)
- Ambiguity and specificity in social issue framing (Chapter 3)
- Constant frame versus a dynamic frame (Chapter 3)
- Bottom-up or top-down framing (Chapter 3)
- Assigning oversight and shared responsibility for resource management (Chapter 4)
- Managing turnover and reaching impact (Chapter 5)
- Organizational agendas and network agendas (Chapter 5)
- Understanding the limits of data and using it anyway (Chapter 6)
- Collecting data for negotiated uses and collecting data for directive purposes (Chapter 6)
- Adapting to change and scaling what works (Chapter 7)
- Addressing resistance and making needed changes (Chapter 7)

These contradictions are never fully resolved, though network leaders can monitor and manage them. Instead, network leaders engage in an ongoing process to navigate each dilemma.

4. Not all networks organized for social impact make a social impact

The central argument of this book is that there are many ways to achieve social impact. The path to social impact depends on making choices that align with the social issues and context. This claim might lead network leaders to conclude that all options in network formation, management, and evolution are equally good. This conclusion is wrong, as axiom four attests. Throughout the book, we identify many dead ends to social impact; these demonstrate that not every choice will lead to it.

In Chapter 2, we argue that social impact might not be the goal of every network. Networks are poor options when social problems are either simple or chaotic. A single organization can address simple problems, given enough resources. Networks are costly models and are more challenging to manage than an organization. As such, they are not a good fit for simple problems.

Similarly, goal-directed networks cannot address chaotic social issues because the environment is changing too rapidly for their actions. In general, goal-directed networks move slower than individual organizations or serendipitous networks. Chaotic social issues require an agile and nimble response.

Finally, networks that address symptoms rather than root causes are unlikely to move the needle on social issues. Root causes are the underlying system-level structures that flower into the symptoms that many social service, education, and environmental conservation groups address. Although these networks perform excellent services, they may find themselves on a treadmill, meeting the needs of different individuals or environments experiencing the same problem.

Chapter 3 suggests that the decisions made early in the network are particularly influential in later network stages. Likewise, some decisions made in this stage of the network are dead ends. Network hosting is unlikely to result in social impact. But, network hosts may lay the groundwork for goal-directed networks. Additionally, they may promote serendipitous networks. However, serendipitous networks result in organizational-level outcomes. Without the binding effect of goals and shared identity, networks are too uncoordinated to achieve the systems-level change that complex or complicated wicked problems require.

Other early-stage dead ends discussed in Chapter 3 include a network's failure to recruit the appropriate people and organizations to their network. Recruitment of individuals and organizational participants is one of the most challenging tasks when setting up a network. In doing so, network instigators ask participants to sacrifice some of their self-interests and possible resources to achieve social good. In many ways, network recruiting is typically a collective action problem.[9] Potential members know that the network will only succeed if enough people say yes and are reluctant to join before seeing that the goal is achievable. However, by holding back, they make it more difficult to recruit other members. Leaders may be tempted to go ahead with a coalition of the willing. But failure to attract key stakeholders limits the social impact that networks can make because it walls off critical elements of a systems-level solution.

Chapter 4 suggests that networks may fail to reach impact due to limitations of financial, human, and technical resources, and time. Network efforts fail when resources run out and when the organizations compete with the network for support. Networks also fall short of impact when they focus on financial resources at the expense of other resources. The pursuit of resources leads leaders to mistake their procurement for social impact. Of course, the responsibility does not lay with network leaders alone; we also suggest that funders thwart network impact with limited grant cycles.

Chapter 5 contends that networks fail to reach social impact when they mistake partner goodwill for a conflict management strategy. Conflicts between organizational partners are inevitable. Also, many networks do not achieve impact because they fail to challenge the systems in which they reside. Systemic inequality cannot be solved through better services to remediate harm.

In Chapter 6, we describe how networks could use data to support various mechanisms for social impact. We note that collecting data to comply with a funder or government's mandates alone undermines social impact in two ways: by failing to provide evidence that activities led to the impact and undermining members' motivation to continue to contribute to those activities. Further, we argue that poor data design and analysis practices incentivize bad behavior, like skimming and setting low goals. Moreover, poor data analysis practices lead networks to make inaccurate assessments about their effectiveness. This erroneous information can undermine the efficacy of programs that reach the most challenging populations or areas.

Chapter 7 addresses the inevitable change that befalls all social impact networks. In that chapter, we argue that network managers should recognize

---

[9] M. Olson, *The Logic of Collective Action: Public Goods and the Theory of Groups* (Cambridge, MA: Harvard University Press, 1965); Gerald Marwell and Pamela E. Oliver, *The Critical Mass in Collective Action: A Micro-Social Theory* (New York: Cambridge University Press, 1993).

the type of change occurring before enacting tactics to navigate it. Networks that fail to heed this language will often see their programs, fundraising, and member retention activities become less effective over time. In the face of a critical crossroads, networks that fail to adapt will die.

So, although there is more than one way to make a social impact, there are also many obstacles that networks must overcome. We began this book by saying that most networks fail to achieve the social impact that they set out to do. Instead, they end up settling for individual-, organizational-, or network-level outcomes. However, some networks can make a significant social impact as a result of their activities.

5. There is more than one path to social impact

There are equally good combinations of management techniques that result in a social impact. In some cases, a configuration of factors is a better fit for the type of social impact, levels of resources, or environment. Throughout this book, we argue for a systems approach. When the network design and management elements are aligned, the whole is more than the sum of the parts. When the parts are not aligned, they create friction that slows a network's progress and limits its potential. Consider the following networks, all of which have been introduced earlier in this book:

- AgeWell Pittsburgh takes a service-based approach to impact as they focus on improving the quality of services for senior citizens.
- The Chattanooga Museum Collaborative sought geography-based and project-based social impact as they moved from sharing back-office functions to their community's physical transformation.
- Multi-Agency Alliance for Children (MAAC) seeks service-based impact as they provide comprehensive services for youth in foster care in the State of Georgia.
- Through Westside Infant-Family Network (WIN), another service-based approach to impact, partners provide mental health services for young children in Los Angeles.
- Summit Education Initiative in Akron, Ohio, pursues geography-based impact to improve educational outcomes for youth in their region.

These networks vary in terms of the social problem they address and the type of impact they seek. Although they took different pathways, as suggested in previous chapters, we also see similar patterns across these networks. Each network had invested leaders, patient funders with a tolerance for risk, specific goals that correspond to a clearly defined problem, and community members' or beneficiaries' support. Evocative of previous network research,[10] financial resources are necessary but not sufficient conditions for network effectiveness; that is, financial resources are essential for a network to be effective, but they are not the only resources needed to reach its goals.

Beyond these necessary but not sufficient conditions, there are many other pathways that a network might follow. Networks make different decisions to suit their respective goals and environments. In AgeWell's case, this meant adopting a specific casework approach to serving their population, which included a willingness to cut programs that were not as effective. Chattanooga Museums Collaborative took an incremental approach to partnership, which enabled them to scale up their impact. MAAC offers a unique governance approach to promote organizational loyalty to the network, even amidst individual turnover. WIN began with funders who supported them as they experimented with different goals and practices. Summit Education Initiative took a systems-alignment approach and aimed for geography-based social impact. Each network worked within the constraints of their environment, developed their partners and community's assets, and created something new to meet their needs. Each of these partnerships demonstrates one of the things we love about networks—the ability to innovate.

In short, networks can and do make a social impact. Although there are typically some common conditions to most of the networks featured in this book, each network develops ways of navigating constraints. Moreover, as axiom five of the model suggests, there is more than one process or configuration that enables them to do so. Some choices are equally as good when addressing a social issue. The type of social impact that networks seek to make and the environment in which they operate determine others.

---

[10] Daniela Cristofoli and Laura Macciò, "To Wind a Skein into a Ball: Exploring the Concept and Measures of Public Network Performance," *Public Management Review* 20, no. 6 (June 2018): 896–922, https://doi.org/10.1080/14719037.2017.1363904; Jörg Raab, Remco S. Mannak, and Bart Cambré, "Combining Structure, Governance, and Context: A Configurational Approach to Network Effectiveness," *Journal of Public Administration Research and Theory* 25, no. 2 (April 1, 2015): 479–511, https://doi.org/10.1093/jopart/mut039; K. G. Provan and H. B. Milward, "A Preliminary Theory of Interorganizational Network Effectiveness: A Comparative Study of Four Community Mental Health Systems," *Administrative Science Quarterly* 40, no. 1 (1995); Alex Turrini et al., "Networking Literature About Determinants of Network Effectiveness," *Public Administration* 88, no. 2 (2010): 528–50, https://doi.org/10.1111/j.1467-9299.2009.01791.x.

Implications for researchers, network instigators, and funders

Throughout the book, we have asked researchers, funders, and practitioners to learn from one another. We believe that researcher-funder-instigator partnerships can advance our knowledge about the pathways that lead to social impact. We offer some implications for research, practice, and funders, but do so, hoping that all readers will learn from them.

Research

Research on networks for social impact, as we have demonstrated throughout this book, is inherently interdisciplinary. We encourage researchers to read broadly, paying attention to the contributions of business, communication, community psychology, public administration, network science, organization studies, social work, and social policy scholars. Moreover, it requires an openness to the trends in the field. Here we suggest four calls for future research.

First, we suggest that research on social impact networks needs to make a turn toward the solution-science. Solution-science has been promoted by both scholars[11] and foundation leaders, like Na'ilah Suad Nair, president of the Spencer Foundation. Both note that understanding the social problem better is foundational knowledge. Social science researchers, writ large, need to understand the levers of change better. They must move beyond understanding the correlates of social problems and social impact; instead, they should identify the mechanisms that create change. Here, our recommendation is to move beyond describing networks to testing interventions to improve networks' social impact. The social network, configurational, and process approaches offer several insights as to which kinds of network configurations and practices are likely and associated with social impact. But we have few tools that enable networks to move from one configuration to another, or to test their effectiveness, given the environment in which they are embedded. We call on researchers to test the effectiveness of interventions to improve the social impact of networks.

Second, in this book, we introduced a typology of social impact. We noted differences in focus, type, scale, and approach. Throughout this book, we have provided examples of networks that have achieved different types of social

---

[11] Duncan J. Watts, "Should Social Science Be More Solution-Oriented?," *Nature Human Behaviour* 1, no. 1 (January 10, 2017): 1–5, https://doi.org/10.1038/s41562-016-0015.

impact. However, there is a shortage of research on what kinds of network processes and configurations are most appropriate for specific social impact types. Such research would be invaluable in resolving some of the conflicting results around network configurations and would inform practice.

Third, and relatedly, there are many measures and best practices available for networks seeking to make a project-based or service-based social impact. However, advocacy networks, or even other types of networks that include advocacy as part of their repertoire, have fewer resources from which to draw. While techniques, like the power-influence matrix, exist to enable these networks to coordinate their efforts, few tools allow them to evaluate their outcomes. In particular, we know little about assessing the impact of networking on policy change, above and beyond the effects of the individual organizations' actions.

Fourth, and finally, individual, organizational, and network outcomes connect to social impact in three ways: aggregation, competition, and temporal interdependence. More research is needed to understand the impact of these types of interrelatedness. When do outcomes at different levels cascade to a larger social impact? When do outcomes at different levels act as countervailing forces, impeding the progress of networks? More research is needed to answer these questions.

Practice

Next, we turn to the implications for practitioners or network instigators. Here we describe the overarching lessons that we believe that instigators can take away from this book. These lessons are in addition to the specifics discussed elsewhere.

First, collaboration is not a good in and of itself. There are both opportunities and high costs of creating and sustaining networks. We caution that building a network may not be worth it in the end. When social problems are simple, networks are a waste of time and money. Without resources, proper management, and a clear focus on a network's intended impact, social impact networks have little chance of making a more significant difference than the organizations working alone.

Second, despite some limitations of network approaches, we remain optimistic about networks' power to make a significant difference in some of the most unrelenting social problems of our time. We remain so because we have identified so many networks making a social impact. These networks recognize that there is no one right way to make a social impact. But outstanding networks for social impact have clear standards for success. They do not confuse attracting resources, network survival, or recognition for social impact. Instead, they track outcomes for their clients, communities, or geographies—demonstrating the long-term benefits of their work.

Third, and finally, network instigators should recognize their power in promoting constrained choice. The research presented here should give them confidence in identifying dead ends and helping networks weigh network dilemmas' trade-offs. When particular paths are appropriate in their context, but not others, they should speak out. And, when there is more than one way forward, they should offer choices. In short, we hope that this book empowers network instigators to provide expert assistance to their networks as they navigate the choppy waters of network emergence, management, and change.

Funders

Finally, we part with some final implications for the funders of networks for social impact. Funders need to recognize their power in creating and sustaining networks. Specifically, they influence the problems, personnel, and progress through the resources they provide. As such, they have the power to significantly undermine or catalyze the social impact that funded networks make.

First, funders can influence the network perception of the problem. A call for proposals affects the type of social networks that will apply or emerge. Social issue framing that is ambiguous encourages networks with diverse organizational participation. This ambiguity fits complex social problems that require the expertise of varied stakeholders but is less useful for networks focusing on complicated social issues. Similarly, when calls frame social issues in terms of their symptoms, networks are likely to form to ameliorate those issues, rather than to engage in the more profound root cause work that could change the underlying system.

Second, funders have the power to influence network personnel. They may influence the choice of conveners or network managers and sometimes are the convener. In such cases, top-down network emergence, with all of its benefits and liabilities, is likely to occur. In other cases, by choosing a network manager to allocate resources, they introduce new power imbalances in the network that are likely to become a source of conflict or apathy. Funders would do well to hold back their mandates for network emergence and instead provide resources. Technical assistance for network champions can energize the entire organizational field.

Third, funders influence network progress through the resources they provide and the reporting requirements they impose. Networks are a more expensive way to achieve social impact. Consequently, they require significant funding for overhead expenses. These may include the financing of a new network administrative organization, evaluation and facilitation staff, and the technologies that will support the collaboration. Often smaller funders will be unable to provide the enterprise-level funding for a new network. In these circumstances, we recommend that grantmakers and government agencies jointly fund networks. Moreover, they should commit to continuing network funding, as long as it continues to progress toward social impact. Funders that go it alone and then move on to other ventures create crossroads moments for networks, sometimes leading to their demise when they are on the cusp of scaling their social impact efforts.

Fourth, funders can influence networks for social impact through their reporting requirements. When funders use reporting to enhance a network's capacity to use data to improve its program efforts, it increases the likelihood that networks will make a social impact. In contrast, when funders require frequent reporting for the sake of demonstrating social impact, they encourage networks to use data for negotiated or compliance purposes. Although both are necessary, funders should prioritize programmatic improvement.

Fifth, and relatedly, funders influence networks for social impact based on their timetable for success. Networks take time to set up, and research[12] suggests that most will not significantly progress on social impact for at least three years (maybe longer). Funders who set timetables where networks must demonstrate results in advance of this time frame encourage networks to displace their goals, create projects unrelated to the root social problems, and concentrate on clients or geographies that are less difficult to serve.

Conclusion

We have been privileged to study and work with many networks for social impact in the last decade. In that time, we have seen networks adopt and replicate practices from one another, demonstrating the power of good ideas and collaborative energy. We have also seen networks develop methods that are new, created as a result of their partners' strengths or in response to needs in their community. As we reflect on these experiences, we are not oblivious to

---

[12] Raab, Mannak, and Cambré, "Combining Structure, Governance, and Context."

the challenges that networks face. But we are optimistic about the future of networks.

We hope readers share this optimism and take that next step in researching, leading, joining, or supporting a network effort. Not only do we think that networks *can* be impactful, we believe that they *have to* be impactful. The big problems of our age are simply too significant for individuals, individual organizations, or individual sectors to tackle alone. Many pathways lead to social impact, and we hope that readers of this book will be encouraged to take action and seek some company on the way.

References

Ackoff, Russell. *Redesigning the Future*. New York: Wiley, 1975.

Agostino, Deborah, Michela Arnaboldi, and Martina Dal Molin. "Critical Crossroads to Explain Network Change: Evidence from a Goal-Directed Network." *The International Journal of Public Sector Management; Bradford* 30, no. 3 (2017): 255–69. http://dx.doi.org. turing.library.northwestern.edu/10.1108/IJPSM-04-2016-0078.

Agranoff, Robert. "Inside Collaborative Networks: Ten Lessons for Public Managers." *Public Administration Review* 66 (2006): 56–65.

———. *Intergovernmental Management: Human Services Problem-Solving in Six Metropolitan Areas*. SUNY Press, 1986.

———. *Managing within Networks: Adding Value to Public Organizations*. Washington, DC: Georgetown University Press, 2007.

Agranoff, Robert, and Michael McGuire. "Big Questions in Public Network Management Research." *Journal of Public Administration Research and Theory* 11, no. 3 (July 1, 2001): 295–326. https://doi.org/10.1093/oxfordjournals.jpart.a003504.

Ahuja, Gautam. "Collaboration Networks, Structural Holes, and Innovation: A Longitudinal Study." *Administrative Science Quarterly* 45 (2000): 425–55. https://doi.org/10.2307/2667105.

Ainsworth, Dale, and Ann E. Feyerherm. "Higher Order Change: A Transorganizational System Diagnostic Model." *Journal of Organizational Change Management* 29, no. 5 (August 8, 2016): 769–81. https://doi.org/10.1108/JOCM-11-2015-0209.

Aldrich, Howard E. *Organizations Evolving*. London: SAGE Publications, 1999.

———. "Visionaries and Villains: The Politics of Designing Interorganizational Relations." *Organization and Administrative Science* 8, no. 1 (1977): 23–40.

Alexander, Malcolm. "Big Business and Directorship Networks: The Centralisation of Economic Power in Australia." *Journal of Sociology* 34, no. 2 (1998): 107–22.

The American Institutes for Research. "Center on Great Teachers & Leaders." Webpage. Accessed October 15, 2019. https://www.gtlcenter.org/.

Andersen, Bjørn, and Tom Fagerhaug. *Root Cause Analysis: Simplified Tools and Techniques*. Milwaukee, WI: ASQ Quality Press, 2006.

Ansell, Chris, and Alison Gash. "Collaborative Governance in Theory and Practice." *Journal of Public Administration Research and Theory: J-PART* 18, no. 4 (2008): 543–71.

Armstrong, Nick, Gillian S. Cantor, Bonnie Chapman, and James D. McDonough. "Adapting the Collective Impact Model to Veterans Services: The Case of AmericaServes." In *Bulletproofing the Psyche: Preventing Mental Health Problems in Our Military and Veterans*, edited by Kate Hendricks Thomas and David L. Albright, 209–27. Santa Barbara, CA: Praeger, 2018.

Ashman, Darcy, and Carmen Luca Sugawara. "Civil Society Networks: Options for Network Design." *Nonprofit Management and Leadership* 23, no. 3 (2013): 389–406. https://doi.org/10.1002/nml.21062.

Atouba, Yannick C. "Let's Start from the Beginning: Examining the Connections Between Partner Selection, Trust, and Communicative Effectiveness in Voluntary Partnerships Among Human Services Nonprofits." *Communication Research*, February 3, 2016, 0093650215626982. https://doi.org/10.1177/0093650215626982.

Atouba, Yannick C., and Michelle Shumate. "International Nonprofit Collaboration Examining the Role of Homophily." *Nonprofit and Voluntary Sector Quarterly* 44, no. 3 (2015): 587–608.

———. "Interorganizational Networking Patterns Among Development Organizations." *Journal of Communication* 60, no. 2 (2010): 293–317. https://doi.org/10.1111/j.1460-2466.2010.01483.x.

———. "Meeting the Challenge of Effectiveness in Nonprofit Partnerships: Examining the Roles of Partner Selection, Trust, and Communication." *VOLUNTAS: International Journal of Voluntary and Nonprofit Organizations*, August 8, 2019. https://doi.org/10.1007/s11266-019-00143-2.

Austin, James E. "Strategic Collaboration Between Nonprofits and Businesses." *Nonprofit and Voluntary Sector Quarterly* 29, no. 1_suppl (March 1, 2000): 69–97. https://doi.org/10.1177/0899764000291S004.

———. *The Collaboration Challenge: How Nonprofits and Businesses Succeed through Strategic Alliances*. San Francisco: John Wiley & Sons, 2010.

Austin, James E., and Maria M. Seitanidi. "Collaborative Value Creation: A Review of Partnering between Nonprofits and Businesses: Part I. Value Creation Spectrum and Collaboration Stages." *Nonprofit and Voluntary Sector Quarterly* 41, no. 5 (2012): 726–58.

Austin, James E., and Maria May Seitanidi. "Collaborative Value Creation: A Review of Partnering between Nonprofits and Businesses. Part 2: Partnership Processes and Outcomes." *Nonprofit and Voluntary Sector Quarterly* 41, no. 6 (2012): 929–68.

Barge, J. Kevin. "Dialogue, Conflict, and Community." In *The SAGE Handbook of Conflict Communication: Integrating Theory, Research, and Practice*, edited by John G. Oetzel and Stella Ting-Toomey, 517–44. Thousand Oaks, CA: SAGE, 2006.

Barker, J. R. "Tightening the Iron Cage—Concertive Control in Self-Managing Teams." *Administrative Science Quarterly* 38, no. 3 (September 1993): 408–37.

Barnett, William P. "The Dynamics of Competitive Intensity." *Administrative Science Quarterly*, 1997, 128–60.

Barney, Jay B. "Looking Inside for Competitive Advantage." *Academy of Management Perspectives* 9, no. 4 (November 1, 1995): 49–61. https://doi.org/10.5465/ame.1995.9512032192.

Bennett, W. Lance, and Alexandra Segerberg. *The Logic of Connective Action: Digital Media and the Personalization of Contentious Politics*. Cambridge: University Press, 2013.

Brown, L. David, and Darcy Ashman. "Participation, Social Capital, and Intersectoral Problem Solving: African and Asian Cases." *World Development*, Implementing Policy Change, 24, no. 9 (September 1, 1996): 1467–79. https://doi.org/10.1016/0305-750X(96)00053-8.

Bryson, J. M. *Strategic Planning for Public and Nonprofit Organizations: A Guide to Strengthening and Sustaining Organizational Achievement (4th Edition)*. San Francisco: Jossey-Bass, 2011.

Bryson, John M., Barbara C. Crosby, and Melissa Middleton Stone. "Designing and Implementing Cross-Sector Collaborations: Needed and Challenging." *Public Administration Review* 75, no. 5 (2015): 647–63. https://doi.org/10.1111/puar.12432.

Bundy, Jonathan, Michael D. Pfarrer, Cole E. Short, and W. Timothy Coombs. "Crises and Crisis Management: Integration, Interpretation, and Research Development." *Journal of Management* 43, no. 6 (2017): 1661–92. https://doi.org/10.1177/0149206316680030.

Burt, Ronald S. "The Network Structure of Social Capital." *Research in Organizational Behavior* 22 (2000): 345–423.

Carboni, Julia L., Saba Siddiki, Chris Koski, and Abdul-Akeem Sadiq. "Using Network Analysis to Identify Key Actors in Collaborative Governance Processes." *Nonprofit Policy Forum; Berlin* 8, no. 2 (2017): 133–45. https://doi.org/10.1515/npf-2017-0012.

Carroll, Archie B. "The Pyramid of Corporate Social Responsibility: Toward the Moral Management of Organizational Stakeholders." *Business Horizons* 34, no. 4 (1991): 39–48.

Castells, Manuel. *Networks of Outrage and Hope: Social Movements in the Internet Age*. Hoboken, NJ: John Wiley & Sons, 2015.

Chevalier, M. "A Wider Range of Perspectives in the Bureaucratic Structure." Ottawa, Ontario, Canada: Commission on Bilingualism and Biculturalism, 1966.

Chin, Robert, and Kenneth Dean Benne. *General Strategies for Effecting Changes in Human Systems*. Human Relations Center, Boston University, 1969.

Choi, Myungweon, and Wendy E. A. Ruona. "Individual Readiness for Organizational Change and Its Implications for Human Resource and Organization Development." *Human Resource Development Review* 10, no. 1 (March 1, 2011): 46–73. https://doi.org/10.1177/1534484310384957.

Christens, Brian D. *Community Power and Empowerment*. New York: Oxford University Press, 2019.

Christens, Brian D., and Paula Tran Inzeo. "Widening the View: Situating Collective Impact among Frameworks for Community-Led Change." *Community Development* 46, no. 4 (August 8, 2015): 420–35. https://doi.org/10.1080/15575330.2015.1061680.

Christens, Brian D., and Paul W. Speer. "Contextual Influences on Participation in Community Organizing: A Multilevel Longitudinal Study." *American Journal of Community Psychology* 47, nos. 3–4 (2011): 253–63.

Clark, Catherine, William Rosenzweigh, David Long, and Sara Olsen. "Assessing Social Impact in Double Bottom Line Ventures." Double Bottom Line Project. Rockefeller Foundation, 2004. https://centers.fuqua.duke.edu/case/wp-content/uploads/sites/7/2015/02/Report_Clark_DoubleBottomLineProjectReport_2004.pdf.

Clarke, Amelia, and Mark Fuller. "Collaborative Strategic Management: Strategy Formulation and Implementation by Multi-Organizational Cross-Sector Social Partnerships." *Journal of Business Ethics* 94, no. 1 (July 1, 2010): 85–101. https://doi.org/10.1007/s10551-011-0781-5.

Clarke, Amelia, and Adriane MacDonald. "Outcomes to Partners in Multi-Stakeholder Cross-Sector Partnerships: A Resource-Based View." *Business & Society* 58, no. 2 (2019): 298–332. https://doi.org/10.1177/0007650316660534.

Coleman, James S. "Social Capital in the Creation of Human Capital." *American Journal of Sociology* 94 (January 1, 1988): S95–120. https://doi.org/10.1086/228943.

Collins, Jim. *Good to Great: Why Some Companies Make the Leap . . . and Others Don't*. New York: Harper Collins, 2001.

Community Tool Box. "Chapter 3. Assessing Community Needs and Resources | Section 8. Identifying Community Assets and Resources." Accessed December 10, 2019. https://ctb.ku.edu/en/table-of-contents/assessment/assessing-community-needs-and-resources/identify-community-assets/tools.

The Compass for SBC. "5 Whys Template." Webpage. Accessed October 15, 2019. https://www.thecompassforsbc.org/sbcc-tools/5-whys-template.

———. "Fishbone Diagram Template." Webpage. Accessed October 15, 2019. https://www.thecompassforsbc.org/sbcc-tools/fishbone-diagram-template.

———. "How to Conduct a Root Cause Analysis." Accessed October 15, 2019. https://www.thecompassforsbc.org/how-to-guides/how-conduct-root-cause-analysis.

———. "Root Cause Tree Template." Webpage. Accessed October 15, 2019. https://www.thecompassforsbc.org/sbcc-tools/root-cause-tree-template.

Cooper, Katherine R. "Disconnect, Collide, Diverge: Tracing Diversity Discourse in Community Collaboration." Presented at the National Communication Association, Convened Virtually, 2020.

———. "Exploring Stakeholder Participation in Nonprofit Collaboration." Dissertation, University of Illinois at Urbana-Champaign, 2014. https://core.ac.uk/download/pdf/29152991.pdf.

———. "Nonprofit Participation in Collective Impact: A Comparative Case." *Community Development* 48, no. 4 (2017): 499–514. https://doi.org/10.1080/15575330.2017.1332654.

————. "Paradox and Process: Navigating Tensions for Network Survival." Presented at the National Communication Association, Baltimore, MD, November 2019.

Cooper, Katherine R. H., Brinton Milward, and Michelle Shumate. "Teaching Simulation: The Toxic Node," 2019. https://www.maxwell.syr.edu/parcc/eparcc/simulations/The_Toxic_Node/.

Cooper, Katherine R., and Michelle Shumate. "Interorganizational Collaboration Explored through the Bona Fide Network Perspective." *Management Communication Quarterly* 26, no. 4 (2012): 623–54.

————. "Policy Brief: The Case for Using Robust Measures to Evaluate Nonprofit Organizations." *Nonprofit Policy Forum* 7, no. 1 (2016): 39–47. https://doi.org/10.1515/npf-2015-0029.

Cooper, Katherine R., Rong Wang, Anne-Marie Boyer, Jack L. Harris, Joshua-Paul Miles, and Michelle Shumate. "The Role of Conveners in Cross-Sector Collaborative Governance." Association for Research on Nonprofit Organizations and Voluntary Associations, San Diego, CA, 2019.

Coughlan, Paul, and David Coghlan. "Action Learning: Towards a Framework in Inter-Organisational Settings." *Action Learning: Research and Practice* 1, no. 1 (April 2004): 43–61. https://doi.org/10.1080/1476733042000187619.

Cristofoli, Daniela, and Laura Macciò. "To Wind a Skein into a Ball: Exploring the Concept and Measures of Public Network Performance." *Public Management Review* 20, no. 6 (June 2018): 896–922. https://doi.org/10.1080/14719037.2017.1363904.

Cristofoli, Daniela, and Josip Markovic. "How to Make Public Networks Really Work: A Qualitative Comparative Analysis." *Public Administration* 94, no. 1 (March 2016): 89–110. https://doi.org/10.1111/padm.12192.

Cristofoli, Daniela, Benedetta Trivellato, and Stefano Verzillo. "Network Management as a Contingent Activity: A Configurational Analysis of Managerial Behaviors in Different Network Settings." *Public Management Review* 21, no. 12 (March 20, 2019): 1775–1800. https://doi.org/10.1080/14719037.2019.1577905.

Cummings, Larry L., and Phillip Bromiley. "The Organizational Trust Inventory." In *Trust in Organizations*, edited by Roderick Kramer and Tom Tyler, 302–30. Thousand Oaks, CA: SAGE, 1996.

Daghfous, Abdelkader. "Absorptive Capacity and the Implementation of Knowledge-Intensive Best Practices." *SAM Advanced Management Journal (07497075)* 69, no. 2 (Spring 2004): 21–27.

Dagnino, Giovanni Battista, Gabriella Levanti, and Arabella Mocciaro Li Destri. "Structural Dynamics and Intentional Governance in Strategic Interorganizational Network Evolution: A Multilevel Approach." *Organization Studies* 37, no. 3 (March 1, 2016): 349–73. https://doi.org/10.1177/0170840615625706.

D'Aunno, Thomas A., and Howard S. Zuckerman. "A Life-Cycle Model of Organizational Federations: The Case of Hospitals." *The Academy of Management Review* 12, no. 3 (1987): 534–45. https://doi.org/10.2307/258519.

Davis, Fred D. "Perceived Usefulness, Perceived Ease of Use, and User Acceptance of Information Technology." *MIS Quarterly* 13, no. 3 (September 1989): 319–40. https://doi.org/10.2307/249008.

Davis, Fred D., Richard P. Bagozzi, and Paul R. Warshaw. "User Acceptance of Computer Technology: A Comparison of Two Theoretical Models." *Management Science* 35, no. 8 (1989): 982–1003.

Dempsey, Sarah E. "Critiquing Community Engagement." *Management Communication Quarterly* 24, no. 3 (2010): 359–90.

Devereaux-Nelson, Robin. *How to Write a Nonprofit Grant Proposal: Writing Winning Proposals to Fund Your Programs and Projects.* 1st ed. New York: CreateSpace Independent Publishing Platform, 2015.

Dewulf, Art, and René Bouwen. "Issue Framing in Conversations for Change: Discursive Interaction Strategies for 'Doing Differences.'" *The Journal of Applied Behavioral Science* 48, no. 2 (2012): 168–93.

Diani, Mario. "Networks and Social Movements." In *The Wiley-Blackwell Encyclopedia of Social and Political Movements*. American Cancer Society. Hoboken, NJ: Wiley-Blackwell, 2013. https://doi.org/10.1002/9780470674871.wbespm438.

Doerfel, Marya L., Yannick Atouba, and Jack L. Harris. "(Un)Obtrusive Control in Emergent Networks: Examining Funding Agencies' Control Over Nonprofit Networks." *Nonprofit and Voluntary Sector Quarterly* 46, no. 3 (June 1, 2017): 469–87. https://doi.org/10.1177/0899764016664588.

Donsbach, Wolfgang, and Michael W. Traugott, eds. *The SAGE Handbook of Public Opinion Research*. 1st ed. Thousand Oaks, CA: SAGE, 2007.

Durlak, Joseph A., and Emily P. DuPre. "Implementation Matters: A Review of Research on the Influence of Implementation on Program Outcomes and the Factors Affecting Implementation." *American Journal of Community Psychology* 41, no. 3 (March 6, 2008): 327. https://doi.org/10.1007/s10464-008-9165-0.

Dweck, Carol. "What Having a 'Growth Mindset' Actually Means." *Harvard Business Review Digital Articles*, January 13, 2016, 2–4.

Eadie, Douglas C. *Changing by Design: A Practical Approach to Leading Innovation in Nonprofit Organizations*. San Francisco: Jossey-Bass, 1997.

Eisenberg, Eric M. "Ambiguity as Strategy in Organizational Communication." *Communication Monographs* 51, no. 3 (September 1, 1984): 227–42. https://doi.org/10.1080/03637758409390197.

Elkington, John. *Cannibals with Forks: Triple Bottom Line of the 21st Century Business*. Oxford: John Wiley & Sons Ltd, 1999.

Emerson, K., and T. Nabatchi. "Evaluating the Productivity of Collaborative Governance Regimes: A Performance Matrix." *Public Performance & Management Review* 38, no. 4 (2015): 717–47.

Entman, Robert M. "Framing: Toward Clarification of a Fractured Paradigm." *Journal of Communication* 43, no. 4 (1993): 51–58. https://doi.org/10.1111/j.1460-2466.1993.tb01304.x.

Fairhurst, Gail T., Wendy K. Smith, Scott G. Banghart, Marianne W. Lewis, Linda L. Putnam, Sebastian Raisch, and Jonathan Schad. "Diverging and Converging: Integrative Insights on a Paradox Meta-Perspective." *The Academy of Management Annals* 10, no. 1 (January 1, 2016): 173–82. https://doi.org/10.1080/19416520.2016.1162423.

Faulk, Lewis, Jurgen Willems, Jasmine McGinnis Johnson, and Amanda J. Stewart. "Network Connections and Competitively Awarded Funding: The Impacts of Board Network Structures and Status Interlocks on Nonprofit Organizations' Foundation Grant Acquisition." *Public Management Review* 18, no. 10 (November 25, 2016): 1425–55. https://doi.org/10.1080/14719037.2015.1112421.

Fetterman, David M., and Abraham Wandersman. *Empowerment Evaluation Principles in Practice*. New York: Guilford Press, 2005.

Fitzpatrick, Jody L., James R. Sanders, and Blaine R. Worthen. *Program Evaluation: Alternative Approaches and Practical Guidelines*. Upper Saddle River, NJ: Pearson Education, 2017.

Forbes, Daniel P. "Measuring the Unmeasurable: Empirical Studies of Nonprofit Organization Effectiveness from 1977 to 1997." *Nonprofit and Voluntary Sector Quarterly* 27, no. 2 (June 1, 1998): 183–202. https://doi.org/10.1177/0899764098272005.

Foster-Fishman, Pennie G., Branda Nowell, and Huilan Yang. "Putting the System Back into Systems Change: A Framework for Understanding and Changing Organizational and Community Systems." *American Journal of Community Psychology* 39, nos. 3–4 (June 1, 2007): 197–215. https://doi.org/10.1007/s10464-007-9109-0.

French, John R. P., and Bertram Raven. "The Bases of Social Power." In *Group Dynamics: Research and Theory*, edited by Dorwin Cartwright and Alvin Zander, 3rd ed., 359–69. New York: Harper & Row, 1968.

Frumkin, P. *On Being Nonprofit*. Boston, MA: Harvard University Press, 2009.

FSG. "Guide to Actor Mapping," December 1, 2015. https://www.fsg.org/tools-and-resources/guide-actor-mapping.

Fu, Jiawei Sophia, Katherine R. Cooper, and Michelle Shumate. "Use and Affordances of ICTs in Interorganizational Collaboration: An Exploratory Study of ICTs in Nonprofit Partnerships." *Management Communication Quarterly* 33, no. 2 (May 1, 2019): 219–37. https://doi.org/10.1177/0893318918824041.

Galaskiewicz, Joseph, Wolfgang Bielefeld, and Myron Dowell. "Networks and Organizational Growth: A Study of Community Based Nonprofits." *Administrative Science Quarterly* 51, no. 3 (September 1, 2006): 337–80. https://doi.org/10.2189/asqu.51.3.337.

Ganesh, Shiv, and Cynthia Stohl. "Collective Action, Community Organizing and Social Movements." In *Sage Handbook of Organizational Communication*, edited by D. K. Mumby and L. L. Putnam, 3rd ed., 743–65. Newbury Park, CA: SAGE, 2014.

Gazley, Beth, and Jeffrey L. Brudney. "The Purpose (and Perils) of Government-Nonprofit Partnership." *Nonprofit and Voluntary Sector Quarterly* 36, no. 3 (September 1, 2007): 389–415. https://doi.org/10.1177/0899764006295997.

Gazley, Beth, and Chao Guo. "What Do We Know about Nonprofit Collaboration? A Comprehensive Systematic Review of the Literature." *Academy of Management Proceedings* 2015, no. 1 (January 1, 2015): 15409. https://doi.org/10.5465/ambpp.2015.303.

Gilchrist, Alison. "Maintaining Relationships Is Critical in Network's Success." *HealthcarePapers* 7, no. 2 (November 2006): 28–31. https://doi.org/10.12927/hcpap.18553 Commentary.

Gray, Barbara. *Collaborating: Finding Common Ground for Multiparty Problems*. San Francisco: Jossey-Bass, 1989.

———. "Strong Opposition: Frame-Based Resistance to Collaboration." *Journal of Community & Applied Social Psychology* 14, no. 3 (2004): 166–76. https://doi.org/10.1002/casp.773.

Gray, Barbara, Peter T. Coleman, and Linda L. Putnam. "Introduction: Intractable Conflict: New Perspectives on the Causes and Conditions for Change." *American Behavioral Scientist* 50, no. 11 (July 1, 2007): 1415–29. https://doi.org/10.1177/0002764207302459.

Gray, Barbara, and Jill Purdy. *Collaborating for Our Future: Multistakeholder Partnerships for Solving Complex Problems*. Oxford, New York: Oxford University Press, 2018.

Gray, Barbara, and Jenna Stites. "Sustainability through Partnerships: A Systematic Review." Ontario, Canada: Network for Business Sustainability, 2013. https://nbs.net/p/sustainability-through-partnerships-a-systematic-revie-e39afcb5-1fe6-4644-90d1-992aaf0918b5.

Greene, Jennifer C. "Communication of Results and Utilization in Participatory Program Evaluation." *Evaluation and Program Planning* 11, no. 4 (January 1, 1988): 341–51. https://doi.org/10.1016/0149-7189(88)90047-X.

Greene, Jennifer G. "Stakeholder Participation and Utilization in Program Evaluation." *Evaluation Review* 12, no. 2 (April 1, 1988): 91–116. https://doi.org/10.1177/0193841X8801200201.

Greve, Cartsen, and Graeme A. Hodge. "Introduction: Public-Private Partnerships in Turbulent Times." In *Rethinking Public-Private Partnerships: Strategies for Turbulent Times*, edited by Cartsen Greve and Graeme A. Hodge, 1–32. Abingdon, Oxon: Routledge, 2013.

Guerra-López, Ingrid J. *Performance Evaluation: Proven Approaches for Improving Program and Organizational Performance*. Hoboken, NJ: John Wiley & Sons, 2017.

Gulati, Ranjay. "Social Structure and Alliance Formation Patterns: A Longitudinal Analysis." *Administrative Science Quarterly* 40, no. 4 (1995): 619–52.

Gulati, Ranjay, and Martin Gargiulo. "Where Do Interorganizational Networks Come From?" *American Journal of Sociology* 104, no. 5 (March 1, 1999): 1439–93. https://doi.org/10.1086/210179.

Guo, Chao, and Muhittin Acar. "Understanding Collaboration among Nonprofit Organizations: Combining Resource Dependency, Institutional, and Network Perspectives." *Nonprofit and Voluntary Sector Quarterly* 34, no. 3 (2005): 340–61.

Hager, Mark A., Joseph Galaskiewicz, and Jeff A. Larson. "Structural Embeddedness and the Liability of Newness among Nonprofit Organizations." *Public Management Review* 6, no. 2 (2004): 159–88.

Hardy, Cynthia, and Nelson Phillips. "Strategies of Engagement: Lessons from the Critical Examination of Collaboration and Conflict in an Interorganizational Domain." *Organization Science* 9, no. 2 (April 1, 1998): 217–30. https://doi.org/10.1287/orsc.9.2.217.

Hart, Stuart L. "A Natural-Resource-Based View of the Firm." *Academy of Management Review* 20, no. 4 (October 1, 1995): 986–1014. https://doi.org/10.5465/amr.1995.9512280033.

Hartley, Jean, and Maria Allison. "Good, Better, Best? Inter-Organizational Learning in a Network of Local Authorities." *Public Management Review* 4, no. 1 (January 2002): 101–18. https://doi.org/10.1080/14616670110117332.

Harvard Business Review Staff. "How Companies Can Profit from a 'Growth Mindset.'" *Harvard Business Review*, November 1, 2014. https://hbr.org/2014/11/how-companies-can-profit-from-a-growth-mindset.

Hayes, John. *The Theory and Practice of Change Management*. London: Palgrave, 2018.

Head, Brian W. "Wicked Problems in Public Policy." *Public Policy* 3, no. 2 (2008): 101–18.

Heald, Morrell. *The Social Responsibilities of Business: Company and Community 1900–1960*. Rutgers, NJ: Transaction Publishers, 1970.

Heath, Renee Guarriello, and Lawrence R. Frey. "Ideal Collaboration: A Conceptual Framework of Community Collaboration." *Communication Yearbook* 28 (2004): 192–233.

Heath, Renee Guarriello, and Matthew G. Isbell. *Interorganizational Collaboration: Complexity, Ethics, and Communication*. Long Grove, IL: Waveland Press, 2017.

Heath, Renee Guarriello, and Patricia M. Sias. "Communicating Spirit in a Collaborative Alliance." *Journal of Applied Communication Research* 27, no. 4 (November 1, 1999): 356–76. https://doi.org/10.1080/00909889909365545.

Henry, Gary T. "Comparison Group Designs." In *Handbook of Practical Program Evaluation*, edited by Kathryn E. Newcomer, Harry P. Hatry, and Joseph S. Wholey, 125–43. Hoboken, NJ: Wiley, 2010.

Herlin, Heidi. "Better Safe Than Sorry: Nonprofit Organizational Legitimacy and Cross-Sector Partnerships." *Business & Society* 54, no. 6 (November 1, 2015): 822–58. https://doi.org/10.1177/0007650312472609.

Hite, Julie M., and William S. Hesterly. "The Evolution of Firm Networks: From Emergence to Early Growth of the Firm." *Strategic Management Journal* 22, no. 3 (March 2001): 275–86. https://doi.org/10.1002/smj.156.

Hoberecht, Susan, Brett Joseph, Jan Spencer, and Nancy Southern. "Inter-Organizational Networks." *OD and Sustainability* 43, no. 4 (2011): 23–27.

Holley, June. *Network Weaver Handbook: A Guide to Transformational Networks*. Athens, Ontario, Canada: Network Weaver Publishing, 2012.

Hood, Jacqueline N., Jeanne M. Logsdon, and Judith Kenner Thompson. "Collaboration for Social Problem Solving: A Process Model." *Business & Society* 32, no. 1 (June 1, 1993): 1–17. https://doi.org/10.1177/000765039303200103.

Horwood, Christiane, Lisa Butler, Pierre Barker, Sifiso Phakathi, Lyn Haskins, Merridy Grant, Ntokozo Mntambo, and Nigel Rollins. "A Continuous Quality Improvement Intervention to Improve the Effectiveness of Community Health Workers Providing Care to Mothers and Children: A Cluster Randomised Controlled Trial in South Africa." *Human Resources for Health* 15, no. 1 (June 13, 2017): 39. https://doi.org/10.1186/s12960-017-0210-7.

Huber, George P. "Organizational Learning: The Contributing Processes and the Literatures." *Organization Science* 2, no. 1 (1991): 88–115.

Hudson, Bob, Brian Hardy, Melanie Henwood, and Gerald Wistow. "In Pursuit of Inter-Agency Collaboration in the Public Sector: What Is the Contribution of Theory and Research?" *Public Management (1461667X)* 1, no. 2 (1999): 235–60.

Human, Sherrie E., and Keith G. Provan. "Legitimacy Building in the Evolution of Small-Firm Multilateral Networks: A Comparative Study of Success and Demise." *Administrative Science Quarterly* 45, no. 2 (2000): 327–65.

Huxham, Chris, and Siv Vangen. "Ambiguity, Complexity and Dynamics in the Membership of Collaboration." *Human Relations* 53, no. 6 (2000): 771–806.

———. "Doing Things Collaboratively: Realising the Advantage or Succumbing to Inertia?" In *Collaborative Governance—A New Era of Public Policy in Australia?*, edited by Janine O'Flynn, John Wanna, Janine O'Flynn, and John Wanna, 29–44. Australia: The Australian National University, 2009. http://epress.anu.edu.au/anzsog/collab_gov/pdf/ch04.pdf.

———. *Managing to Collaborate: The Theory and Practice of Collaborative Advantage*. London: Routledge, 2013.

Huybrechts, Benjamin, and Helen Haugh. "The Role of Networks in Institutionalizing New Hybrid Organizational Forms: Insights from the European Renewable Energy Cooperative Network." *Organization Studies* 39, no. 8 (August 2018): 1085–1108. https://doi.org/10.1177/0170840617717097.

Ihm, Jennifer, and Elizabeth A. Castillo. "Development and Transformation of Collaborative Networks in Events." *Journal of Convention & Event Tourism* 18, no. 3 (July 3, 2017): 205–24. https://doi.org/10.1080/15470148.2017.1322021.

Ingold, Karin, and Manuel Fischer. "Drivers of Collaboration to Mitigate Climate Change: An Illustration of Swiss Climate Policy over 15 Years." *Global Environmental Change* 24 (January 1, 2014): 88–98. https://doi.org/10.1016/j.gloenvcha.2013.11.021.

Inkpen, Andrew C. "Learning Through Joint Ventures: A Framework of Knowledge Acquisition." *Journal of Management Studies* 37, no. 7 (2000): 1019–44. https://doi.org/10.1111/1467-6486.00215.

Isett, Kimberley Roussin, and Keith G. Provan. "The Evolution of Dyadic Interorganizational Relationships in a Network of Publicly Funded Nonprofit Agencies." *Journal of Public Administration Research and Theory: J-PART* 15, no. 1 (2005): 149–65.

Joecks, Jasmin, Kerstin Pull, and Karin Vetter. "Gender Diversity in the Boardroom and Firm Performance: What Exactly Constitutes a 'Critical Mass?'" *Journal of Business Ethics* 118, no. 1 (November 1, 2013): 61–72. https://doi.org/10.1007/s10551-012-1553-6.

Joseph, Miranda. *Against the Romance of Community*. Minneapolis: University of Minnesota Press, 2002.

Kagan, Sharon Lynn. *United We Stand: Collaboration for Child Care and Early Education Services*. New York: Teachers College Press, 1991.

Kania, John, and Mark Kramer. "Collective Impact." *Stanford Social Innovation Review*, 2011. https://ssir.org/articles/entry/collective_impact#.

———. "The Equity Imperative in Collective Impact." *Stanford Social Innovation Review*, 2015. https://ssir.org/articles/entry/the_equity_imperative_in_collective_impact.

Kanter, Rosabeth Moss. "Collaborative Advantage: Successful Partnerships Manage the Relationship Not Just the Deal." *Harvard Business Review* July–August (1994): 96–108.

Kapucu, Naim. "Interagency Communication Networks During Emergencies: Boundary Spanners in Multiagency Coordination." *The American Review of Public Administration* 36, no. 2 (June 1, 2006): 207–25. https://doi.org/10.1177/0275074005280605.

Keast, Robyn, Myrna P. Mandell, Kerry Brown, and Geoffrey Woolcock. "Network Structures: Working Differently and Changing Expectations." *Public Administration Review* 64, no. 3 (2004): 363–71. https://doi.org/10.1111/j.1540-6210.2004.00380.x.

Keck, Margaret E., and Kathryn Sikkink. "Transnational Advocacy Networks in International and Regional Politics." *International Social Science Journal* 51, no. 159 (1999): 89–101. https://doi.org/10.1111/1468-2451.00179.

Kenis, Patrick, and Jörg Raab. "Back to the Future: Using Organization Design Theory for Effective Organizational Networks Introduction: The Discovery and Study of Organizational Networks." *Perspectives on Public Management and Governance* 3, no. 2 (2020): 109–23.

Kerr, Norbert L., and R. Scott Tindale. "Group Performance and Decision Making." *Annual Review of Psychology* 55, no. 1 (January 12, 2004): 623–55. https://doi.org/10.1146/annurev. psych.55.090902.142009.

Kilduff, Martin, and Wenpin Tsai. *Social Networks and Organizations.* Thousand Oaks, CA: SAGE, 2003.

Klijn, Erik-Hans, Bram Steijn, and Jurian Edelenbos. "The Impact of Network Management on Outcomes in Governance Networks." *Public Administration* 88, no. 4 (December 2010): 1063–82. https://doi.org/10.1111/j.1467-9299.2010.01826.x.

Klimaat, Ministerie van Economische Zaken en. "Organisatie—Over het Klimaatakkoord— Klimaatakkoord." Webpage, April 18, 2018. https://www.klimaatakkoord.nl/klimaatakkoord/ organisatie.

———. "Over het Klimaatakkoord - Klimaatakkoord." Webpage, February 19, 2019. https:// www.klimaatakkoord.nl/klimaatakkoord.

Klimes-Dougan, Bonnie, Gerald J. August, Chih-Yuan Steven Lee, George M. Realmuto, Michael L. Bloomquist, Jason L. Horowitz, and Todd L. Eisenberg. "Practitioner and Site Characteristics That Relate to Fidelity of Implementation: The Early Risers Prevention Program in a Going-to-Scale Intervention Trial." *Professional Psychology: Research and Practice*, Children's Mental Health 40, no. 5 (October 2009): 467–75. https://doi.org/10.1037/a0014623.

Koppenjan, Joop, and Erik-Hans Klijn. *Managing Uncertainties in Networks. A Network Approach to Problem Solving and Decision Making.* London: Routledge, 2004.

Koschmann, Matthew A., Timothy R. Kuhn, and Michael D. Pfarrer. "A Communicative Framework of the Value of Cross-Sector Partnerships." *The Academy of Management Review* 37, no. 3 (2012): 332–54.

Koza, M. P., and A. Y. Lewin. "The Coevolution of Network Alliances: A Longitudinal Analysis of an International Professional Service Network." *Organization Science* 10, no. 5 (September 1999): 638–53.

Kraatz, M. S. "Learning by Association: Interorganizational Networks and Adaptation to Environmental Change." *Academy of Management Journal* 41, no. 6 (1998): 621–43.

La Piana, David, and Michaela Hayes. "M&A in the Nonprofit Sector: Managing Merger Negotiations and Integration." *Strategy & Leadership* 33, no. 2 (2005): 11–16.

Lane, Peter J., Balaji R. Koka, and Seemantini Pathak. "The Reification of Absorptive Capacity: A Critical Review and Rejuvenation of the Construct." *The Academy of Management Review* 31, no. 4 (2006): 833–63. https://doi.org/10.2307/20159255.

Larkin, Richard F., and Marie DiTommaso. *Wiley Not-for-Profit GAAP 2018: Interpretation and Application of Generally Accepted Accounting Principles.* Hoboken, NJ: John Wiley & Sons, 2018.

Larson, Andrea. "Network Dyads in Entrepreneurial Settings: A Study of the Governance of Exchange Relationships." *Administrative Science Quarterly* 37, no. 1 (March 1992): 76–104. https://doi.org/10.2307/2393534.

Lawless, Michael W., and Rita A. Moore. "Interorganizational Systems in Public Service Delivery: A New Application of the Dynamic Network Framework." *Human Relations* 42, no. 12 (1989): 1167–84.

Lazerson, Mark. "A New Phoenix?: Modern Putting-Out in the Modena Knitwear Industry." *Administrative Science Quarterly* 40, no. 1 (1995): 34–59. https://doi.org/10.2307/2393699.

Le, Vu. "Why Communities of Color Are Getting Frustrated with Collective Impact." *Nonprofit AF* (blog), November 29, 2015. https://nonprofitaf.com/2015/11/why-communities-of-color-are-getting-frustrated-with-collective-impact/.

Le Pennec, Morgane, and Emmanuel Raufflet. "Value Creation in Inter-Organizational Collaboration: An Empirical Study." *Journal of Business Ethics* 148, no. 4 (April 1, 2018): 817–34. https://doi.org/10.1007/s10551-015-3012-7.

Lee, Chongmyoung, and Richard M. Clerkin. "Exploring the Use of Outcome Measures in Human Service Nonprofits: Combining Agency, Institutional, and Organizational Capacity Perspectives." *Public Performance & Management Review* 40, no. 3 (February 1, 2017): 601–24. https://doi.org/10.1080/15309576.2017.1295872.

———. "The Adoption of Outcome Measurement in Human Service Nonprofits." *Journal of Public and Nonprofit Affairs* 3, no. 2 (July 31, 2017): 111–34. https://doi.org/10.20899/jpna.3.2.111-134.

Lewis, Laurie. "Collaborative Interaction: Review of Communication Scholarship and a Research Agenda." In *Communication Yearbook*, edited by Christina Beck, 30:197–247. Mahwah, NJ: Lawrence Erlbaum, 2006.

Liket, Kellie C., Marta Rey-Garcia, and Karen E. H. Maas. "Why Aren't Evaluations Working and What to Do About It: A Framework for Negotiating Meaningful Evaluation in Nonprofits." *American Journal of Evaluation* 35, no. 2 (June 1, 2014): 171–88. https://doi.org/10.1177/1098214013517736.

Locke, Edwin A., and Gary P. Latham. "Building a Practically Useful Theory of Goal Setting and Task Motivation: A 35-Year Odyssey." *American Psychologist* 57, no. 9 (September 2002): 705–17. https://doi.org/10.1037/0003-066X.57.9.705.

———. "New Directions in Goal-Setting Theory." *Current Directions in Psychological Science* 15, no. 5 (October 1, 2006): 265–68. https://doi.org/10.1111/j.1467-8721.2006.00449.x.

Longoria, Richard A. "Is Inter-Organizational Collaboration Always a Good Thing?" *Journal of Sociology and Social Welfare* 32 (2005): 123–38.

Lucidarme, Steffie, Greet Cardon, and Annick Willem. "A Comparative Study of Health Promotion Networks: Configurations of Determinants for Network Effectiveness." *Public Management Review* 18, no. 8 (September 2016): 1163–217. https://doi.org/10.1080/14719037.2015.1088567.

Maas, Karen, and Kellie Liket. "Social Impact Measurement: Classification of Methods." In *Environmental Management Accounting and Supply Chain Management*, edited by Roger Burritt, Stefan Schaltegger, Martin Bennett, Tuula Pohjola, and Maria Csutora, 171–202. Eco-Efficiency in Industry and Science. Dordrecht: Springer Netherlands, 2011. https://doi.org/10.1007/978-94-007-1390-1_8.

Mandell, Myrna P., and Toddi A. Steelman. "Understanding What Can Be Accomplished Through Interorganizational Innovations." *Public Management Review* 5, no. 2 (June 2003): 197–224. https://doi.org/10.1080/1461667032000066417.

Marangunić, Nikola, and Andrina Granić. "Technology Acceptance Model: A Literature Review from 1986 to 2013." *Universal Access in the Information Society* 14, no. 1 (March 1, 2015): 81–95. https://doi.org/10.1007/s10209-014-0348-1.

March, James G. "Exploration and Exploitation in Organizational Learning." *Organization Science* 2, no. 1 (1991): 71–87.

Margolin, Drew B., Cuihua Shen, Seungyoon Lee, Matthew S. Weber, Janet Fulk, and Peter Monge. "Normative Influences on Network Structure in the Evolution of the Children's Rights NGO Network, 1977–2004." *Communication Research* 42, no. 1 (February 1, 2015): 30–59. https://doi.org/10.1177/0093650212463731.

Mariotti, Francesca, and Rick Delbridge. "Overcoming Network Overload and Redundancy in Interorganizational Networks: The Roles of Potential and Latent Ties." *Organization Science* 23, no. 2 (April 2012): 511–28. https://doi.org/10.1287/orsc.1100.0634.

Marquardt, Michael J. H., Skipton Leonard, Arthur M. Freedman, and Claudia C. Hill. "Fundamentals of Action Learning and How It Works." In *Action Learning for Developing Leaders and Organizations: Principles, Strategies, and Cases*, 21–49. Washington, DC: American Psychological Association, 2009. https://doi.org/10.1037/11874-002.

Marwell, Gerald, and Pamela E. Oliver. *The Critical Mass in Collective Action: A Micro-Social Theory*. New York: Cambridge University Press, 1993.

McAdam, Doug. "Conceptual Origins, Current Problems, Future Directions." In *Comparative Perspectives on Social Movements: Political Opportunities, Mobilizing Structures, and Cultural Framings*, edited by Doug McAdam, John D. McCarthy, and Mayer N. Zald, 23–40. New York: Cambridge University Press, 1996.

McGuire, Michael, and Robert Agranoff. "The Limitations of Public Management Networks." *Public Administration* 89, no. 2 (2011): 265–84.

McKinsey & Company. "7 Elements of Nonprofit Capacity Building." Reston, VA: Venture Philanthropy Partners, 2001. http://bonner.pbworks.com/w/file/fetch/106093761/Effective%20Capacity%20Building%20in%20Nonprofit%20Organizations.pdf.

McKnight, John L., and John Kretzmann. *Mapping Community Capacity*. Institute for Policy Research, Northwestern University Evanston, IL, 1996.

Meyer, Alan D., Geoffrey R. Brooks, and James B. Goes. "Environmental Jolts and Industry Revolutions: Organizational Responses to Discontinuous Change." *Strategic Management Journal* 11 (1990): 93–110.

Meyer, Alan D., Anne S. Tsui, and C. R. Hinings. "Configurational Approaches to Organizational Analysis." *The Academy of Management Journal* 36, no. 6 (1993): 1175–95. https://doi.org/10.2307/256809.

Milam, Jessica MacDonald, and Renee Guarriello Heath. "Participative Democracy and Voice: Rethinking Community Collaboration Beyond Neutral Structures." *Journal of Applied Communication Research* 42, no. 4 (October 2, 2014): 366–86. https://doi.org/10.1080/00909882.2014.911944.

Milward, H. Brinton, Katherine R. Cooper, and Michelle Shumate. "Who Says a Common Agenda Is Necessary for Collective Impact?" *Nonprofit Quarterly*, 2016. https://nonprofitquarterly.org/who-says-a-common-agenda-is-necessary-for-collective-impact/.

Milward, H. Brinton, and Keith G. Provan. *A Manager's Guide to Choosing and Using Collaborative Networks*. Vol. 8. IBM Center for the Business of Government Washington, DC, 2006.

Morris, John Charles, William Allen Gibson, William Marshall Leavitt, and Shana Campbell Jones. *The Case for Grassroots Collaboration: Social Capital and Ecosystem Restoration at the Local Level*. Lanham, MD: Lexington Books, 2013.

National Council of Nonprofits. "Fiscal Sponsorship: Who Does What?" Infographic. Accessed December 14, 2019. https://www.councilofnonprofits.org/sites/default/files/images/fiscal-sponsorship-infographic.png.

National Network of Fiscal Sponsors. "Guidelines for Comprehensive Fiscal Sponsorship." Website. Accessed December 14, 2019. http://www.fiscalsponsors.org/pages/best-practices-fiscal-sponsorship.

Nee, Eric. "A Flexible Framework for Going Beyond Collective Impact." *Stanford Social Innovation Review*, 2020. https://ssir.org/articles/entry/a_flexible_framework_for_going_beyond_collective_impact.

Newcomer, Kathryn E., Harry P. Hatry, and Joseph S. Wholey. *Handbook of Practical Program Evaluation*. Hoboken, NJ: Wiley, 2010.

Nobbie, Patricia Dautel, and Jeffrey L. Brudney. "Testing the Implementation, Board Performance, and Organizational Effectiveness of the Policy Governance Model in Nonprofit Boards of Directors." *Nonprofit and Voluntary Sector Quarterly* 32, no. 4 (December 1, 2003): 571–95. https://doi.org/10.1177/0899764003257460.

Nonprofit Quarterly. "How Dashboards Can Help Your Nonprofit Achieve Its Goals," (recorded webinar). December 6, 2018. https://nonprofitquarterly.org/how-dashboards-can-help-your-nonprofit-achieve-its-goals/.

Nooteboom, Bart. "Trust, Opportunism and Governance: A Process and Control Model." *Organization Studies* 17, no. 6 (November 1, 1996): 985–1010. https://doi.org/10.1177/017084069601700605.

Noy, Darren. "Power Mapping: Enhancing Sociological Knowledge by Developing Generalizable Analytical Public Tools." *The American Sociologist* 39, no. 1 (2008): 3–18.

O'Brien, Nina F., Andrew Pilny, Yannick Atouba, Michelle Shumate, Janet L. Fulk, and Peter R. Monge. "How Does NGO Partnering Change Over Time? A Longitudinal Examination of Factors That Influence NGO Partner Selection." *Nonprofit and Voluntary Sector Quarterly*, in press.

Olson, M. *The Logic of Collective Action: Public Goods and the Theory of Groups.* Cambridge, MA: Harvard University Press, 1965.

O'Toole, Laurence J. "Implementing Public Innovations in Network Settings." *Administration & Society* 29, no. 2 (May 1, 1997): 115–38. https://doi.org/10.1177/009539979702900201.

———. "Networks and Networking: The Public Administrative Agendas." *Public Administration Review* 75, no. 3 (May 2015): 361–71. https://doi.org/10.1111/puar.12281.

Paquin, Raymond L., and Jennifer Howard-Grenville. "Blind Dates and Arranged Marriages: Longitudinal Processes of Network Orchestration." *Organization Studies* 34, no. 11 (November 1, 2013): 1623–53. https://doi.org/10.1177/0170840612470230.

Pepper, M. P. J., and T. A. Spedding. "The Evolution of Lean Six Sigma." *The International Journal of Quality & Reliability Management; Bradford* 27, no. 2 (2010): 138–55. http://dx.doi.org.turing.library.northwestern.edu/10.1108/02656711011014276.

Peterson, N. Andrew, and Marc A. Zimmerman. "Beyond the Individual: Toward a Nomological Network of Organizational Empowerment." *American Journal of Community Psychology* 34, no. 1 (September 1, 2004): 129–45. https://doi.org/10.1023/B:AJCP.0000040151.77047.58.

Pfeffer, Jeffrey, and R. Gerald Salancik. *The External Control of Organizations: A Resource Dependence Perspective.* New York: Harper & Row, 1978.

Polanyi, Michael. *The Tacit Dimension.* London: Routledge, 1966.

Poole, Marshall Scott. "On the Study of Process in Communication Research." *Annals of the International Communication Association* 36, no. 1 (2013): 371–409.

———. "Systems Theory." In *The SAGE Handbook of Organizational Communication: Advances in Theory, Research, and Methods,* edited by Linda L. Putnam and Dennis K. Mumby, 49–74. Thousand Oaks, CA: SAGE, 2014.

Popp, J. K. H., Brinton Milward, MPA, Gail MacKean, MPA, Ann Casebeer, and A. Lindstrom. "Inter-Organizational Networks." Collaboration across Boundaries Series. Washington, DC: IBM Center for the Business of Government, 2014.

Porter, Michael E., and Mark R. Kramer. "Philanthropy's New Agenda: Creating Value." *Harvard Business Review* 77, no. 6 (1999): 121–30.

Powell, Kristen Gilmore, Sarah L. Gold, N. Andrew Peterson, Suzanne Borys, and Donald Hallcom. "Empowerment in Coalitions Targeting Underage Drinking: Differential Effects of Organizational Characteristics for Volunteers and Staff." *Journal of Social Work Practice in the Addictions* 17, no. 1–2 (April 3, 2017): 75–94. https://doi.org/10.1080/1533256X.2017.1304947.

Powell, W. W. "Neither Market nor Hierarchy: Network Forms of Organization." *Research in Organizational Behavior* 12 (1990): 105–24.

Powell, Walter W., K. W. Koput, and L. SmithDoerr. "Interorganizational Collaboration and the Locus of Innovation: Networks of Learning in Biotechnology." *Administrative Science Quarterly* 41, no. 1 (March 1996): 116–45.

Prahalad, C. K., and Gary Hamel. "The Core Competence of the Corporation." *Harvard Business Review*, May 1, 1990. https://hbr.org/1990/05/the-core-competence-of-the-corporation.

Provan, K. G., and H. B. Milward. "A Preliminary Theory of Interorganizational Network Effectiveness: A Comparative Study of Four Community Mental Health Systems." *Administrative Science Quarterly* 40, no. 1 (1995): 161–90.

Provan, Keith G., Jonathan E. Beagles, and Scott J. Leischow. "Network Formation, Governance, and Evolution in Public Health: The North American Quitline Consortium Case." *Health Care Management Review* 36, no. 4 (2011): 315–26. https://doi.org/10.1097/HMR.0b013e31820e1124.

Provan, Keith G., Amy Fish, and Joerg Sydow. "Interorganizational Networks at the Network Level: A Review of the Empirical Literature on Whole Networks." *Journal of Management* 33, no. 3 (June 1, 2007): 479–516. https://doi.org/10.1177/0149206307302554.

Provan, Keith G., and Kun Huang. "Resource Tangibility and the Evolution of a Publicly Funded Health and Human Services Network." *Public Administration Review* 72, no. 3 (2012): 366–75. https://doi.org/10.1111/j.1540-6210.2011.02504.x.

Provan, Keith G., Kimberley R. Isett, and H. Brinton Milward. "Cooperation and Compromise: A Network Response to Conflicting Institutional Pressures in Community Mental Health." *Nonprofit and Voluntary Sector Quarterly* 33, no. 3 (September 2004): 489–514. https://doi.org/10.1177/0899764004265718.

Provan, Keith G., and Patrick Kenis. "Modes of Network Governance: Structure, Management, and Effectiveness." *Journal of Public Administration Research and Theory* 18, no. 2 (April 1, 2008): 229–52. https://doi.org/10.1093/jopart/mum015.

Provan, Keith G., and H. Brinton Milward. "A Preliminary Theory of Interorganizational Network Effectiveness: A Comparative Study of Four Community Mental Health Systems." *Administrative Science Quarterly* 40, no. 1 (1995): 1–33. https://doi.org/10.2307/2393698.

Purdy, Jill M. "A Framework for Assessing Power in Collaborative Governance Processes." *Public Administration Review* 72, no. 3 (2012): 409–17. https://doi.org/10.1111/j.1540-6210.2011.02525.x.

Putnam, Linda L., Gail T. Fairhurst, and Scott Banghart. "Contradictions, Dialectics, and Paradoxes in Organizations: A Constitutive Approach." *The Academy of Management Annals* 10, no. 1 (January 1, 2016): 165–71. https://doi.org/10.1080/19416520.2016.1162421.

Raab, Jörg, Remco S. Mannak, and Bart Cambré. "Combining Structure, Governance, and Context: A Configurational Approach to Network Effectiveness." *Journal of Public Administration Research and Theory* 25, no. 2 (April 1, 2015): 479–511. https://doi.org/10.1093/jopart/mut039.

Raeymaeckers, Peter. "From a Bird's Eye View? A Comparative Analysis of Governance and Network Integration among Human Service Organizations." *Journal of Social Service Research* 39, no. 3 (2013): 416–31.

Raeymaeckers, Peter, and Patrick Kenis. "The Influence of Shared Participant Governance on the Integration of Service Networks: A Comparative Social Network Analysis." *International Public Management Journal* 19, no. 3 (2016): 397–426.

Rawlins, Brad. "Give the Emperor a Mirror: Toward Developing a Stakeholder Measurement of Organizational Transparency." *Journal of Public Relations Research* 21, no. 1 (January 2009): 71–99. https://doi.org/10.1080/10627260802153421.

Rescher, Nicholas. *Process Metaphysics: An Introduction to Process Philosophy*. New York: Suny Press, 1996.

Rittel, Horst W. J., and Melvin M. Webber. "Dilemmas in a General Theory of Planning." *Policy Sciences* 4, no. 2 (1973): 155–69.

Rogers, Everett M., and David G. Cartano. "Methods of Measuring Opinion Leadership." *The Public Opinion Quarterly* 26, no. 3 (1962): 435–41.

Rose, T. R. "Research Project Report: Evolution, Development, and Maintenance of the Southern Alberta Child and Youth Health Network." *Center for Health and Policy Studies at the University of Calgary*, 2004.

Rothman, Robert. *Data Dashboards: Accounting for What Matters*. Georgia: Alliance for Excellent Education, 2015.

Salamon, Lester M., and Helmut K. Anheier. "Social Origins of Civil Society: Explaining the Nonprofit Sector Cross-Nationally." *Voluntas: International Journal of Voluntary and Nonprofit Organizations* 9, no. 3 (September 1, 1998): 213–48. https://doi.org/10.1023/A:1022058200985.

Schad, Jonathan, Marianne W. Lewis, Sebastian Raisch, and Wendy K. Smith. "Paradox Research in Management Science: Looking Back to Move Forward." *The Academy of Management Annals* 10, no. 1 (January 1, 2016): 5–64. https://doi.org/10.1080/19416520.2016.1162422.

Schurr, Paul H, Laurids Hedaa, and Jens Geersbro. "Interaction Episodes as Engines of Relationship Change." *Journal of Business Research* 61, no. 8 (August 2008): 877–84. https://doi.org/10.1016/j.jbusres.2007.09.006.

Schwantes, Marcel. "6 Things Good CEOs Always Do to Connect with Employees." Inc.com, April 14, 2017. https://www.inc.com/marcel-schwantes/7-things-good-ceos-always-do-to-connect-with-employees.html.

Seeds for Change. "Consensus Decision Making." Accessed June 24, 2019. http://www.seedsforchange.org.uk/consensus.

Seitanidi, M. May. *The Politics of Partnerships: A Critical Examination of Nonprofit-Business Partnerships*. London: Springer Science & Business Media, 2010.

Seitanidi, Maria May, and Andrew Crane. "Implementing CSR through Partnerships: Understanding the Selection, Design and Institutionalisation of Nonprofit-Business Partnerships." *Journal of Business Ethics* 85 (2009): 413–29.

Selsky, John W. "Lessons in Community Development: An Activist Approach to Stimulating Interorganizational Collaboration." *The Journal of Applied Behavioral Science* 27, no. 1 (1991): 91–115. https://doi.org/10.1177/0021886391271005.

Selsky, John W., and Barbara Parker. "Platforms for Cross-Sector Social Partnerships: Prospective Sensemaking Devices for Social Benefit." *Journal of Business Ethics* 94, no. 1 (July 1, 2010): 21–37. https://doi.org/10.1007/s10551-011-0776-2.

Shah, Reshma H., and Vanitha Swaminathan. "Factors Influencing Partner Selection in Strategic Alliances: The Moderating Role of Alliance Context." *Strategic Management Journal* 29, no. 5 (2008): 471–94. https://doi.org/10.1002/smj.656.

Shapiro, Valerie B., J. David Hawkins, and Sabrina Oesterle. "Building Local Infrastructure for Community Adoption of Science-Based Prevention: The Role of Coalition Functioning." *Prevention Science* 16, no. 8 (November 1, 2015): 1136–46. https://doi.org/10.1007/s11121-015-0562-y.

Shapiro, Valerie B., Sabrina Oesterle, Robert D. Abbott, Michael W. Arthur, and J. David Hawkins. "Measuring Dimensions of Coalition Functioning for Effective and Participatory Community Practice." *Social Work Research* 37, no. 4 (December 2013): 349–59. https://doi.org/10.1093/swr/svt028.

Shortell, Stephen M., Charles L. Bennett, and Gayle R. Byck. "Assessing the Impact of Continuous Quality Improvement on Clinical Practice: What It Will Take to Accelerate Progress." *The Milbank Quarterly* 76, no. 4 (1998): 593–624.

Shumate, Michelle, and Katherine R. Cooper. "Collective Impact: What We REALLY Know." Evanston, IL: Network for Nonprofit and Social Impact at Northwestern University, May 23, 2016, http://nnsi.northwestern.edu/cireport.

Shumate, Michelle, Jiawei Sophia Fu, and Katherine R. Cooper. "Does Cross-Sector Collaboration Lead to Higher Nonprofit Capacity?" *Journal of Business Ethics* 150, no. 2 (June 1, 2018): 385–99. https://doi.org/10.1007/s10551-018-3856-8.

Shumate, Michelle, Janet Fulk, and Peter R. Monge. "Predictors of the International HIV/AIDS INGO Network over Time." *Human Communication Research* 31 (2005): 482–510. https://doi.org/10.1111/j.1468-2958.2005.tb00880.x.

Shumate, Michelle, and Zachary Gibson. "Interorganizational Network Change." In *Oxford Handbook of Organization Change and Innovation*, edited by Marshall Scott Poole and Andrew Van de Ven, 2nd ed. Oxford: Oxford University Press, 2021.

Shumate, M., and Liz Livingston Howard. "Making the Most of the Chicago Benchmarking Collaborative." *Kellogg School of Management Cases* (2018). https://store.hbr.org/product/making-the-most-of-the-chicago-benchmarking-collaborative/KE1066.

Shumate, Michelle, Liz Livingston Howard, and Waikar Sachin. "Driving Strategic Change at The Junior League (A)." *Kellogg School of Management Cases* (2017). https://doi.org/10.1108/case.kellogg.2016.000101.

Shumate, Michelle, Yuli Patrick Hsieh, and Amy O'Connor. "A Nonprofit Perspective on Business–Nonprofit Partnerships: Extending the Symbiotic Sustainability Model." *Business & Society*, 2016, 0007650316645051. https://doi.org/10.1177/0007650316645051.

Shumate, Michelle, and Amy O'Connor. "The Symbiotic Sustainability model: Conceptualizing NGO-Corporate Alliance Communication." *Journal of Communication 63* (2010): 577–609.

——"Corporate Reporting of Cross-Sector Alliances: The Portfolio of NGO Partners Communicated on Corporate Websites." *Communication Monographs* 77 (2010): 238–61. https://doi.org/10.1080/03637751003758201.

Silver, Samuel A., Rory McQuillan, Ziv Harel, Adam V. Weizman, Alison Thomas, Gihad Nesrallah, Chaim M. Bell, Christopher T. Chan, and Glenn M. Chertow. "How to Sustain Change and Support Continuous Quality Improvement." *Clinical Journal of the American Society of Nephrology* 11, no. 5 (May 6, 2016): 916–24. https://doi.org/10.2215/CJN.11501015.

Silvia, Chris. "Collaborative Governance Concepts for Successful Network Leadership." *State and Local Government Review* 43, no. 1 (2011): 66–71.

Smith, Elizabeth A. "The Role of Tacit and Explicit Knowledge in the Workplace." *Journal of Knowledge Management; Kempston* 5, no. 4 (2001): 311–21. http://doi.org/10.1108/13673270110411733.

Snowden, David J., and Mary E. Boone. "A Leader's Framework for Decision Making." *Harvard Business Review*, PMID 18159787, November 2007, 69–76.

Spires, Anthony J. "Lessons from Abroad: Foreign Influences on China's Emerging Civil Society." *The China Journal*, no. 68 (2012): 125–46. https://doi.org/10.1086/666577.

Stadler, Christian, Tazeeb Rajwani, and Florence Karaba. "Solutions to the Exploration/Exploitation Dilemma: Networks as a New Level of Analysis." *International Journal of Management Reviews* 16, no. 2 (April 2014): 172–93. https://doi.org/10.1111/ijmr.12015.

Steffek, Jens. "Explaining Cooperation between IGOs and NGOs – Push Factors, Pull Factors, and the Policy Cycle." *Review of International Studies* 39, no. 4 (October 2013): 993–1013. https://doi.org/10.1017/S0260210512000393.

Stephens, Kimberlie J., Janet Fulk, and Peter R. Monge. "Constrained Choices in Alliance Formations: Cupids and Organizational Marriages." *Human Relations* 62, no. 4 (April 1, 2009): 501–36. https://doi.org/10.1177/0018726708101982.

Stirman, Shannon, Cassidy A. Gutner, Paul Crits-Christoph, Julie Edmunds, Arthur C. Evans, and Rinad S. Beidas. "Relationships between Clinician-Level Attributes and Fidelity-Consistent and Fidelity-Inconsistent Modifications to an Evidence-Based Psychotherapy." *Implementation Science* 10, no. 1 (August 13, 2015): 115. https://doi.org/10.1186/s13012-015-0308-z.

Stone, Melissa M., and Susan Cutcher-Fershenfeld. "Challenge of Measuring Performance in Nonprofit Organizations." In *Measuring the Impact of the Nonprofit Sector*, edited by Patrice Flynn and Virginia A. Hodgkinson, 33–57. New York, NY: Kluwer Academic/ Plenum Publishers, 2001.

Susskind, Lawrence, Sarah McKearnan, and Jennifer Thomas-Larmer. "Conducting a Conflict Assessment." In *The Consensus Building Handbook*, edited by Lawerence E. Susskind, Sarah McKernen, and Jennifer Thomas-Larmar, 99–136. Thousand Oaks, CA: SAGE, 1999.

Tarrow, Sidney. *Power in Movement: Social Movements in Contentious Politics.* Cambridge: Cambridge University Press, 1998.

Taylor, Maureen, and Marya L. Doerfel. "Building Interorganizational Relationships That Build Nations." *Human Communication Research* 29, no. 2 (2003): 153–81.

———. "Evolving Network Roles in International Aid Efforts: Evidence from Croatia's Post War Transition." *Voluntas: International Journal of Voluntary and Nonprofit Organizations* 22, no. 2 (2011): 311–34.

Teegen, Hildy, Jonathan P. Doh, and Sushil Vachani. "The Importance of Nongovernmental Organizations (NGOs) in Global Governance and Value Creation: An International Business Research Agenda." *Journal of International Business Studies* 35, no. 6 (November 1, 2004): 463–83. https://doi.org/10.1057/palgrave.jibs.8400112.

Thomson, Ann Marie, and James L. Perry. "Collaboration Processes: Inside the Black Box." *Public Administration Review* 66 (2006): 20–32.

Torchia, Mariateresa, Andrea Calabrò, and Morten Huse. "Women Directors on Corporate Boards: From Tokenism to Critical Mass." *Journal of Business Ethics* 102, no. 2 (August 1, 2011): 299–317. https://doi.org/10.1007/s10551-011-0815-z.

Turrini, Alex, Daniela Cristofoli, Francesca Frosini, and Greta Nasi. "Networking Literature about Determinants of Network Effectiveness." *Public Administration* 88, no. 2 (2010): 528–50. https://doi.org/10.1111/j.1467-9299.2009.01791.x.

United Nations. "Human Development Report 2003." United Nations. Accessed November 23, 2019. http://hdr.undp.org/en/content/human-development-report-2003.

Uzzi, Brian. "Social Structure and Competition in Interfirm Networks: The Paradox of Embeddedness." *Administrative Science Quarterly*, 1997, 35–67.

Van Horn, M. Lee, Abigail A. Fagan, J. David Hawkins, and Sabrina Oesterle. "Effects of the Communities That Care System on Cross-Sectional Profiles of Adolescent Substance Use and Delinquency." *American Journal of Preventive Medicine* 47, no. 2 (August 1, 2014): 188–97. https://doi.org/10.1016/j.amepre.2014.04.004.

Van Tulder, Rob, and Nienke Keen. "Capturing Collaborative Challenges: Designing Complexity-Sensitive Theories of Change for Cross-Sector Partnerships." *Journal of Business Ethics* 150, no. 2 (2018): 315–32.

Vangen, Siv, and Nik Winchester. "Managing Cultural Diversity in Collaborations: A Focus on Management Tensions." *Public Management Review* 16, no. 5 (July 4, 2014): 686–707. https://doi.org/10.1080/14719037.2012.743579.

Varda, Danielle M. "Data-Driven Management Strategies in Public Health Collaboratives." *Journal of Public Health Management and Practice* 17, no. 2 (April 2011): 122. https://doi.org/10.1097/PHH.0b013e3181ede995.

Venkatesh, Viswanath, and Hillol Bala. "Technology Acceptance Model 3 and a Research Agenda on Interventions." *Decision Sciences* 39, no. 2 (2008): 273–315. https://doi.org/10.1111/j.1540-5915.2008.00192.x.

Venkatesh, Viswanath, and Fred D. Davis. "A Model of the Antecedents of Perceived Ease of Use: Development and Test." *Decision Sciences* 27, no. 3 (1996): 451–81.

Vergne, Jean-Philippe, and Rodolphe Durand. "The Missing Link Between the Theory and Empirics of Path Dependence: Conceptual Clarification, Testability Issue, and Methodological Implications." *Journal of Management Studies* 47, no. 4 (2010): 736–59. https://doi.org/10.1111/j.1467-6486.2009.00913.x.

Verweij, Stefan, Erik-Hans Klijn, Jurian Edelenbos, and Arwin Van Buuren. "What Makes Governance Networks Work? A Fuzzy Set Qualitative Comparative Analysis of 14 Dutch Spatial Planning Projects." *Public Administration* 91, no. 4 (2013): 1035–1055.

Waddell, Steve. "Complementary Resources: The Win-Win Rationale for Partnership with NGOs." In *Terms of Endearment: Business, NGOs and Sustainable Development*, edited by Jem Bendell, 193–206. Sheffield, UK: Greenleaf publishing, 2000.

Waddock, Sandra A. "A Typology of Social Partnership Organizations." *Administration & Society* 22, no. 4 (February 1, 1991): 480–515. https://doi.org/10.1177/009539979102200405.

———. "Building Successful Social Partnerships." *Sloan Management Review; Cambridge* 29, no. 4 (Summer 1988): 17.

Wang, Rong, Katherine R. Cooper, and Michelle Shumate. "Alternatives to Collective Impact: The Community Systems Solutions Framework." *Stanford Social Innovation Review*, Winter 2020. https://ssir.org/articles/entry/community_system_solutions_framework_offers_an_alternative_to_collective_impact_model.

Wang, Weijie. "Exploring the Determinants of Network Effectiveness: The Case of Neighborhood Governance Networks in Beijing." *Journal of Public Administration Research and Theory* 26, no. 2 (April 1, 2016): 375–88. https://doi.org/10.1093/jopart/muv017.

Watts, Duncan J. "Should Social Science Be More Solution-Oriented?" *Nature Human Behaviour* 1, no. 1 (January 10, 2017): 1–5. https://doi.org/10.1038/s41562-016-0015.

Weber, Edward P., and Anne M. Khademian. "Wicked Problems, Knowledge Challenges, and Collaborative Capacity Builders in Network Settings." *Public Administration Review* 68, no. 2 (2008): 334–49. https://doi.org/10.1111/j.1540-6210.2007.00866.x.

Wernerfelt, Birger. "A Resource-Based View of the Firm." *Strategic Management Journal* 5, no. 2 (1984): 171–80. https://doi.org/10.1002/smj.4250050207.

Williamson, O. "Economics of Organization: The Transaction Cost Approaches." *American Journal of Sociology* 87 (1981): 548–77.

———. *Markets and Hierarchies*. New York: Free Press, 1975.

Winig, Laura. "Social Media and the Planned Parenthood/Susan G. Komen for the Cure Controversy." *Harvard Kennedy School of Government* Case Number 1975.0 (2012). https://case.hks.harvard.edu/social-media-and-the-planned-parenthood-susan-g-komen-for-the-cure-controversy/.

Witesman, Eva, and Andrew Heiss. "Nonprofit Collaboration and the Resurrection of Market Failure: How a Resource-Sharing Environment Can Suppress Social Objectives." *VOLUNTAS: International Journal of Voluntary and Nonprofit Organizations* 28, no. 4 (August 1, 2017): 1500–1528. https://doi.org/10.1007/s11266-016-9684-5.

Wolff, Tom. "Ten Places Where Collective Impact Gets It Wrong." *Global Journal of Community Psychology and Practice* 7, no. 1 (2016). https://www.gjcpp.org/en/resource.php?issue=21&resource=200.

Woo, DaJung. "Exit Strategies in Interorganizational Collaboration: Setting the Stage for Re-Entry." *Communication Research*, June 4, 2019, 0093650219851418. https://doi.org/10.1177/0093650219851418.

Wood, Donna J., and Barbara Gray. "Toward a Comprehensive Theory of Collaboration." *The Journal of Applied Behavioral Science* 27 (1991): 139–62. https://doi.org/10.1177/0021886391272001.

Zajac, Edward J., and Cyrus P. Olsen. "From Transaction Cost to Transactional Value Analysis: Implications for the Study of Interorganizational Strategies*." *Journal of Management Studies* 30, no. 1 (1993): 131–45. https://doi.org/10.1111/j.1467-6486.1993.tb00298.x.

Zimmerman, Marc A. "Empowerment Theory." In *Handbook of Community Psychology*, edited by Julian Rappaport and Edward Seidman, 43–63. Boston, MA: Springer, 2000.

Zoller, Heather M. "'A Place You Haven't Visited before': Creating the Conditions for Community Dialogue." *Southern Communication Journal* 65, no. 2–3 (March 1, 2000): 191–207. https://doi.org/10.1080/10417940009373167.

Index